In Memory of the late Jim Kemmy (1936-1997)

Long-serving Labour TD for Limerick East and twice Mayor of Limerick, Jim was a friend of all humanity and a committed internationalist. Long may his legacy live with us.

Barry McLoughlin

Fighting for Republican Spain 1936-38

Frank Ryan and the Volunteers from Limerick in the International Brigades

With biographical data on 230 Irish members
of the International Brigades

ISBN 978-1-291-96839-2

First printing:
August 2014

Publisher:
Barry McLoughlin
finbarr.mcloughlin@univie.ac.at

Cover design & layout:
Christian Lendl

Cover images:
Members of the International Brigades learning to fire the Maxim Machine Gun
Source: Collection Hans Griebaum, Vienna

Map of Belchite
Source: Book of the 15th Brigade, Madrid, 1938

Printed by

Table of Contents

Acknowledgements

Limerick is City of Culture 2014 and during the festivities it is planned to unveil a monument to the volunteers from the city and county who fought for the Spanish Republic in the years 1936-38. Now the six Limerick men who fought for Republican Spain belong to everybody. This is my contribution to the memory of volunteers for democracy who are, with one exception, all but forgotten.

The most prominent of the six Limerick men who fought for Spanish democracy was Frank Ryan from Elton, Co. Limerick, a figure who has fascinated me for decades, not least his lonely death in Germany during World War 2. In fact, his personality was one of the main reasons why I completed a M.A. thesis about German-Irish Relations 1939-45 under Professor T. Desmond Williams of UCD in 1979. Immediately afterwards I emigrated to Vienna on a Ph.D. scholarship, completed my doctorate in 1990 and at present teach Irish History and Contemporary History at Vienna University.

For twelve years (1991-2002) I was often in Moscow researching the crimes of Stalinism. While at the fount of knowledge, so to speak, I also looked at Irish material in the Comintern archive RGASPI. On several occasions my friend Emmet O'Connor was my companion, and we also tried to find what material we could on Irish volunteers in the International Brigades (IB).

For the last few years we both have been mulling over the idea of writing a comprehensive study on the Irish who fought for Republican Spain, for which the Moscow files are essential. The Limerick memorial idea prompted me to interrupt the greater project and write an account of the IB soldiers from the area, an undertaking which had to be completed in some haste in order that this publication could be available before the weekend devoted to the Limerick brigaders, 12-14 September 2014.

Many people helped me in the writing of this study. Without the assistance of my brother Michael and that of my friends Christian Lendl (layout), Diarmuid Duggan (maps), Emmet O'Connor and Richard Baxell, this book could not have been prepared in such a short time. I received further valuable support from the following:

Jim Carmody, Guillem Casan, Frank Clissmann, Maeve Clissmann, Neil G. Cobbett, Enric Comas, Ciaran Crossey, Nicholas Cummins, Fred Firsov, John Halstead, Wladislaw Hedeler, Julian Hendy, Michael Kennedy, Piotr Kwasniewski, Anna Martí, Ger McCloskey, Declan McLoughlin, Mike McNamara, Myron Momryk, Harry Owens, Amina Parkes, Danny Payne, Sean Quinn, Svetlana Rosental', Des Ryan, Eamon Ryan, Mary Davis Ryan, Mary Sheehan, Eleanor Updale, Alan Warren, David Yorke.

The commemoration of the "Limerick Six" is an opportunity to remind ourselves of the links of our city to foreign wars and Spanish culture. This book is dedicated to the memory of Jim Kemmy. My conversations with him were always lively debates. It is a pity I did not meet him often enough.

Barry McLoughlin, August 2014
(*finbarr.mcloughlin@univie.ac.at*)

List of abbreviations

ATGWU	Amalgamated Transport and General Workers' Union (Ireland)
C.I.D.	Criminal Investigation Department (of Irish police)
C.O.	Commanding officer
Comintern	Communist International
CBS	Christian Brothers schools
Co.	Company (military)
CP	Communist Party
CPAUS	Communist Party of Australia
CPCan	Communist Party of Canada
CPGB	Communist Party of Great Britain
CPI	Communist Party of Ireland
CPUSA	Communist Party of the United States of America

CYMS	Catholic Young Men's Society (Ireland)
DIFP	Documents on Irish Foreign Policy (Royal Irish Academy)
ESB	Electricity Supply Board (Ireland)
FG	Fine Gael party
GAA	Gaelic Athletic Association
GHQ	General Headquarters
IB	International Brigades
ICA	Irish Citizen Army
ICF	Irish Christian Front (Ireland)
ILP	Independent Labour Party (UK)
INTO	Irish National Teachers' Organisation
IRA	Irish Republican Army
IRC	Irish Republican Congress
ITGWU	Irish Transport and General Workers' Union
IWM	Imperial War Museum (London)
IWW	Industrial Workers of the World (USA)
LAI	League against Imperialism
LP	Labour Party (UK)
MG	Machine-gun
MML	Marx Memorial Library, London
NAI	National Archives of Ireland, Dublin
NAUK	National Archives of the United Kingdom, Kew, London
NILP	Northern Ireland Labour Party
NLHMM	National Labour History Museum, Manchester
O.C.	Officer commanding
OKW	Oberkommando der Wehrmacht

PCE	Spanish Communist Party
RGASPI	Russian State Archive for Social and Political History (Moscow)
RIC	Royal Irish Constabulary
RWG	Revolutionary Workers' Groups (Ireland)
SIM	Counter-intelligence branch of Spanish Republican Army
SPNI	Socialist Party of Northern Ireland
SWML	South Wales Miners' Library
TGWU	Transport and General Workers Union (UK)
TUC	Trades Union Council (UK)
UCD	University College Dublin (National University)
WCML	Working Class Movement Library, Salford UK
WUI	Workers' Union of Ireland
YCL	Young Communist League

Battles of the British Battalion in the Spanish Civil War

Belchite & Quinto, August - September 1937

Ebro, July - September 1938

Boadilla and La Coruna Road, December 1936

Calaceite, April - March 1938

Segura de los Banos, February 1938

Jarama, February 1937

Brunete, July 1937

Teruel, December 1937- February 1938

Tarazona

Madrigueras

Albacete

Lopera, December 1936

Albacete was the base of the International Brigades. The British Battalion trained first at Madrigueras and later, together with the Americans and the Canadians, at Tarazona.

Introduction

Limerick is not a place one would associate with radical left-wing politics before the arrival of Jim Kemmy on the local and national scene over forty years ago. During the War of Independence the record of the city battalions of the IRA was indifferent, and one of their leaders, Captain Tom Keane, executed in the New Barracks (Sarsfield Barracks) in June 1921, is now virtually a forgotten figure. The IRA in the east of Co. Limerick invented the concept of the "Flying Column" and it held its own under heavy losses when fighting in flat countryside unsuited to intensive guerrilla warfare.

Between the end of the Civil War in 1923 and the outbreak of World War 2 there is little or no evidence of left-wing organisations in the city. The Limerick "Soviet" of 1919 was essentially a commendable display of solidarity against arbitrary military rule, nothing more. The "Soviets" in the creamery industry in the following years were workers' struggles against wage cuts. The press gave the stoppages a Russian-language title that stuck, but these self-organisation efforts of local labour left no long-term legacy.

Six men from Limerick city and county fought in the International Brigades during the Spanish Civil War. None of them was resident in their native place when they decided to play their part in the struggle against international fascism, and it does not seem that any of the three survivors returned on a permanent basis to where they had been born and bred. The most famous among them was Frank Ryan, the Republican from Elton, Co. Limerick. He figures prominently in the following pages because he was the accepted and highly popular leader of the Irish volunteers in Spain, and on account of his sojourn in Nazi Germany, where he died in 1944. This aspect of his life still gives rise to (often groundless) speculation and sensationalism. We know little about the others, primarily because they left Limerick at an early age and their siblings are no longer with us. We should not forget that participation in the Spanish war on the "Red side" was a fact many Irish Catholic families chose to keep to themselves. The files on the Limerick men held in the Moscow archive RGASPI contain scant information.

Dublin was the point of departure to Spanish battlefields for Frank Ryan, and England for Paddy Brady, Joe Ryan and Gerrard Doyle. Jim Woulfe travelled from Canada to Spain, and Emmet Ryan had been living in France when he crossed the Pyrenees to join the Brigades. Woulfe was killed in action and Emmet Ryan was executed by his own unit, the British battalion of the 15th Brigade. Brady was repatriated with a bad shoulder wound in 1937, as was Joe Ryan, primarily, I believe, because he was deemed to be too young and was possibly demoralized. Gerrard Doyle was taken prisoner with many others of the British battalion in March-April 1938. He was repatriated to Britain six months later and remained there. Their biographies are summarized in Chapter 7.

Why is interest in the International Brigades still strong or even growing? Two reasons spring to mind. First, the volunteers are seen as idealists, "premature anti-fascists" (in the language of those who discriminated against the *brigadistas* during WW2 in the U.S. and British armed forces), "men of no property" who put their lives on the line to stop the rise of fascism in Europe at a time when the democratic governments were appeasing the dictators Hitler and Mussolini. Second, the affection for the Brigades stems from romantic attachment to left-wing causes, a sentiment which wins new adherents at times of general economic downturn and its attendant austerity.

The story of the International Brigades was for many years generally the work of supporters of the Soviet Union. This situation has changed greatly over the last two decades because the files on the International Brigades held in the Moscow archive RGASPI (3,365 voluminous folders) were de-classified during the presidency of Boris Yelzin. Many of the scholarly works mentioned in "Sources" at the end of this book are witness to the process of "historicization", i.e. the Spanish war or the history of the International Brigades is now less a controversial political topic in English-speaking countries but more a subject that can be studied *sine ira et studio*. The participants are no longer alive and new information is becoming available all the time. Our knowledge of the volunteers' lives and of the context of their actions in Spain is now far more extensive, and our judgment more differentiated than was previously the case. This is a welcome development. One can now say that the story of the Brigades belongs to everybody, not to any political party or movement. It has become part of the national narrative in Ireland and Britain, a fitting reminder that international solidarity had real meaning 80 years ago.

The motivations of those English-speakers who enlisted for service in Republic Spain cannot be encompassed in one word or one sentence. For some, going to fight in Spain was an escape from personal problems, for others it was better than vegetating as one of the countless unemployed in Britain's devastated industrial and mining regions. The number of such volunteers has probably been underestimated because those disillusioned by war rarely write memoirs or give interviews decades later to researchers. Not a few volunteers would have taken the journey to the Spanish frontier because of group friendships, or to avenge a brother or a close friend who had fallen in the war. The majority, it appears, had some affiliation to the official labour movement, and, having experienced injustice themselves or seen it around them since childhood, decided to join the Brigades. This stance was coupled with outrage about the failure of parliamentary democracy to alleviate the effects of mass pauperization during the world Depression. The politically interested had read about the destruction of free trade unions and left parties in Germany and Italy and were disturbed by the sympathy for fascism at the highest levels of society or by the marching of fascists on the streets of Britain and Ireland.

From one-half to two-thirds of the volunteers were seasoned militants, members of the British Communist Party (CPGB) and participants in the famous Hunger

Marches. In Ireland a common path to political radicalism began in the ranks of the illegal IRA, those members of the "Legion of the Rearguard" who became active in politics in the early 1930s. About a dozen had fought in the Irish Civil War of 1922/23 and, in some cases, had subsequently served in other armies. The Irish Republicans fighting in Spain brought a collective mentality and an understanding of the necessity for military discipline. They provided the British battalion with commanding officers such as Peter Daly and Paddy O'Daire, or company leaders like Jack Nalty, Johnny Power and Paddy O'Sullivan. The Irish reached positions of prominence in the 15th Brigade over and above what might be expected on the basis of their numbers: 230, about one-tenth of the British enlistment. What is not generally realized is that just over half of the Irish IB soldiers went to Spain from Britain. They were often emigrants from rural and small-town Ireland, men who had become politicised in exile, in the workplace, on hunger marches, through trade union struggles and in battles against the Blackshirts.

What can be ruled out for all volunteers is the supposition that they went to fight in Spain for mercenary reasons. The pay was negligible, 10 pesetas a day for a common infantryman and amounted to less than half of what a private soldier was receiving at the time in the Irish Free State Army or the British Army. Most volunteers gave half their pay to the Spanish 'Red Aid'.[1] Furthermore, there was constant speculation on the money markets against the Republican currency which fell in value throughout 1937 and 1938, levelling out at the bottom at about 70 pesetas to the £. Not that the rank-and-file were interested in the currency rates because they knew that was virtually nothing to buy. British and Irish recruits, apprised of the arduous terms of service and the dangers involved before leaving Dublin or London, knew that there would be no military pension if they were invalided out of Spain.

In Republican Spain tobacco was in short supply and almost unobtainable in late 1938, and alcohol, while cheap, rarely included beer. The Irish and the British, not used to hard liquor, drank their anis or cognac too quickly, with disastrous results. The wine on offer gave some comfort, but often lacked "kick", not unlike the "vang blang" served up to the Tommies by bar-owners on the make twenty years earlier in France. It is interesting that the sustenance of British and Irish

---

[1] Imperial War Museum (IWM), Interview 803, George Leeson, reel 1.

soldiers for generations – hot, sweet tea – is rarely mentioned in volunteers' memoirs. Tea could have been a substitute for wine rations but the ceremonious "brew-up" was probably the privilege of the quarter-master and his mates: coffee, not tea, was the morning drink of the Spaniards, even when it was an ersatz concoction won from acorns. Milk was almost unobtainable and reserved for mothers with children, and the distribution of condensed milk from abroad was an occasion to be remembered by brigaders in their war memoirs. Considering that the International Brigades towards the end were composed of Spanish recruits to the extent of seventy to eighty per cent, banning alcohol from the Brigades was not feasible. Another reason why the "cuppa" was absent from the daily life of the brigaders was the primitive state of the infrastructure in rural Spain: the lack of water or potable water. Most water supplies were drawn from rivers and wells that dried up in summer. Sewage schemes were also underdeveloped so that the local water supply was often contaminated. Peter O'Connor, a teetotaler, drank water instead of *vino* and caught typhoid on two occasions during his seven months in Spain.[2] The water shortage meant that the men could not wash as often as was hygienically necessary, leading to the torment of lice and fleas. Inadequate sanitary conditions were the root cause of dysentery and several forms of fever. Illnesses could spread quickly because the men suffered from malnutrition and lack of vitamins, and broke out periodically in painful boils and rashes. A diet of beans, other vegetables and mule-meat fried in often rancid olive oil caused chronic stomach disorder. Towards the end of the Brigades' engagement the food shortage was acute in the entire Republican Zone. The volunteers on the Ebro, fighting in tattered uniforms, had to go without food or drink for the first four days of the battle. When it was over, Tom Murphy from Monaghan, a former soldier in the Irish Guards, weighed only eight stone.[3] Soldiers dreamed of a "good feed" with their hoarded pesetas. The English volunteer John Peet, while on sick-leave in Barcelona in the summer of 1938, spent twelve days' pay in a black-market restaurant for a meal of two fried eggs and two thin slices of bread.[4]

---

[2] Peter O'Connor, A Soldier of Liberty: Recollections of a Socialist and Anti-fascist Fighter, Dublin 1996

[3] IWM, Interview 805, Tom Murphy, reel 2.

[4] D. Corkill/S. Rawnsley, The Road to Spain. Anti-Fascists at War 1936-1939, Dunfermline 1981, pp. 109-110.

The Spanish republican army had to fight with one arm tied behind its back.[5] It not only lacked arms because of the Non-Intervention policy of the European democracies and the USA but often the right kind of weapons. Even the most modern of the Soviet fighters, so successful in defending the skies above Madrid or routing the Italians at the Battle of Guadalajara, were obsolescent by the summer of 1937. The Republic never had enough heavy artillery pieces or mortars, its machine-guns were either unserviceable French pieces from World War 1 or the heavy Russian Maxim-1910, a cumbersome weapon which features at some length in the chapter about Maurice Emmet Ryan. It is probable that the Soviets, when cheating the Republicans on the exchange rate for armaments and holding the Republic's gold reserves as security, foisted "out of service" weaponry on the Spaniards.[6] The standard weapon of the IB infantry, various types of the Russian Mosin Nagant rifle, had been zeroed-in with the long chisel-tipped bayonet attached. Most volunteers found the bayonet a nuisance, used it as a tent peg or threw it away at some stage, which meant that the sighting was then askew. The weapon was built for the Artic winter, not for torrid Spanish summers and the wooden shaft often split in the heat. Its bolt was too short so that clearing the jammed weapon was a problem.[7]

The most prized and efficient Russian weapon in the Brigades was the brand-new 45 mm anti-tank gun, and the British battalion had three pieces. But these had been disabled or destroyed by April 1938. The Soviet advisers were terrified that the weapon might fall into enemy hands, and were just as solicitous about their aircraft or tanks. One of the weaknesses of the Republican command was that the Russians decided when and how their aircraft and tanks were to be employed, not the Chief-of Staff of the Republican Army Vicente Rojo. All-arms coordination was thus not a primate of Republican tactics. Soviet arms deliveries dropped sharply after the late summer of 1937, with roughly only one third of the total

---

[5] The following passages about the Republican forces' fighting worth are taken from general reading, more specifically the works of Alpert, Beevor and Hugh Thomas mentioned in "Sources".

[6] The standard work on Republican Spain' efforts to acquire arms is Gerald Howson's Arms for Spain (London 1998). See pp. 146-152 for the manipulative practices of the Soviet arms sellers.

[7] See the interview with John Dunlop in: Ian McDougall (ed.), Voices from the Spanish Civil War. Personal Recollections of Scottish Volunteers in Republican Spain 1936-39, Edinburgh 1986, pp. 117-168.

supplies arriving after December 1937.[8] Stalin had more pressing matters nearer home, namely the Japanese advance in China. Soviet shipments to Mao Tse Tung from autumn 1936 to 1938 equalled, if not surpassed, Moscow's shipments to Spain.[9]

Neither the republicans nor the fascists used Blitzkrieg attacks with armour in Spain, and almost all attacks of Republican tanks used *en masse* ended in a debâcle. Military tactics were quite conventional on both sides, too many frontal assaults with appalling losses. The Republicans were hampered by their proclivity to interrupt an offensive in order to capture an enemy strong point instead of driving around it and onwards. Practically all Republican successes were temporary ones, for the forces involved did not possess sufficient reserves in men or equipment to sustain a long campaign. The Republican People's Army was desperately short of trained commissioned officers because the majority had opted for Franco or was retired by the Madrid Ministry for National Defence on grounds of suspect loyalty. Trained NCOs in the anti-fascist army were also few and far between. Spain had been neutral in World War 1, so officers, republican or fascist, had limited experience of modern warfare. Fighting the Rif rebels in Morocco in the 1920s was a doubtful yardstick of military capability: Spanish units were periodically annihilated there and the rebels could be subdued finally in 1925 only with the help of the French military.

The Republican military leaders that did emerge in the course of the war were generally Communists, former Spanish Army NCOs such as Enrique Lister, Juan Modesto and El Campesino. Their military training was slight and they detested one another. Lesser known republican commanders were often students or recently graduated physicians or scientists who had learned their craft "on the job".

As regards the 15th Brigade, the few former professional officers could not stay the course: Tom Wintringham lost the support of the CPGB leadership and was repatriated prematurely; George Nathan, perhaps the most gifted, was killed at Brunete; and Clifford Wattis returned to Britain in April 1938 and "spilled the

---

[8] Iurii Rybalkin, Sovetskaia voennaia pomoshch' respublikanskoi Ispanii (1936-1939), Moscow 2000, pp. 44-45.
[9] *http://www.hpu.edu/CHSS/History/GraduateDegree/MADMSTheses/files/Julie_Zeiss_MADMS_THESIS_COMPLETED_APRIL_2009.pdf*. Accessed 29.05.2014.

beans" about Communist domination in the Brigades. His preference for promotion on the basis of record in battle rather than political affiliation was shared by many volunteers and they thus criticized the very opposite that frequently prevailed. Volunteers from countries that had a long tradition of compulsory military service for young men (in Britain only in the years 1916-1918, and never in Ireland) had a larger cadre of ex-officers and NCOS with experience.

To go by reports collated by Soviet advisers and sent to Moscow there was considerable tension between native Spanish and foreign units in the Brigades. The Polish divisional commander General Walter unequivocally blamed the volunteers from abroad for their "chauvinism".[10] The proponents of "international solidarity" chose to forget that men are nationalists before they become "internationalists". That applied to some former Irish Republicans in Spain who had inflated ideas about their revolutionary antecedents or their role in the freedom struggle of 20 years before. The English, it could be argued, were also patriotic, but in a more subdued fashion. The Irish probably bored the more stolid of their English comrades with countless renditions of rebel songs ("too much self-pity or strains of morbidness about them when they were not just funny").[11] Some Britons responded "with varying degrees of enthusiasm" to the lines of "James Connolly" (God curse you, England, you cruel-hearted monster...Another martyr for old Ireland"...).[12]

Relations between André Marty, the choleric, paranoid and callous chief of the Brigades based in Albacete, and party representatives were turbulent to say the least: he had leading German IB personnel expelled from Spain in 1938.[13] In addition there was much resentment on the part of professional Republican Army officers at the presumptiveness of foreigners, who were politically well-connected but military neophytes.[14] Towards the end of the war, many Spaniards in their

---

[10] See his reports in: Ronald Radosh/Mary B. Habeck (eds), Spain Betrayed. The Soviet Union and the Spanish Civil war, New Haven and London 2001.

[11] Working Class Movement Library, Salford (WCML), Ms. Bob Clark, p. 41.

[12] Fred Thomas, Tilting at Windmills. A Memoir of the Spanish Civil War, Michigan State University Press 1996, pp. 58-59.

[13] See: Angela Berg, Die Internationalen Brigaden im Spanischen Bürgerkrieg 1936-1939, Essen 2005.

[14] See: Luigi Longo (Gallo), Die Internationalen Brigaden in Spanien, German edition West-Berlin n.d, Italien original edition Rome 1956.

pride were thoroughly tired of the foreigners. Famous is the remark of the Colonel Juan de Blanco Yagüe (it provoked his demotion), one of Franco's more capable and bloodthirsty commanders. At a banquet in Burgos in mid-April 1938, he praised the fighting spirit of the Republicans, termed his German and Italian allies "beasts of prey", and then suggested clemency for the captured foe, which of course was ignored.[15]

The attrition of the conflict, the all-pervasive war-weariness, also deeply affected the International Brigades. Numbers peaked in 1937 but there were never enough recruits from abroad to replace the heavy losses. The Soviets were never any good at keeping (truthful) statistics so the following figures from Red Army and Soviet party archives are often contradictory or incomplete. After the Battle of Brunete (July 1937), for example, the strength of the 15th Brigade shrunk from 2,144 to 885: 293 killed, 735 wounded, 167 deserted.[16] By early August 1937 over 18,000 foreigners had arrived, but only 10,000 were still in service – killed, wounded, deserted and evacuated to other areas totaled over 8,000.[17] The official total up to the end of April 1938 for all foreigners arrived in Spain was 31,569, but those still serving up the line were exactly half that figure (15,992) – 5,000 had been repatriated because of their severe wounds and 4,600 were dead or missing.[18] By some accounts the earlier recruits were not properly registered so that a maximum total of 35,000 IB volunteers seems plausible. In late August 1938, by which time Moscow had agreed in principle to the withdrawal of the IB from Spain, the number of foreigners in the "extremely exhausted" brigades had fallen to around 10,000, half of whom were at the front.[19] International volunteers were now only a fraction, around a quarter of both figures. When the last Republican offensive, the Battle of the Ebro, began in late July, the English, Scots, Welsh and Irish in the British battalion numbered 283 out of 558 men in five companies.[20] At the end of the slaughter, two months later, the non-

---

[15] Hugh Thomas, The Spanish Civil War, 3rd edition Penguin Books London 1977, pp. 819-820.
[16] Radosh/Habeck, Spain Betrayed p. 238.
[17] Ibid., pp. 258-259.
[18] Ibid., p. 468.
[19] Ibid., p. 469.
[20] MML, IB, archive box C 24/2. I am grateful to Jim Carmody (London) for his notes on the battalion strength.

Spaniards in the battalion could muster only 58 men barely able to stand, let alone fight.[21]

Considering all these facts – lack of equipment and food, incompetent tactical decisions, little prospect of getting out alive due to delays in repatriation – it is little short of a wonder that so many kept on fighting. Few, if any, regular armies could boast of such endurance under similar conditions. But the International Brigades was not a normal military corps: there were general assemblies to discuss "problems", a social welfare officer-cum-confessor in attendance if the Political Commissar was good, and a wide tolerance of bitching and "answering back to superior officers". Such behavior was known as "playing the old soldier" in the British Army, in the jargon of the British commissars in Spain it was termed "strong rank-and-file tendencies". And of course most men were politically committed: they knew what they were fighting for.

There was a sinister side, specifically "getting rid of troublemakers" (assassination), as the case of Sergeant Emmet Ryan demonstrates. As in all wars, there was widespread political corruption behind the lines where dandified officers held "cushy" jobs since they had "protection" in the higher echelons because of their good "party record".

Some men went to Spain as committed Communists, became totally disillusioned and deserted. Seemingly apolitical volunteers often had excellent records and steered clear of the politicos, concentrating on the tasks in hand. There are no hard and fast rules about how men will react in battle conditions and we should be forbearing towards those who were not "up to it". The more perspicacious realized the war was definitely lost when Republican Spain was carved in two in April 1938. Others saw the beginning of the end after Brunete.[22]

Irish readers, and especially those from Limerick, may find fault that the volunteers from Thomond flit in and out of the narrative, overshadowed again and again by Frank Ryan. I can only repeat what I said about lack of sources and plead the difficulties I have of accessing information about Limerick when sitting at my desk in Vienna. Attempting to give an authentic picture of the men's situation is perhaps more important than additional biographical facts.

---

[21] Bill Alexander, British Volunteers for Liberty. Spain 1936-39, London 1982, p. 215.

[22] For example, the Lurgan-born Syd Quinn who was repatriated in autumn 1937 – IWM Interview 801 Sydney Quinn, reel 3.

1

Frank Ryan and the Ireland of 1936

The great majority of the Irish volunteers in the International Brigades had found their political orientation in the social and political struggles of the 1930s. A smaller group had taken part in the War of Independence and the Civil War. As Communists, Socialists or leftwing Republicans they faced a myriad of foes: extreme right-wingers, religious bigots, the Catholic Church, the political establishment and the political police.[1]

Once the Irish State had been established in 1922, the Church sought to exert influence in social and political fields which would have been inadmissible under the British. Pliant and like-thinking administrators bowed to the crozier, passing legislation that banned divorce, contraception and "immoral literature". There were few protests. Not all episcopal directives were successful. Fulminations against late night dancing (till 3 or 4 am), excessive drinking or the insatiable appetite of the faithful for salacious British Sunday papers were ineffective. Many bishops, perturbed by the crash of empires and the rise of revolutionary

---

[1] For the origin and activities of Catholic Action in Ireland, see: Fearghal McGarry, Irish Politics and the Spanish Civil War, Cork 1999, pp.113-116.

movements after 1918, by fashion trends and the emancipation of women had a pessimistic world-view, implying that their younger members of their flock would prove prey to all or some of these dangers.[2] Whether declaiming about "faith and morals", which arguably could cover all aspects of life, or political non-conformity, Ireland's bishops were determined to exercise "social control" over the faithful. In many aspects, their efforts can be seen as proof of a totalitarian mind-set, with church activists acting as a kind of Orwellian "thought-police". But Ireland was a state of law inherited from the British, not a totalitarian entity like Germany, Italy or the Soviet Union. Not all bishops or priests were intolerant zealots, nor arguably was their influence on politics as pervasive in the 1930s as it would be twenty years later.

Catholic-inspired violence against the Irish Left, 1933-1936

In political terms, the Church was vociferously anti-communist, but then as later did not differentiate between shades of leftwing opinion. The most hysterical clerical attacks against the Left occurred between 1933 and 1936. After the Irish Civil War Catholic forces were relatively quiescent on Communism and Ireland because Jim Larkin Senior, although nominally head of the Irish section of the Communist International (Comintern), showed reluctance to transform his Irish Worker League into a proper CP. Instead, behind the scenes in Moscow, he sought funds for his trade union, The Workers' Union of Ireland (WUI), and Soviet backing for the removal of British-based unions from the Irish Free State. Since he was unsuccessful in both endeavors, he cut links with Moscow in 1929. Church authorities would have been reluctant to launch a major *ad personam* attack against this gifted and vituperative polemicist, still immensely popular in Dublin, not least for his use of memorable Christian imagery during the 1913 Lockout.[3] However, there had been one instance of a mob attack on Communists before Larkin's return to Ireland from America. In January 1922, Liam O'Flaherty, without the permission of the Communist Party of Ireland (CPI) leadership, seized the Rotunda Concert Hall (now The Gate Theatre). O'Flaherty wanted to draw the attention of the city fathers to the plight of Dublin's

---

[2] J.H. Whyte, Church and State in Modern Ireland, 1923-1979, 2nd edition, Dublin 1980.
[3] Emmet O'Connor, Reds and the Green. Ireland, Russia and the Communist Internationals, 1919-43, Dublin 2004; Ibid., James Larkin. Radical Irish Lives, Cork 2002.

unemployed, but had to withdraw his men with the help of IRA police after a crowd had attacked the building and torn down the red flag on its roof.[4]

This situation changed radically after 1931.[5] On the heels of *Quadragesimo Anno* (15 May 1931), the Papal encyclical condemning class warfare and propagating the corporate state, lay groups soon known collectively as "Catholic Action" and the weekly *The Standard* increased calls for state and lay activity against known radicals. The international religious background was the persecution of the Orthodox religion in Soviet Russia (closure of churches, arrest of clergymen and believers), which ran in conjunction with the mass repression of the peasantry in 1929-31. Stalin temporarily suspended the worst excesses following the global publication of a Papal protest (by Pius XI, 2 February 1930) but resumed the persecution in mid-1931, scaling it down again for reasons of *Realpolitik* in 1934 (exchange of ambassadors with the USA, Hitler's appointment as Reichskanzler).[6] Irish abhorrence of Communism was thus primarily grounded in the militant atheism of the USSR and less in Soviet economic policy. The specifically Irish backdrop to the targeting of political radicals by Church and State was the feeling of panic in leading Government circles in 1931 that a revolutionary upsurge was taking place. Amid mass unemployment and grinding poverty, the IRA was gaining adherents and moving to the left; Irish communists, foremost young cadres just back from Moscow's International Lenin School, were regrouping in a serious attempt, supervised by the Communist Party of Great Britain (CPGB), to establish a section of the Comintern. General Eoin O'Duffy, Garda Commissioner, primed the Irish bishops who condemned a series of left organisations in a 1931 pastoral. The Cosgrave Government banned the groupings outright and introduced emergency legislation (military tribunals).[7]

---

[4] Peter Costello, Liam O'Flaherty's Ireland, Dublin 1996, pp. 39-40; Barry McLoughlin, Left to the Wolves. Irish Victims of Stalinist Terror, Dublin-Portland (Oregon) 2007, pp. 232-233.

[5] Emmet O'Connor, „Anti-Communism in twentieth century Ireland", Twenty Century Communism, 6, 2014, pp. 59-81.

[6] Michail Vital'evič Škarovskij, „Die Russische Kirche unter Stalin in den 20er und 30er Jahren des 20. Jahrhunderts", in: Manfred Hildermeier (Ed.), Stalinismus vor dem Zweiten Weltkrieg. Neue Wege der Forschung, München 1998, pp. 233-253.

[7] Patrick Murray, Oracles of God. The Roman Catholic Church and Irish Politics, 1922-37, Dublin 2000; Brian Hanley, The IRA 1926-1936, Dublin 2002.

The Cumann naGaedheal cabinet could argue that the IRA had recently killed a Garda inspector and a juror, making trials by jury of subversives impossible.[8]

The Church ban, reminiscent of the October 1922 letter from Maynooth against the "godless" IRA, may not have had the desired effect, at least not on the older radicals who were accustomed to excommunication and police harassment after 1922. A sinister development, however, was pogrom-style violence against Communists and left Republicans.

In 1933 the Lenten Pastorals of the bishops concentrated on the "dangers of Communism". Prominent in the propaganda campaign was Bishop Fogarty of Killaloe who tried to scarify even boys at confirmation ceremonies in his diocese.[9] In March 1933, a "Catholic" crowd made three sustained attacks on offices of the Irish Communists (Revolutionary Workers Groups - RWG), at Connolly House, 64 Great Strand Street in Dublin. The prime instigators were Catholic priests fulminating during Lenten missions. On the third attempt the attackers left the building gutted and also attacked Charlotte Despard's Workers' College in Eccles St., but were dispersed by threats of gunfire from IRA volunteers. It was clearly a coordinated onslaught, initiated by Catholic Action, supported by the Blueshirts, with The Catholic Young Men's Society (CYMS) and the "St. Patrick's Anti-Communist League" playing the part of "outraged" Christian zealots. That one of the buildings under brick-attack was the headquarters of Larkin's WUI showed the political, as against the religious, motivation of the mobs.[10] The Communist Party of Ireland managed to re-constitute itself at a clandestine congress in June 1933 but often had to suspend its activities because of Church-inspired persecution.

In truth the greatest peril to the Communists was not the organs of the State, it was danger to life and limb posed by Catholic fanatics and toughs from the slums. There was a recurrence of anti-communist violence in 1936. In the first

---

[8] Eunan O'Halpin, Defending Ireland. The Irish State and its Enemies since 1922, Oxford 1999, pp. 77-80.
[9] Limerick Chronicle, 28.02.1933, 27.05.1933.
[10] O'Connor, Reds and the Green, pp. 185-187. For personal memories of the attacks, see: Patrick Byrne, Memoirs of the Republican Congress, London (Four Provinces Books) n.d., pp. 9-11; Joe Monks, With the Reds in Andalusia, London 1985, pp. 9-11. The best analysis of the 1933 attacks is by Brian Hanley – "The Storming of Connolly House", History Ireland, vol. 7 (2), Summer 1999, pp. 5-7.

clash on 11 January, members of the Dublin CYMS attempted to disrupt a meeting in Rathmines Town Hall organized by the CPI. Harry Pollitt, Britain's foremost Communist, was guest speaker. The disrupters received a drubbing from young men "with red rags pinned in their buttonholes" and were removed.[11] One unimpeachable Catholic, the Benedictine monk Father Tom Sweetman from Gorey, was of the opinion that "you cannot put religion into a man's head with a broken chair" and called the disturbance "in the name of Catholic Action... misdirected zeal".[12] Rosamund Jacob, an agnostic Quaker and Frank Ryan's most intimate female friend, indicated the danger to civil liberties posed by CYMS fanatics.[13] Jacob commented as follows on the statement of the Dublin secretary of the CYMS speaking in Letterkenny that his organization could see to it "that nothing would happen in any sphere of life in Ireland of which the Church did not approve":

> *Non Catholics ... will note ... that they would have no liberty to do anything of which the Catholic Church might disapprove. They would be forced to conform to the ideas of a Church to which they do not belong. Is this "Catholic Action"? It is certainly a very plain threat of religious tyranny.*[14]

The CPI invited CPGB guests soon again to Dublin, for the 20th anniversary celebration of the 1916 Rising. It was a courageous move, obviously for recruiting purposes. In billing Willie Gallacher, Britain's only Communist MP, as a prominent speaker, Dublin's communists were taking a risk, or engaging in "braggadocio" according to Frank Ryan.[15] And the CYMS, smarting from the drawn match in January, tried to stop Gallacher from entering the country. The Dept. of Justice replied that

> *There is no law authorizing such action on the part of the Government even if it were thought desirable as a matter of policy to take such action. I am to add that existing law provides reciprocally for unrestricted freedom of movement between Great Britain and Saorstát Éireann for the citizens of*

---

[11] Irish Independent, 25.01.1936, letters to the editor.
[12] Irish Independent, 15.01.1936, letters to the editor.
[13] For their relationship see: Fearghal McGarry, Frank Ryan. Historical Association of Ireland. Life and Times Series No. 17, Dundalk 2002, pp. 5-7.
[14] Irish Press, 04.02.1936, letters to the editor.
[15] Sean Cronin, Frank Ryan. The Search for The Republic, Dublin 1980, p. 66.

both countries, and that this arrangement is not one which could be lightly set aside.[16]

The Catholic actionists pressurized Dublin Vocational Education Committee, the landlord of Rathmines Town Hall, into refusing the premises for a communist meeting on Easter Monday evening, 13 April. The CPI therefore switched venues, to College Green, which guaranteed that the meeting would be a mass one. The other hall-owners were so intimidated that the Communist felt that they had no alternative but to address the public in the open air rather than bowing to mob-rule. A bad omen was the attack on Communist and Republican groups on the Easter Sunday march to Glasnevin, a running of the gauntlet that IRA men behind did nothing to stop.[17] The police feared a serious flare-up on Easter Monday evening, and while noting the determination of the organizers and the CYMS, did not advocate a ban.[18] The speakers were a veritable "Who's Who" of the Irish Left and included Jack Nalty later killed in Spain. The 4,000-5,000 strong hostile crowd, many of them "of the respectable type…a fair percentage of females" set up a chorus of booing when Peadar O'Donnell rose to speak. He made two attempts from a lamp-post to address the multitude, and was subject to a hail of bottles before being rescued by the police (he requested their protection) and brought to College Green Garda Station.[19] On the way to safety, O'Donnell was struck in the face. Eugene Downing, who later fought in Spain and returned an invalid, bled from the mouth and was ferried home in a Special Branch car.[20] That was the second time that the men in blue had rescued Downing. He had escaped the "Animal Gang" not long before, when he, Gerry Doran and Kevin Blake (both served later in Spain) were chased down O'Connell Street by rightwing desperadoes after a meeting in Cathal Brugha Street. At the bridge, a lone Garda intervened and brought the trio to Store Street Station and safety.[21] Bob Doyle, another future fighter for Republican Spain, had to face the

---

[16] National Archives of Ireland (NAI), JUS 8/28,CYMS to Sean T. O'Kelly, 06.04.1936; Minister for Justice to CYMS, 08.04.1936.

[17] O'Connor, Reds and the Green, p. 212.

[18] NAI, JUS 8/28, Inspector John McGloin, Special Branch, to Chief Inspector DMP, 09.04.1936.

[19] Ibid., John McGloin to Chief Inspector DMP, 14.04.1936.

[20] Ibid., Garda Maher to Chief Inspector, "B" District DMP, 13.04.1936.

[21] *www.irelandscw.com/ibvol-ED1930s.htm*, letter from Eugene Downing to Geraldine Abrahams, 26.02.2002.

"Animal Gang" on a daily basis in 1934. Knowing that they would again assault him after work, he contacted his brother Peter:

> *I knew they would be waiting again when I knocked off, so I sent a message to my brother Peter, who came down with my loaded .45 revolver. With Peter, whom they didn't know, walking behind, I turned the corner into Abbey Street and spotted the gang coming out of a lane towards me armed with sticks and iron bars. I shouted to Peter who got out in the middle of the road, firing three shots over their heads. The gang scattered in all directions and we made our escape. After that, whenever I passed the corner near Capel Street where a couple of the gang lived, I'd have a hand held inside my jacket as if holding a gun, and they would sing 'Who's Afraid of the Big Bad Wolf?' but they never tried it on [me] again.*[22]

The rioters of Easter Monday evening in 1936 went on to cause minor damage to the Republican Congress offices at 57 Middle Abbey Street, but courageous Gardai prevented the rampant rabble from breaking and entering the headquarters of the WUI in Marlborough Street or the new CPI office on Lower Ormond Quay.[23] As in reporting the Spanish Civil War soon afterwards, *The Irish Independent* was adamantly hostile to left or liberal opinion concerning the April disorders in Dublin. After the Easter riots and in the course of the Spanish conflict Fianna Fáil's *The Irish Press* and the liberal *Irish Times* gave the open-minded citizenry a platform. In connection with the Easter Monday disruptions, one letter-writer wrote of his "feeling…of nausea" listening to the "users of foul language" singing "Faith of Our Fathers":

> *What would have been the feelings of Pearse … or Connolly, who gave his life for this country's political freedom, if they had looked on and watched a rabble hurling obscenities and broken bottles in the name of religion at a group of men speaking on behalf of an utterly negligible section of our people?*[24]

---

[22] Bob Doyle, Brigadista. An Irishman's Fight against Fascism. Notes and Additional Text by Harry Owens, Dublin 2006, pp. 40-41.

[23] NAI, JUS 8/28, "C" District to Chief Inspector, Dublin City Area, 14.04.1936; "B" District to Chief Inspector, DM Division, 14.04.1936.

[24] Irish Press, 15.04.1936, readers' views. That day's issue also carried the official statement of the CPI on the riots.

Representatives of the liberal intelligentsia condemned such violence as a danger to free speech, noting "the growing tendency in this country towards a similar elimination of the right of every free Irishman or woman to form his or her own opinions and to express them openly."[25] Once they had caught breath, so to speak, the leaders of Irish Republican Congress (IRC) let off a salvo against the "defenders of faith and morals" and their gurrier friends. Frank Ryan and George Gilmore, joint secretaries of the IRC, saw the real culprits in the "Cosgrave Party", the organizers of "this disguised Imperialist-Fascist challenge to the rights of the people".[26] The CPI went underground again, suspending meetings and withdrawing its candidates from the Dublin municipal elections held in June 1936.

News from the outbreak of the Spanish Civil War in mid-July caused a furore in Ireland, dominating politics for the next twelve months. The anger of Irish Catholics is understandable, even if it was manipulated by reactionary forces, clerical and lay. Among the 200,000 men and women killed extra-judicially behind the lines in Spain, approximately three quarters were shot by advancing Franco units in "cleansing operations" (*limpieza*) that targeted persons of both sexes who had any connection with Republicanism, left-wing parties or trade unions, and regardless of whether they were captured in arms or not. Fascist killings were planned and continued as long as the war lasted, and a further 20,000 Republicans were executed in the years following Franco's victory in March 1939. Unlawful killings on the Republican side totaled approximately 50,000 – many executions in both zones were never recorded so the figures published to date are under-estimates. One can say that the repression by the Francoists was "from above", and in the Republican zone "from below", i.e. in the main carried out spontaneously by armed bands, usually anarchist, including criminals released from prison.[27]

Widespread violence commenced shortly after the victory of the Popular Front parties at the February 1936 Cortes elections. At that time, not unlike Russia

---

[25] Irish Times, letters to the editor, 17.04.1936. The protest was signed, among others, by Owen Sheehy Skeffington, his aunt Katharine Cruise O'Brien (the mother of Conor Cruise O'Brien) and the writer Dorothy McArdle.

[26] Letters to the editor, Irish Press and Irish Times, 01.05.1936.

[27] See the standard work in English on the subject - Paul Preston, The Spanish Holocaust. Inquisition and Extermination in Twentieth-Century Spain, London 2012, here pp. xi-xx.

between the revolutions of March and November 1917, a social revolution took grip in the impoverished regions in the South, tit-for-tat killings in the cities were daily occurrences and the Church and its servants, as in all Spanish revolts, were targeted. Many local "scores" were settled with unpopular employers or hated large landowners. In 1936, Spain had over 115,000 clergy, of whom 45,000 were nuns. Thirty per cent of the monks and 18 per cent of lay clergy were killed in the Republican areas. The fatalities for nuns numbered 296 (1.3 per cent). In all, at least 8,000 priests, monks and nuns were murdered.[28] The greater part of these atrocities, which were linked to the destruction of churches and sacred objects, had ceased by the end of 1936. Foreigners found it difficult to understand the depth of popular hatred against the Spanish church, forgetting their forefathers, too, had taken the New Testament seriously, like English Protestants who harkened after a golden, pre-feudalist age before the Normans and before Church and State in England became one. "The anger of the Spanish Anarchist against the Church", one long-term English resident in Spain wrote, "is the anger of an intensely religious people who felt they have been deserted and deceived."[29] The Spanish poor resented the symbiosis of Church and monarchy and the reactionary stance of Spain's episcopacy in social questions, especially its monopoly of the education system.

When Franco's coup was staged in mid-July, the Spanish Government consisted entirely of middle-class men, Left or Right Republicans, who had neither the requisite energy nor the authority to pursue the war effectively or restore public order. Following the formation of a new administration by Largo Caballero in September and a new cabinet which included six socialists, two communists, five bourgeois leaders (and later two anarchists), steps were taken to clamp down on the executions squads of the worker militias. It is therefore inaccurate to speak, then or later, of a "Communist" government. It was an anti-fascist coalition to the end, even if the Spanish Communist Party (PCE) gained in influence, especially in the army, largely because of its members' discipline and Soviet aid. When violent incidents committed by the left were being carried out from the February 1936 elections onwards, the Communists, having won only 14 of the

[28] Ibid., p. 235.
[29] Gerald Brenan, The Spanish Labyrinth. An Account of the Social and Political Background to the Spanish Civil War, Cambridge, 1976 edition, pp. 188-197, here p. 189.

473 Cortes seats, were a minor political group and dwarfed in electoral terms by the Socialists, and by the anarchists in numbers of militants.[30]

Most Irish people knew little about Spain, apart from romanticised history from Elizabethan times, lyrically if somewhat inappropriately expressed in the line "and Spanish ale shall give you hope" by James Clarence Mangan ("My Dark Rosaleen"). Conditions in that country – 50 per cent illiteracy on the land, half that figure in the big cities[31] and appalling under-employment and unemployment among hundreds of thousands of landless peasants mainly in the South – resembled those of rural Ireland in the 18th Century and should have awoken sympathy for the Spanish poor in the Irish electorate. But in the propaganda battle in Ireland, the febrile emotions on the clerical side concentrated on atrocities against the Church to the exclusion of everything else.

A new organization, the Irish Christian Front (ICF), founded in August 1936, mobilized Irish Catholics against "godless Spain". Its leading figures were the renegade Fianna Fáil TD (Member of Irish Parliament) Patrick Belton, now a Fine Gael (FG) deputy and a wealthy builder and farmer in his own right, and Alex McCabe, an ex-TD from Sligo. McCabe was a supporter of O'Duffy's lunatic fringe party during WW2 and was interned for two years, while Belton, a pronounced anti-Semite and supporter of Italian fascism, lost his Dáil seat in July 1937 to a Labour candidate. Their enterprise flourished for a while, bringing massive crowds on to the streets of Dublin (30 August, 25 October) and Cork (20 September), whipping up an atmosphere of frenzy in which hecklers or opponents were in danger of their lives. However, the inaugural meeting in Waterford in late September was a damp squib – seven priests and two lay persons attended.[32] Less than two weeks later, however, more than 10,000 assembled in Ballybricken for an ICF rally and were welcomed by the president of the trades council.[33]

In Limerick city in late July, Fr. Fox of the Redemptorists, as he told the members of the Arch-Confraternity, was worried about manifestations of

---

[30] Hugh Thomas, The Spanish Civil War, 3rd edition, London 1977, pp. 156-157.
[31] Ibid., p. 56.
[32] McGarry, Irish Politics and the Spanish Civil War, p. 117.
[33] Emmet O'Connor, A Labour History of Waterford, Waterford Trades Council 1989, p. 241.

"paganism": mixed bathing on "the Shannon contiguous to the city".[34] However, Spain soon became the main theme of Catholic correspondents, with labour circles positioning themselves unequivocally in the divine camp. Limerick Trades Council passed a motion condemning the Spanish church burnings,[35] a stance that soon received the blessing of the Confraternity fathers.[36] Members of the ATGWU working in a clerical capacity for the ESB at Ardnacrusha disaffiliated from their British-based union because of its pro-Republican attitude in the Spanish war.[37] But the limits of ICF influence emerged when it was seen to be prejudicial to civil rights or critical of de Valera's strictly neutral position in Spain, i.e. supporting Non-Intervention or refusing to give Franco's regime diplomatic recognition. At a meeting of Limerick County Council in mid-October, members, who had earlier condemned Spanish atrocities against the Church, were asked to vote in support of a motion passed by Leitrim County Council that called on the Government to take legal proceedings against the CPI and Republican Congress, in a word, to proscribe them. Fianna Fáil councillors for Co. Limerick professed their full confidence in the Government to combat subversion, with one speaker adding that Communism was practically non-existent in the country,[38] and that earlier attempts at banning it, such as the October 1931 measures, had "acted as a boomerang". The Leitrim motion was dismissed by 15 votes 8.[39]

Sean Lemass, acting for Justice Minister Gerry Boland in the Dáil on 4 November, was equally dismissive:

> The information at my disposal points to the conclusion that the Communist organization in Dublin is insignificant in numbers and influence. Nothing has come to my notice to make me think that the public interest would be served by prosecuting this organization for sedition.[40]

---

[34] Limerick Leader, 29.07.1936.

[35] Limerick Leader, 24.08.1936.

[36] Limerick Leader, 05.09.1936.

[37] Limerick Leader, 19.09.1936.

[38] The CPI had about 135 members in 1934, and this figure declined further in 1936, largely due to apathy and recruitment for the International Brigades (O'Connor, Reds and the Green, pp. 194, 214).

[39] Limerick Leader, 24.10.1936.

[40] http://oireachtasdebates.oireachtas.ie/debates%20authoring/debateswebpack.nsf/takes/dail193611 0400016?opendocument. Accessed 10.04.2014. Lemass and his Cabinet colleagues were

Limerick was one of the few areas in the country where a Labour TD (member of parliament), the railway carpenter Michael Keyes, stood on a platform of the ICF. On a wet Sunday, 15 November 1936, the mayor and Fianna Fáil Deputy Dan Bourke, and nine other councilors, alongside the notables from the Chamber of Commerce, faced a large crowd that stretched from Tait's Clock to the British Legion Memorial in Pery Square. Keyes, while asking for public support for Belton's front, deftly drew attention to Irish social conditions which were "a disgrace to humanity".[41] Some drenched listeners might have asked themselves why Limerick's leading Blueshirts or ICF propagandists from Dublin were suddenly showing such concern for Limerick's labouring classes, whom all speakers expressly addressed.[42]

On the eve of the Christian Front mass-meeting, there had been another bad-tempered debate in Limerick County Council about Spain. Referring to a motion passed in the chamber three years before calling on the Government to ban the recently inaugurated CPI, a Fine Gael speaker proposed a motion of support for Franco's troops "who are nobly, unselfishly and heroically fighting on behalf of Christianity and morality". His opponents, obviously annoyed at the prospect of another fruitless wrangle, alleged that the ploy was really an attack on the Government's foreign policy. The FG motion was defeated by 17 votes to 10.[43] The refusal of Republican councilors to be stampeded into advocating any interference into Spanish affairs aroused the ire of the Canon of St. Munchin's. He reminded readers of Spanish aid against "wicked Queen Bess of England", insulted the council as a whole (""the learned and refined County Council of Limerick") and two councillors by name.[44] However, some Church dignitaries were uncomfortable with the politicisation of religion, as one Tipperary Canon wrote anonymously to the *Limerick Leader.*[45]

Speakers from outside were brought to Limerick in order to keep the campaign of hysteria and misinformation about contemporary events in Iberia on the boil, or at least simmering. On the last day of November, in the Grand Central Cinema,

---

criticized for this neutralist stance in a leading article in „The Kilkenny Journal" (14.11.1936). Lemass passed on the cutting to the Dept. of Justice (NAI, JUS 8/426).
[41] Limerick Leader, 21.11.1936.
[42] Limerick Leader, 16.11.1936.
[43] Limerick Leader, 21.11.1936.
[44] Ibid.
[45] Limerick Leader, 28.11.1936.

at least somebody with experience of Spain spoke: Fr. Stenson, a former Vice-Rector of the Irish College in Salamanca. Giving a highly partisan précis of Spain's history (the invading Moslems had turned Spain into a "brothel"), Stenson saw the root of all modern Spanish evil in the machinations of the Masonic lodges, especially since the establishment of the Republic in 1931.[46] Here he was in agreement with Church doctrine since the 1790s. However, Free Masonry on the Continent owed much to the egalitarian aspirations of the French Revolution, while in Ireland it was seen as a Protestant plot or network to hobble Catholic businesses. Many Spanish politicians since the 19th century were Masons, usually anti-clerical and anti-religious. The Army, moreover, was honeycombed with Masonic lodges since the 1820s, and even three of Franco's leading generals were Free Masons.[47]

One month later, at a lecture sponsored by the Young Ireland Hurling Club and presided over by the chairman of the Limerick GAA Board, Fr. P.G. Byrne, an Augustinian priest, imparted very definite views to his listeners in the Savoy Cinema. He held the Spanish Government responsible for the outrages against the clergy, stated that Franco's rising was justified and upbraided the Irish Government for not recognizing the Franco military dictatorship in Burgos.[48] The latter point of criticism was one of the reasons for the relatively rapid demise of Ireland's Christian Front. Belton's increasing criticism of de Valera made many shy off. Most leading politicians and prominent Church men steered clear of involvement in or with an organization without statutes or elected leadership. The ICF was gradually perceived as a political racket, a cranks' ramp, for which the description "politicised religion is the last refuge of a scoundrel" seems apt. Arguably it was the ignominious return of O'Duffy's *bandera* from Spain in June 1937, and the news that the bulk of the money collected in late 1936 in Irish parishes for the Franco regime (£43,331) had ended up in the pocket of Paddy Belton, that finished off the ICF as an influential force in Irish politics.[49] A final factor, difficult to quantify, was images of the dead women and children killed in fascist air-raids on Madrid, Guernica and Barcelona published in newspapers or shown in cinema newsreels.

---

[46] Limerick Leader, 05.12.1936.
[47] Thomas, Spanish Civil War, pp. 13, 43.
[48] Limerick Leader, 14.12.1936.
[49] McGarry, Irish Politics and the Spanish Civil War, pp. 125-134.

What made the Spanish Civil War a lasting episode in Irish history was not so much the propaganda or the mass-meetings of concerned Catholics but rather the participation of political enemies on both sides in the Spanish conflict. In August Cardinal McRory, rather prematurely and unilaterally, promised a Franco emissary that the Church would help to raise a volunteer force to fight for the Spanish insurgents.[50] Over 600 subsequently sailed to Spain, returning in discord half a year later. Placing Eoin O'Duffy, Ireland's best-known fascist, as expeditionary corps commander was an additional challenge to Irish republicans and anti-fascists. In November the Left began recruiting for volunteers to aid the Spanish Republic, and Frank Ryan was to lead the first group from Ireland to Spain. They left Ireland two weeks before Christmas 1936.

From Elton to España: Frank Ryan 1902-1936

As a historical figure Frank Ryan enjoys iconic status. He is seen as a sort of Gaelic hero who died far from his native land under sad and mysterious circumstances. Ryan was immensely popular during the period 1923-36, an IRA activist, as able with the pen as with the loud-hailer or microphone, a striking figure in Dublin at a time when mass-meetings were common. Ryan was over average height, broad-shouldered with an upright shock of dark hair that made him stand out in a crowd. He was often in the thick of street battles with cane in hand, at the head of marchers trying to break through police-cordons. Ryan was courageous, a natural leader of men, but he was also well-liked by women because, apart from his good looks, he organized *ceilis* under the auspices of *Conradh na Gaeilge*, in which he was a prominent figure. With close friends he liked to ramble in the Dublin Mountains, adjourning to a friend's house afterwards, or to the pub for a pint.[51] Proinnsias, as some of his friends called him, retained a strong sense of loyalty to the IRA even after leaving it in 1934. Frank Ryan knew many Irish communists, shared some of their views but never showed an interest in "signing up". He said as much in a lecture at Mrs Despard's Workers' College in 1932:

> *He urged the need for a new revolutionary party in Ireland. He would not belong to a Communist party because in his mind Communism meant*

---

[50] Ibid., Part I, Chapter 1 and Part II, Chapter 5.
[51] C.S. Andrews, Man of No Property, Dublin, 2001 edition, p. 72.

ignoring Ireland and concentrating on certain aims to the exclusion of national aspirations.[52]

As is the experience of all intelligent political activists, Frank Ryan refined his views over time, seeing the complete liberation of Ireland in a world-wide framework, in the global struggle against British Imperialism. Coupled with his militant anti-imperialism was a growing interest in socialism, but he seems never to have had any great interest in Marx, or in the writings of Lenin and Stalin for that matter. Like many hard-core IRA men before and since, Ryan gradually realized that "the gun" was not the solution to win an All-Ireland republic: the movement had to "politicise" itself and reject the arid abstentionism of Sinn Fein after the secession of de Valera and his supporters in 1926. While de Valera and most of his admirers finally embraced constitutionalism, Ryan was reluctant to follow suit, hoping for a regrouping of Republican radicals and Marxists in a joint effort, if not at revolution, then at least to push Fianna Fáil to the left.

The organization which gave Ryan an insight into anti-colonial struggles and the opportunity to exchange views with like-minded foreigners was the Comintern-sponsored League Against Imperialism (LAI, 1927-1935). He attended, with Donal O'Donoghue, an executive meeting of the organization in Brussels in December 1927 and held an anti-imperialist rally in Dublin the following August. Peadar O'Donnell and Sean McBride were present at the LAI Second World Congress in Frankfurt-am-Main in July 1929.[53] In Frankfurt, O'Donnell spoke at the gathering and met the German students Helmut Clissmann and Jupp Hoven.[54] Hoven later founded the *Jung Preussischer Bund*, a grouping that had split from more right-wing German paramilitary bodies and positioned itself at the end of the Weimar Republic on the left, supporting the candidacy of the Communist leader Ernst Thälmann at the German Presidential Election in Spring 1932. The motivation of Clissmann and Hoven (and his brothers) to interest themselves in the "Celtic" minorities of Western Europe was in all probability the highly contested annexation of the "lost cantons" of Malmedy, Eupen and Sankt Vith to Belgium as a result of the Versailles Treaty of 1919.

---

[52] Irish Press, 05.12.1932.

[53] Kate O'Malley, Ireland, India and Empire. Indo-Irish Radical Connections 1919-64, Manchester 2008, pp. 31-37.

[54] Joachim Lerchenmüller, Keltischer Sprengstoff. Eine wissenschaftliche Studie über die deutsche Keltologie von 1900-1945, Tübingen 1997, pp. 322.

The area, just south of Aachen, the home area of Clissman and the Hoven brothers, had been Prussian since 1815. The League of Nations plebiscite in 1920 in the three cantons was a farce – opponents of Belgian annexation had to register with the authorities and were thereafter intimidated from questioning the incorporation of the area into the Belgian state (1925).[55]

Ardnacrusha 1931. L. to R. Helmut Clissmann, Frank Ryan, Victor Hoven, Heinz Hoven

Clissman and Hoven came to Ireland on a private visit in 1930/31 and befriended Frank Ryan. Clissmann later studied history at TCD, returning to Ireland again as an academic exchange student and teacher of German. Both played a major role in rescuing Ryan from Burgos Prison in 1940, and in looking after him subsequently. The Irish section of the LAI was clearly dominated by left-wing Republicans, who organized the anti-Poppy demonstrations under this internationalist banner. Fianna Fáil ministers also showed in interest in struggles within the British Empire, especially India. In July 1932 de Valera met V.J. Patel, Gandhi's "second commander", for two long meetings, and leading Republicans, including Frank Ryan visited him in his hotel. Patel was guest speaker at a public

---

[55] Ina Schmidt/Stefan Breuer/Ernst Jünger/Friedrich Hielscher (eds), Briefe von Ernst Jünger 1917-1985, Stuttgart 2005, pp. 386-387.

meeting organized by the LAI in College Green.[56] Subhas Chandra Bose, who would recruit an army to fight on the side of the Japanese against the British in World War 2, visited Dublin in February 1936. He met the Lord Mayor, Government ministers and Labour leaders. Frank Ryan welcomed him at a meeting of the Universities Republican Club and at a banquet in the Shelbourne Hotel.[57]

Westland Row church 1931. First row from right Helmut Clissmann, Jupp Hoven. Second row, first right Frank Ryan

Despite his varied interests, Frank Ryan was a "traditionalist" in the importance he attached to the restoration of the Irish language, and for his interest in the GAA. And while very young he organized the misguided disruption of Sean O'Casey's *Plough and the Stars* at the Abbey Theatre in 1926.[58] In fact, the three leading men on the Republican left in interwar Ireland – Ryan, Peadar O'Donnell and George Gilmore – were strong individualists with different scales of priorities. Although he could speak Irish from childhood, O'Donnell was not a

---

[56] O'Malley, Ireland, India, pp. 65-74.
[57] Ibid., pp. 90-104.
[58] McGarry, Frank Ryan, p. 14. Todd Andrews, Ryan's friend and an equally implacable Republican at the time, disapproved of the disturbances. See his second volume of autobiography: Andrews, Man of No Property, Dublin, 2001 edition, pp. 49-52.

language "enthusiast", nor was Gilmore. O'Donnell often dropped out of activities to write, having the financial backing of his rich wife Lile who ran a nursing home in Dublin. He seems to have been a Communist party member in the early 1920s, and while no longer a card-carrying cadre later, remained close to Moscow's disciples – the secretary of the CPI, Sean Murray, was his closest friend. George Gilmore, one of three Protestant brothers from South Dublin, shared a long IRA record with Ryan and O'Donnell, but he never joined the CPI, although his diction and writings would suggest otherwise. Ryan differed from the others in that he refused to relegate Pearse in his pantheon to the advantage of Connolly. As a "street-fighting man" Ryan was arguably the better known of the trio in Dublin's vibrant street life.

So Ryan had an unusual amalgam of public personae, for he was also a learned man though not an intellectual in the accepted sense, a gifted publicist and speaker, talents he shared with O'Donnell. For all that, Frank Ryan was primarily a man of action, a tireless organizer but who was also vociferously intolerant of those he deemed to be his enemies. There is no denying that he was a "hard man" with a strong militaristic instinct, willing to put his well-being, his health, even his life, at risk for what he believed in. Few men are built like that, and it is difficult to see Frank Ryan as a conventional politician if fate would have made such a role possible.

Ryan grew up in the shadows of the Galtee Mountains, in the triangle where the counties of Cork, Limerick and Tipperary meet.[59] Born at Bottomstown, Elton, near Knocklong, on 11 September 1902, Frank was the fifth and last son of nine children. His father Vere Foster Ryan had met his future wife Annie Slattery when both were teaching in Clare, her home county. Two of Frank's brothers, Maurice and Vincent, studied medicine and emigrated to Yorkshire and Liverpool, respectively. The eldest son, Jeremiah Joseph, studied to be a teacher like his parents. Another brother, John, emigrated to the USA, where he died of bronchial trouble in 1932. Of the four sisters three became nuns. Catherine, the fourth child and four years older than Frank, was his favourite. She also fell prey to TB, dying in 1937. The youngest child, Eilís, who also suffered from lung trouble as a child, received a university education financed by her parents on the

---

[59] This account of Frank Ryan's childhood is based on an interview given by Eilís Ryan to Aodh Ó Canainn, published in Saothar, 21, 1996, pp. 129-143.

understanding that they could come and live with her on retirement. This was not unusual in rural Ireland, since the "master" lost his rented house on reaching pension age. Before moving to Dublin in 1937, the old couple lived with their eldest son Jeremiah Joseph at 6, Lower Mallow Street in Limerick city.[60]

Eilís, who never married, became the family chronicler. Frank suggested she drop her childhood name Lizzie/Elizabeth for the Irish version and insisting on conversing with her in Irish only. The Ryan parents belonged to the aspiring nationalist middle-class, kept a servant girl and imparted a love of learning to their children. Vere Foster Ryan and his wife Annie held fairly conventional political views, admiring Parnell and hoping for a Home Rule settlement. None of Frank's siblings seem to have been actively involved in politics, and Eilís, who was in Cumann na mBan, stated that their strict father, while not approving, "always backed Frank up".

Frank Ryan had to battle with a physical disability from an early age: impaired hearing. The origin was probably some contagious illness and his mother noticed it when teaching her sons to play the piano. He had specialist attention and his condition improved, but deteriorated during his internment in 1922/23. He learned to lip-read and could "hear perfectly well on the phone, in a train or a tram or amid the noise of traffic."[61] Frank sometimes preferred not to hear what he was being told or asked to do, and seemed to some to be a detached onlooker, wrapped in his own silent world. Cearbhall Ó Dalaigh, a contemporary of Frank Ryan at university remembers:

> [He was] *very gentle and gently spoken, somewhat of an aristocrat in its best sense, a military bearing, warm, yet aloof. A Sir Galahad. He had an easy charm.*[62]

After primary school Frank was sent to St. Colman's College in Fermoy, Co. Cork, the secondary school for the Diocese of Cloyne and a strong hurling nursery. Believing he had a vocation for the Church, his parents transferred him to Rockwell College. Ryan's sojourn among the Holy Ghost Fathers was short: he

---

[60] At least in 1931/32. See Limerick City electoral list (pdf, p. 152):
http://www.limerickcity.ie/Library/LocalStudies/RegistersofElectors/ScannedRegistersofElectorsforLimerickCity1931to1950/Thefile,9539,en.pdf
[61] Michael McInerney, Frank Ryan Profile - 1, Irish Times, 07.04.1975.
[62] Ibid.

complained about the food, organised a strike and was expelled. The priests at St. Colman's took back the popular pupil. One of the teachers, Fr. Roche, infected the returnee with his strong Republican convictions, and Frank and his brother Maurice would clamber over the school wall at night and drill with the local IRA. Whether Frank was also a member of the local IRA unit around Elton before the Truce, or if he took part in any military action prior to that, is open to dispute.[63]

Ryan matriculated, entering UCD in the autumn of 1921 to study Irish on a scholarship from Limerick County Council. In the summer holidays he was attached to the Elton Company of the IRA, and rejecting the Treaty, took up arms around the time of the siege of Kilmallock in late July-early August 1922. According to Sean Cronin, his first biographer, Ryan's unit ran into a Free State Army patrol in the Knockmealdown Mountains and he was wounded in a brief fire-fight and captured.[64] While a prisoner in Knocklong creamery, Frank was allowed see his favourite sister Catherine who was leaving home to enter a convent. After a spell in Limerick Gaol, the prisoners were brought to Cork and thence to Dublin by sea. Interned in Hare Park, Curragh Camp, from 29 November 1922,[65] Frank brought out an Irish-language paper for his fellow-prisoners, and he was released one year later almost to the day.

At least 12,000 Republicans were interned during the Civil War. That is sizeable number of radicals in a country with a small population, embittered men who did not all emigrate. Their hatred of the Cosgrave government focused on the 77 official executions (73 after trial by military tribunal) and extra-judicial killings by Free State forces, especially in Kerry, Dublin and Sligo. That this abhorrence was shared by many is one of the reasons why abstentionist Sinn Fein did surprisingly well and won 44 seats at the August 1923 General Election. The Government party, Cumann na nGaedheal, achieved a disappointing 63 seats.

Ryan resumed his studies at UCD (Limerick County Council restored his scholarship) and graduated with a M.A. in Celtic Studies in 1925. He was active in UCD Republican Club, the university IRA Company, and in Conradh na Gaeilge. Like other young Irishmen, Ryan feared his parents' admonitions that he

---

[63] McGarry, Frank Ryan, p. 4.
[64] Sean Cronin, Frank Ryan. The Search for The Republic, Dublin 1980, pp. 20-21.
[65] Irish Military Archives, Prisoners' Location Index Books CW/P/01/01 and 02

had not got a "steady job". He dropped the idea of teaching, after failing an interview for a post because he could not hear the interviewer's questions, and following his sacking from Mountjoy School because of involvement in a riot on "Poppy Day" 1926 – he was to the forefront in tearing down Union Jacks.[66]

Since Frank Ryan was a principal actor in these protests for over ten years, it is worthwhile breaking the chronology in order to go into the 11 November marches and riots in some detail. The annual armistice commemorations in Dublin, in particular the marching of ex-soldiers in military formation and the use of military commands by men using their former British Army officer rank, was a source of annoyance to both Republicans and the authorities. The flaunting of the Union Jack from buildings, by spectators, its display in shop windows and on motor vehicles always provoked violent response. In 1924, a British Legion meeting in College Green had resulted in a mass brawl.

The following year the police directed the closing meeting of the British Legion to the junction of Lower Leeson Street and St. Stephen's Green, just a stone's throw away from UCD in Earlsfort Terrace. Republican students, including Frank Ryan, infiltrated the crowd, letting off stink-bombs. The outnumbered students were retiring towards the university when C.S. (Todd) Andrews, one of few republican militants in UCD, was confronted by a revolver-wielding man, whom he struck and disarmed. It turned out that Andrews's victim was a C.I.D. detective, but honour was saved on all sides because of the intervention of the College President, Dr. Coffey: the policeman got his weapon back, while Andrews, Ryan and a third student were released, no charges being proffered.[67] By 1928, the situation had escalated to such an extent that Colonel Neligan of the Special Branch, the very real bogey-man of Frank Ryan and his friends, wrote to Garda Commissioner O'Duffy:

> The "commemoration" is becoming the excuse for a regular military field-day for these persons. I direct our attention to the formation of companies under persons calling themselves Captain and Majors, and the companies are going to march in military formation … if the Irregulars [IRA] adopted

[66] McGarry, Frank Ryan, pp. 16-17.
[67] Andrews, Man of No Property, pp. 54-56.

these tactics they would be arrested under the Treasonable Offences Act, 1925.[68]

Commissioner Eoin O'Duffy concurred, expressing concern that the presence of Baden Powell boy scouts in the Legion ranks provoked *Fianna Éireann*, the youth section of the IRA, to follow suit. O'Duffy was also worried by the prospect of British *fascisti* joining the British Legion columns.[69] His misgivings were justified in that some column commanders overdid the use of British Army drill commands in, for example, Ennis:

> *The Armistice parade ... was a definite Imperialistic display, and not a Commemoration to the War dead, as it ought to have been. The continuance of exhibitions of this kind which are hateful in the eyes of nine tenths of the people will undoubtedly court trouble...I respectfully beg to renew my recommendation to have permission for such displays refused in future years.*[70]

In Dublin the 1928 marches went off comparatively peacefully, due to strong police cordons and C.I.D. intelligence. The Dublin IRA under George Gilmore, however, landed two coups: the blowing up of the "King Billy" statue in College Green, now the site of the Thomas Davis sculpture ensemble ("Urination Once Again"), and of a memorial to King Edward VIII in Herbert Park.[71] The 1929 commemorations were prefaced by the destruction of the British Legion hall in Inchicore by a bomb.[72] Frank Ryan's best-known "Poppy Day" protest speech was in 1932, when the IRA was in an exuberant mood following the defeat of Cumann na nGaedheal, and before relations between the IRA and de Valera's administration soured. Once again Commissioner O'Duffy was expecting an "imperialistic display" and he recommended to the Minister for Justice (Gerry Boland) that the carrying of Union Jacks should be banned, and the wearing of Union Jack badges on the part of "Poppy" sellers who should be allowed to ply their wares on two days only. He found particularly offensive the waving of

---

[68] NAI, JUS 8/684, Neligan to Commissioner, 07.11.1928.
[69] Ibid., Commissioner to the Secretary, Dept. of Justice, 08.11.1928.
[70] Ibid., Chief Superintendent, Ennis, to Commissioner „C", 12.11.1928.
[71] Ibid., Chief Superintendent to Secretary Dept. of Justice, 21.11.1928
[72] Ibid., Runaidhe to Secretary, Dept. of Defence, 09.11.1929.

Union Jacks by spectators (often young girls) and the singing of "God Save the King" at the end of the two minutes silence for the Great War dead.[73]

In 1932, the protestors against "Poppy Day" erected two platforms in the open street spaces near TCD. Over 150 Gardai were present, monitoring a crowd of about 15,000.[74] The speeches were triumphalist and belligerent. Peadar O'Donnell saw the situation in Ireland in Bolshevik terms (the Army Comrades' Association being the "White Army"), and Frank Ryan harangued the crowd with a tirade that became infamous:

> *No matter what anybody says to the contrary, while we have hands, fists and boots to use, and guns if necessary, there will be no free speech for traitors.*[75]

Rosamund Jacob's description of Ryan on the platform puts one in mind of Cúchullain in of his "battle frenzies":

> *I never heard him so fierce … he got into 2 or 3 rages, and roared as if he must be heard to the far edge of the throng, which was huge (they had an amplifier) and he has a powerful voice. It seemed perfectly spontaneous, a sort of real battle fury that grew and burst, and it was nearly frightening to hear him. He seemed to swell up and get taller and broader …*[76]

Ryan did show sympathy for the ex-soldiers ("Those men fought for an ideal"), but the emotions he aroused prompted some at the end of the meeting to carry out cowardly attacks against people wearing poppies: a bus conductor and four young people, two of whom were female.[77] In 1934 and 1935, Frank Ryan was active in organizing speeches and parades in co-operation with ex-serviceman, concentrating on their plight, such as slum conditions and unemployment. There was a consensus that attacks on British Legion parades were counter-productive.[78] At the 1936 "Poppy" protest meeting, the last Frank Ryan was to attend, listeners had fallen to about 600, a sign of the marginalization of the Left. His remarks demonstrate that he had matured further in his attitude to ex-participants in the Great War:

---

[73] Ibid., Eoin Ua Dubhaigh to the Minister, memorandum, 21.09.1932.
[74] Ibid., G. Brennan to Commissioner, 15.11.1932.
[75] Irish Independent, 11.11.1932.
[76] McGarry, Frank Ryan, p. 17.
[77] Irish Times, 11.11.1932.
[78] Irish Press, 12.11.1934, 11.11.1935.

I ask you to give the benefit of the doubt to those who wear poppies tomorrow. Many will wear them in memory of dear friends who were deluded into dying for fine ideals in a horrible capitalist war. Respect them for their love of their people. I would condemn in the strongest terms any attacks on these people by those who, by attempting to be patriots, merely make themselves thugs.[79]

The efforts of Frank Ryan to find a steady job after rejecting teaching as a career were difficult. Todd Andrews, who remembers Ryan as "always penniless", organized a position for him with the Irish Travel Association in 1928. This predecessor of *Bord Fáilte* brought out a periodical funded from advertisements, but Ryan was put to work on a book, *Guide to Ireland*. It slowly dawned on Andrews that Ryan was a leading IRA man (he was adjutant to the Dublin Brigade) so he warned his friend not to use the office as a depot for IRA documents. Ryan did not follow this advice. C.I.D. man Peter Ennis, on a lightning raid in October, uncovered a cache of papers in Ryan's room at work. The affair descended into a farce, when Ennis came back after his lunch and asked Andrews to confirm that Ryan had admitted that the documents were his. Andrews denied ever having heard such a thing. Ryan was arrested but released after a night in the cells because there were no impartial witnesses.[80] A prosecution did, however, take place. Faced with the charge of membership in the IRA, Ryan denied it and refused to recognize the court. The jury disagreed and Ryan remained in custody in Mountjoy Gaol until the second trial in February 1929. Ryan defended himself, and Superintendent Ennis was without a witness to confirm that he had found the documents and not planted them in Ryan's desk. The verdict was an acquittal.[81]

Ryan spoke amiably with Ennis and his hard-bitten detectives after the trial.[82] The Limerick man was not a good hater, despite his Republican bombast or the rough handling he was subjected to on resisting arrest. The C.I.D. had little time for sentimentality and arrested Ryan several times in December 1929 and then released him – a "cat and mouse tactic" used against several Republicans in order to induce their employers to sack them. The tactic misfired after compensation

---

[79] Irish Press, 11.11.1936.
[80] Andrews, Man of No Property, pp. 71-72.
[81] McGarry, Frank Ryan, pp. 19-20; Cronin, Frank Ryan, p. 24.
[82] McGarry, Frank Ryan, p. 7.

claims from the aggrieved and criticism of police methods by sensible judges. Ryan was thus acquitted, again, in 1930.[83]

With his career as a tourism writer terminated, Frank Ryan's financial worries eased in 1929, when he was appointed as successor to Peadar O'Donnell as editor of *An Phoblacht*. As a Staff Captain attached to GHQ, Ryan received a salary. It was probably meagre because the newspaper, although successful – 8,000 printed copies in January 1930, a highpoint of over 25,000 in May 1932, before falling to 11,000 in January 1934 – swallowed around 50 per cent of the organisation's total expenses, up to £1,500 a year.[84] The C.I.D. were frequent visitors to the paper's printers, Fodhla Printing Works in Rutland Place, during the crackdown against the IRA in autumn 1931, seizing copies and visiting wholesale newsagents to stop distribution.[85] On entering his office in St. Andrews Street on 8 December, Frank Ryan was accosted by detectives and led away after a fracas.[86]

He faced the Military Tribunal set up under the recently passed Article 2A of the Constitution on four charges (membership of the IRA; publishing a seditious article; refusing to give information on IRA weapons, ammunition and documents; refusing to give information on his association with proscribed left-wings groups). Because Ryan refused to plead on 13 January, he was found guilty of contempt and sentenced to three months' detention, with the prospect of a heavier sentence once his trial had been completed.[87] Arbour Hill was a notorious military "glass house" where prisoners were kept in solitary confinement and without reading matter. Seventeen IRA men were incarcerated. George Gilmore was naked in his cell, save for a blanket, because he refused to wear prison garb. Ryan went on partial hunger strike against the brutal treatment at the hands of the hated military policemen. Then fate intervened in the shape of Frank Aiken, the Minister for Defence in the new government, who visited the prisoners individually on 9 March. All were freed the next day and feted by a huge crowd in College Green.[88] Eilís remembers the celebrations:

---

[83] Ibid., p. 20-21.
[84] Hanley, The IRA, p. 53.
[85] Irish Press, 11.09.1931.
[86] Irish Press, 09.12.1931.
[87] NAI, TSCH S 2863, Attorney General vs. Frank Ryan (includes lists of the prisoners).
[88] Cronin, Frank Ryan, pp. 40-42.

They came out looking green in the face, they'd been on hunger-strike. We went to a céilí that night and he [Frank] asked me to dance. He wasn't able to stand up, he was that weak. My aunt in Kilfenora brought him down there for about ten days. She gave him so much to eat, eggs and everything, it put new life in him.[89]

The euphoria that came with liberation did not last. The IRA could not agree on a strategy towards Fianna Fail, the leadership settling for the supposition that if extra-parliamentary Republicans supported de Valera, he would not hinder their military expansion. Events would show, however, that de Valera would tolerate only one army in the State. One of the most prescient observers of this fragile relationship was George Gilmore. He tried to resign from the Army Council as early as September 1932 with the argument that anti-Free State opinion was now "hopelessly pro-Dev" and that Fianna Fáil would "hold the field for a long time to come", adding that there was little the IRA could do about it. Equally farseeing was his opinion that the IRA "were in for a pretty hard time".

At the January 1933 Extraordinary Army Convention, Gilmore, Ryan and O'Donnell were defeated in their attempt to radicalize the rank-and-file for political action.[90] Ryan resigned the editorship of *An Phoblacht* in April, and his deputy, Hannah Sheehy-Skeffington, relinquished her position a week later.[91] The reason for the double éclat was Army Council interference, even the dictation to Ryan of the contents of the leading article.[92]

After a long break, Ryan received short-lived employment as director of organisation in *Fianna Éireann*[93] before the final organisational, if not emotional, break with the IRA after the next Army Convention, held in a ballet school on St. Stephen's Green on St. Patrick's Day 1934. Ryan and his friends had canvassed many IRA commanders in advance of the assembly and would have won a slight majority in favour of a radical social programme had not the votes of Executive and Army Council officers tipped the balance.[94]

---

[89] Interview, Saothar 1996, p. 134.
[90] Hanley, IRA, p. 130.
[91] Irish Press, 22.04.1933.
[92] Cronin, Frank Ryan, p. 46.
[93] Irish Press, 30.01.1934, 19.03.1934.
[94] J. Bowyer Bell, The Secret Army. A History of the IRA 1916-1970, London 1970, pp. 112-115.

The defeated gathered at Athlone on 7-8 April, without the participation of delegates from Munster who could not be contacted in time. A "call" was issued in favour of a worker-small farmer-small trader alliance against Irish capitalism. The argument was basically that the IRA had failed to support the majority of the population suffering from the economic distress.[95] Calling themselves Irish Republican Congress and issuing a periodical of the same name, the dissidents who had either resigned or had been expelled by the IRA met in Rathmines Town Hall on 29-30 September 1934, together with like-minded trade unionists. The delegates, however, knew beforehand that the "Organising Bureau", while agreeing on the objective (workers' and small farmers' republic) was split on how to reach that goal: a new Workers' Republican Party or a United Front of all "progressive" forces. There was a vote taken on the two resolutions, the "frontists" winning by 14 votes.[96] The losers rejuvenated the Irish Citizen Army and later joined the Labour Party, while the upholders of a broad alliance took to agitation on slum dwellings, strikes and the plight of the landless.[97] Meanwhile, clashes between IRA men and the Blueshirts were daily occurrences, even though the IRA had banned its members from taking part in such actions. Article 2a of the Constitution was revived in August 1933 and Arbour Hill began to fill up with civilian prisoners once more.

Frank Ryan, one of the tireless Congress activists and the editor of its paper, took no part in the anti-Blueshirt riots. Indeed, even before he left the IRA, in a speech at Naas in October 1933, he implied that violence against the O'Duffyites was counter-productive:

> *We Irish people are too soft-hearted. We do not prosecute traitors, on the contrary we protect them. That thing was done down at Killmallock* [the Irish Free State Army had to be called out to separate supporters of the IRA and the Army Comrades' Association[98]], *when these people calling themselves the 'White Army'– white to the 'gills'– had to be protected from*

---

[95] Irish Press, 10.04.1934.

[96] See: George Gilmore, The Republican Congress (New York 1935), reprinted by The Cork Workers' Club, 1974, 1987, especially pp. 45-57.

[97] Brian Hanley, „The Irish Citizen Army after 1916", Saothar 28, 2003, pp. 37-47.

[98] The incident took place on 9 October 1932, and 31 rioters were charged, including two leading Blueshirts for drawing revolvers (Limerick Chronicle, 04.02.1933).

the people by the military. That is a hopeful sign, but these people are getting far too much publicity and the people should ignore them.[99]

Congress managed to find some support in Belfast, but, as is well-known, when a Congress delegation from the North carried a banner at the Bodenstown commemoration in 1934, they were set upon by southern IRA men ordered to enforce a "no banners" remembrance meeting. The Bodenstown fracas repeated itself in 1935.[100]

His estrangement from the IRA did not prevent Frank Ryan from protesting about conditions for Republican men held in Arbour Hill, especially the suicide there of a fellow-Limerick man Sean Glynn.[101] In two campaigns Ryan interceded on behalf of Congress activists, some of whom he would later take to Spain. For supporting the workers in the labour dispute in O'Mara's chain of bacon shops by posting solidarity pickets, 23 Congress members were charged with besetting the premises, obstruction and threatening behavior. They were fined £5 each or a month in gaol in January 1935. Four of the group committed to serve their term in Mountjoy served in Spain: Charlie Donnelly, Denis Coady and Jack Nalty were fatalities, Eugene Downing survived.[102]

The second cause supported by Ryan was the re-instatement of Frank Edwards (another *Brigadista*) who had been sacked from his post as a primary school teacher in Waterford by Monsignor Byrne, the acting bishop, because of his leading role in the IRC.[103] Ryan was no more successful in this cause célèbre than in his general activities, working long hours for next to nothing to bring out the IRC paper. In early 1936 his health broke down. At only 33 years of age, Ryan had coronary problems which would finally kill him. He put himself in the medical care of his brother Vincent, a physician in Dewsbury, Yorkshire. Ryan's lungs, despite his heavy smoking, were in order, but his heart was enlarged and his blood pressure too high. Admonished by his brother to go easy on cigarettes and whiskey (which Frank rarely drank) and live regular hours, he returned to

---

[99] Irish Press, 31.10.1933.
[100] See the IRC protest, signed by Ryan and Gilmore in: Irish Press, 29.06.1935.
[101] Irish Press, 14.11.1935, 30.05.1936, 16.09.1936; Cronin, Frank Ryan, pp. 71-72.
[102] Irish Press, 14.01.1935.
[103] Irish Press, 23.01.1935., 26.01.1935, 19.11.1935. See the interview with Frank Edwards in: Uinseann Mac Eoin, Survivors, second edition Dublin 1987, pp. 1-20.

Dublin after Easter 1936, relieved, and perhaps scared.[104] Telling Eilís of Vincent's diagnosis, he asked, "I'm all right now, but what will I be like in ten years?"[105]

The Congress movement was foundering: a new left-wing party for workers and farmers or a broad-based Republican front. Neither slogan had a political future. At this juncture there was little place for a socialist party to the left of the Irish Labour Party, as the meagre results attained by Congress candidates at elections would show. And some kind of Republican front favoured by Irish Communists – a forerunner of the Popular Front adopted by the Communist International only in 1935 – did not make sense in Ireland: a united front against what, against a purportedly fascist movement already in decline? Apart from the leaders and ideologues harbouring extreme-right wings ideas borrowed from the Continent (primarily from "Catholic" dictators such as Salazar and Dollfuss), the foot-soldiers of the Blueshirts were more exercised by the austerities accompanying the economic war with Britain than anything else. Fianna Fáil, having shown its republican credentials by removing most of the constitutional trappings linking Ireland to the British Empire, was firmly in control by the mid-1930s, gaoling Blueshirt and IRA perpetrators of violence. The Irish Free State was a stable democracy, developing its classical three party system. The banning of the IRA in 1936 and the acceptance of the new 1937 Constitution rounded off the process of stabilisation. Indeed, a substantial left-wing republican political party was not to emerge for another ten years, with the founding of Clann na Poblachta in 1946.

In the 1930s Ryan renewed his contacts with his old alma mater. The Republican Clubs of UCD and TCD had formed a 'Student Vanguard against Fascism' in May 1934. The inaugural meeting at 41 Parnell Square was in danger of disintegrating into fisticuffs between Blueshirts, who inexplicably had been invited, and Republicans, until the 20-year-old Charlie Donnelly, soon to sit on the Executive of the IRC, took over the chair. Frank Ryan escorted the Blueshirts from the building before the real discussion started.[106] It speaks for Ryan's inherent decency that he withdrew his demand that the disrupters should leave on hearing that they had been invited:

[104] Cronin, Frank Ryan, pp. 65-66.
[105] Interview, Saothar 1996, p. 134.
[106] Joseph Donnelly, Charlie Donnelly. The Life and Poems, Dublin 1987, p. 29.

If it is a fact that all students were invited to this meeting, I admit that I was acting very discourteously in requesting any students to leave the room. On the other hand, it is absolutely absurd if it is to be understood that at an anti-Fascist meeting Fascists will be allowed. They cannot help obstructing the meeting whatever way they can.[107]

In public perception, University College Dublin was intrinsically linked for many years with Cumann na nGaedheal and its successor Fine Gael. Ryan had been banned from taking part in a debate opposing the formation of an Officers' Training Corps at the College in the late 1920s. The college club doors were closed to him again in January 1935, when the students' Cumann Gaedhealach advertised a debate on the motion that "socialism was the only solution to Irish difficulties". In a petty gesture, President Coffey banned the debate on specious grounds: the subject "was of a propagandistic nature" and Frank Ryan was not suitable as chairman because he was in dispute with the Bishop of Waterford in the Frank Edwards controversy.[108] The son of the 1916 hero "the O'Rahilly" called the ban "puerile", having "no effect other than to make the National University the laughing-stock of educated Europe".[109]

At the end February 1936, the Congress periodical ceased publication, and its successor, "The Irish People" survived only for a few issues. In the summer of 1936 Frank Ryan's employment ceased when Co-Op Printers went to the wall. The final blow had been expenses generated by the participation of Ryan and Gilmore in the Dublin local elections of June 1936, in which Gilmore had polled relatively well and Ryan badly.[110] Gilmore received 730 votes, Ryan only 418, i.e. one-fifth and one-tenth of the quota.[111] Their political programme was an incompatible strange mix for all but committed radicals: on the one hand, a call for new houses, free school books and rent-reductions, demands shared by official Labour, on the other the end to coercion against the IRA which had been banned during the Dublin canvassing after two gruesome killings.[112]

---

[107] Irish Press, 12.05.1934.
[108] Irish Press, 23.01.1935.
[109] Irish Press, 24.01.1935. The student Republican clubs also protested (Irish Press, 07.02.1935)
[110] Cronin , Frank Ryan, pp. 68-69.
[111] I thank Emmet O'Connor for the results.
[112] Irish Press, 15.06.1936, 22.06.1936, 26.06.1936, 27.06.1936.

Republican Congress was relatively slow to respond to events in Spain. In fact, it was reactive, referring to events in Ireland rather than the international aspects of fascism. In mid-September 1936, at a poorly attended Congress meeting, the text of a telegram to Largo Caballero, the Spanish premier, was formulated: it supported Catalan and Basque autonomy, but switched immediately to Irish conditions, condemning the Irish Christian Front and *The Irish Independent* as agencies of fascism. One wonders what Caballero made of this imbalanced statement of solidarity.[113]

At the time both George Gilmore and Peadar O'Donnell were in Spain. Gilmore wanted to bring over a Basque representative to Ireland. He found Fr. La Borda, and the priest spoke in Ireland in early 1937. The Irishman was fortunate to survive an air-crash in a thunder-storm near Bilboa with a broken leg. O'Donnell, on holiday in Spain with his wife, was a witness to church burnings and public executions. He was perturbed, knowing the mileage the Irish Right would get out of such lawlessness.[114] Otherwise he seems to have admired the verve and commitment of the anarchists in Barcelona, that city of the "Antichrist". Both veteran Republicans were against the suggestion to send a volunteer contingent to fight the Spanish fascists. This view was widely held in the wider Republican community in Ireland, and is not to be discounted: at a time when the Spanish authorities in the Republican Zone were just beginning to turn the undisciplined and foolhardy militia men into soldiers, Gilmore and O'Donnell had seen enough able-bodied, idle men in Spain. In any case, what Spanish Republicans needed was not untrained cannon-fodder but experts and military equipment. In its first call to its foreign sections in mid-August 1936, the Comintern urged the sending of experts, especially pilots, to the Spanish fronts; only one month later, on 18 September, were the communist parties instructed to send volunteers.[115] So even if the Republican Congress leaders had sat on their hands, the CPI would have begun recruiting.

Frank Ryan, too, was initially reluctant to commit the IRC to a Spanish expedition. He was more concerned with keeping the movement together in Ireland, and America, where forces in the Irish Republican organization *Clan na Gael* were expelling members of the IRC. Ryan was heavily criticized for his

---

[113] Irish Press, 16.09.1936.

[114] Michael McInerney, Peadar O'Donnell. Irish Social Rebel, Dublin 1974, pp. 171-175.

[115] Fridrikh Firsov, Sekretye kody istorii kominterna 1919-1943, Moscow 2007, pp.197-199.

stance on Spain by Charlie Donnelly home on holiday from Britain. The younger man, active in the London branch of Congress, had an incisive mind, was studying military strategy and saw the Spanish fascist coup primarily in a European, less in an Irish context.[116] In mid-September, Ryan still thought that "the frontline trenches of Spain are right here".[117] What pushed Frank Ryan towards commitment to Spain were the activities of the Irish Right: the ongoing preparations to send the Blueshirt contingent, which departed in November and December, and the rebukes of the Church. Ryan and his comrades took issue with a statement made by Cardinal McRory in Dundalk on 20 September that the Spanish Civil War was a struggle between communism and atheism. The Congress replied two days later in a spirited statement from Ryan:

> *We Republicans deny that religion is at stake in Spain, just as we denied –*
> *in the teeth of ecclesiastical condemnation – that religion was at stake when*
> *we were fighting in arms to defeat the Cosgrave Government in 1922-23.*
> *Our stand in 1922-23 is already vindicated; history will vindicate our*
> *stand on the Spanish question today. Finally, may I assure our Eminence*
> *that, as a Catholic, I will 'take my religion from Rome', but as an Irish*
> *Republican, I will take my politics neither from Maynooth nor Moscow.*[118]

"His Eminence" was incensed and urged the Government to proscribe Congress.[119] Recruitment for the International Brigades commenced shortly afterwards in Ireland. It was probably a joint effort between Congress and the Communists Sean Murray and Bill Gannon. The Dublin IRA supplied the majority of the first group that left Dublin with Ryan on Friday, 11 December. Chief of Staff Tom Barry banned volunteers from becoming "Wild Geese", but the injunction proved fruitless in many cases.[120] By December there were at least four Irishmen already fighting in the International Brigades which had been formed two months earlier: Bill Scott, a bricklayer from Inchicore, William ('Blue') Barry, who had come from Melbourne, Tommy Patten, from Achill (a Congress activist in London), and John Meehan from Galway.

---

[116] Donnelly, Charlie Donnelly, pp. 42-43.
[117] Cronin, Frank Ryan, p. 79.
[118] Ibid., pp. 79-80.
[119] McGarry, Frank Ryan, p.p. 45-46
[120] Bowyer Bell, Secret Army, p. 133.

Ryan tried to keep his departure a secret from his family, but Eilís, who heard rumours about his leading the group to Spain, learned from a friend that he was leaving that night. She turned up at Westland Row Station before the train to the Dunlaoghaire-Holyhead ferry left. Frank got out of the carriage, and he placed his rosary beads into her hand, saying, "Tell mother and father that I am not a 'red'. I am going to fight for democracy in Spain."[121]

He was interviewed by *The Irish Press* before leaving and gave a differentiated picture of his motivation:

> *It is the demonstration of the sympathy of revolutionary Ireland with the Spanish people in their fight against international Fascism. It is also a reply to the intervention of Irish fascism in the war against the Spanish Republic which, if unchallenged, would remain a disgrace on our own people. We want to show that there is a close bond between the democracies of Ireland and Spain. Our fight is the fight of the Spanish people, as it is of all peoples who are the victims of tyranny.*[122]

The press reporter mentioned some figures that were inaccurate – the "Irish battalion" would soon number 200, or that a further 80 men (40 travelling via Dublin, 30 Larne-Stranraer and 10 Rosslare-Fishguard) were also on their way to Spain that weekend.[123] According to my own calculation about 25, including Frank Edwards, travelled together with Ryan, more joined the party in London, including a handful from the southern counties and others, like Joe Monks, already resident in England. By mid-January 1937 a total of 100 Irish-born volunteers had arrived in Spain – the highest number for the whole war. But there was no "Connolly Column", no Irish company or battalion, and Ryan realised over time that the numbers were too low for an exclusively Irish unit since the losses in the early days were horrific.[124]

---

[121] Interview, Saothar 1996, p. 135.
[122] Irish Press, 14.12.1936.
[123] Ibid.
[124] The Irish in the Lincoln Brigade formed a "James Connolly Centuria", but the unit does not seem to have received official recognition from the IB leadership.

2

The Battles of 1937

Walter Greenhalgh from Manchester, a member of the Young Communist League, met Frank Ryan's group on the ferry from Britain to France. The Irish were in high spirits, singing rebel songs in the bar. For Walter, who became a close friend of the Irish leader, Ryan was "a big, soft Irishman and yet he could command attention without raising his voice". The English were processed in Paris at the Communist trade union offices at Place du Combat (now Place du Colonel Fabien) and their departure from Gare St. Lazare with French volunteers was a joyous, open affair. Their destination was Perpignan.[1]

Greenhalgh and his friend Jud Colman met Ryan's group[2], who had legally crossed the Spanish border on buses in the night on 14 December, at the

---

[1] IWM Interview 11187 Walter Greenhalgh, reel 2.
[2] The men who crossed the border into Spain with Frank Ryan were: Frank Conroy, Anthony Fox, Leo Green, Michael May, Michael Nolan, Thomas Wood, Joe Monks, Jim Prendergast, Frank Edwards, Michael Lehane, Gerald Doran, John Goff, Paddy Smith. The first six were

assembly point of the Internationals, the fortress of Figueras. Ryan was martially attired in highly polished boots and a leather coat he had bought in London. Douglas ("Dave") Springhall, the English *responsable* was similarly attired. Their men were housed in the spacious dungeons. There was still blood on the walls, traces of the last stand resistance of rebels officers killed at the outbreak of the conflict. The sanitation was primitive, turds littered the floors of the large vaults.[3] One Irishman partook excessively of the local vino and was the cause of an altercation with the furious commander of the castle who fired his pistol into the ceiling, waking everybody. In a smattering of languages, Ryan calmed the Spanish officer and personally led the culprit to the guardroom.[4]

After stopovers in Barcelona and Valencia, both groups arrived in Albacete, the main base of the Internationals, in the early morning of 17 December. The town was the provincial capital of La Mancha, in flat, dusty country where indigent peasants had worked the land for absentee landlords. The training base for the English and Irish was in the nearby village of Madrigueras. It was a depressing place, ankle-deep in mud in the winter but the desperately poor inhabitants who seemed to live mainly by gathering saffron (won from the fields of crocus bulbs surrounding the village) were grave and civil. One of the greatest problems was that, once the perfunctory day's training was over, the volunteers had little to do and drifted to the few bars that sold highly alcoholic drinks such as anis and brandy. Some of the more politically committed were determined to learn the language and had their rations cooked by families they had befriended.[5]

None of the English officers or political functionaries had the requisite military experience to equip them for modern warfare. Peter Kerrigan, the irascible Scottish Political Commissar responsible for the British and Irish at the Albacete base, had served in the ranks of the British Army as a lorry driver in Ireland and Egypt from 1918 to 1920.[6] Springhall, Political Commissar of the Anglo-Irish battalion in the process of formation at Madrigueras, was a graduate of the International Lenin School in Moscow (as were most British-born political

---

soon fatalities, and all the others sustained wounds. See: Joe Monks, With the Reds in Andalusia, London 1985, p. 50.

[3] IWM Interview 801 Sydney Quinn, reel 1.

[4] Monks, Reds in Andalusia, p. 2; IWM Interview Walter Greenhalgh, reel 2.

[5] IWM Interview 803 George Leeson, reel 2.

[6] IWM Interview 810 Peter Kerrigan, reel 1.

commissars) and had been expelled from the Royal Navy for political reasons at the age of nineteen in 1920.[7] Tom Wintringham, head of training at Madrigueras, had at least served at the front in WW1, as a balloon officer. He was well-mannered, unpretentious and generally liked.[8] That cannot be said of Wilfred Macartney, the first commander of the British battalion, who had a criminal record and was obviously a high-class misfit, fraudster and martinet.[9]

Macartney was born in Scotland in 1899 as the son of a millionaire who had made a fortune laying tramlines in Europe and the Americas. Wilfred came into a fortune on the death of his father shortly before the First World War, in which he served as an infantry officer. Macartney was taken prisoner by the Germans in October 1918 but soon escaped. By the mid-1920s he had dissipated his inheritance and was sent to prison for nine months in 1926 for breaking the window of a jeweller's shop. While in prison it is said he met two Communists and was converted to the "cause". Shortly after his release, he was involved in a Soviet spy-ring in London and was sentenced to ten years in January 1928 for acquiring a RAF manual in breach of the Official Secrets Act.[10] Why the CPGB leadership in London chose him to command the British battalion is still a mystery. What would have damned Macartney in the eyes of all Irish volunteers (they did not know initially), was his enlistment in the Auxiliary Division of the RIC in 1920 and his dismissal (soon reversed) from that body for excessive drinking.[11]

Frank Ryan organized 43 of the Irish for service in the Marseillaise Battalion of the 14th (Franco-Belge) Brigade and they left for the Cordoba Front on Christmas Eve. The Irishmen, mostly Dubliners, were posted to the battalion's No. 1 Company of 145 English-speakers. They were naturally surprised that Ryan was not accompanying them on the journey south. That Ryan was not

---

[7] RGASPI, f. 17, o. 98, d. 751, autobiography 10.02.1929.
[8] Jason Gurney, Crusade in Spain, London 1976 edition, p. 63.
[9] In 1940 Macartney was found guilty of obtaining credit by fraud and the Special Branch believed he had spent £2,000 at the Savoy Hotel in three years. (NAUK, KV 2/648) British secret service sources were later of the view that his idea was "to feather his own nest...a born crook."(Information from Richard Baxell, 21.07.2013, quoting from Special Branch files.)
[10] National Archives of the United Kingdom (NAUK), KV2/647, 648; Daily Record (Glasgow), 18.09.1999 (accessed under *www.thefreelibrary.com* 20.01.2011); The Times (London), 19.11.-08.12.1927, 17.-20.01.1928.
[11] F.P. Crozier, Impressions and Recollections, London 1930, pp. 264-265. I am grateful to Richard Baxell for the extract.

given field command was probably not due to his non-Communist status but more to his function as a captain attached to the Political Commissariat of the Brigades that now "loaned" him to the 12th Brigade of Germans and Italians during the fighting around University City in Madrid. His hearing impairment was naturally an impediment in a battle situation. In any case, he was of more value to the Irish acting from behind the scenes. In his place Christopher ('Kit') Conway from Co. Tipperary, a Communist, led the preponderantly Irish No. 1 platoon at Cordoba.[12]

The commander of No. 1 Company with the "Marseillaise" volunteers was a legendary figure, George Nathan, who was killed seven months later at Brunete. George Samuel Montague Nathan was christened into the Church of England but his father was a Jewish butcher in London's East End. Young George learned the victualler's trade but soon lied about this age and joined the reserve of the Duke of Cornwall Light Infantry at sixteen in 1913, enlisting in the regular army some months later. He was a corporal in that regiment when it entrained for France. He rose through the ranks and was commissioned as Second Lieutenant in the Royal Warwickshire Regiment in April 1917. During the Battle of Arras at Easter 1917, after his men had taken 30 German prisoners, Nathan was wounded and fell into German hands. On his return to Britain in December 1918, he was promoted to 1st Lieutenant and served with his old regiment in India.

Nathan retired from the Army in August 1920 (joining the Reserve of Officers) in order to join the Auxiliary Division of the RIC. After his service in Ireland, Nathan resigned his commission and joined the West Yorkshire Regiment as a private soldier. He bought himself out in October 1922, but probably unable to find work, re-enlisted, this time in the Royal Fusiliers, in October 1925.[13] Nathan was a homosexual and because of this he was dismissed from the service "with ignominy" in 1926. At his trial at the depot in Hounslow, he was sentenced on 28 April 1926 to 35 days "hard labour" for the offence of "indecency".[14] Afterwards he tried his luck at farming in Canada, returned to

---

[12] Monks, Reds in Andalusia, p. 7; Cronin, Frank Ryan, pp. 90-91.
[13] NAUK, WO 374/50047, officer file G.S.M. Nathan. I am indebted to Julian Hendy for locating this file. Nathan's record of service is also reproduced on that excellent homepage *www.cairogang.com*.
[14] NAUK, WO 86/93, Court Martials ledger, 1924-1927. Neil G. Cobbett of NAUK kindly drew my attention to this source.

Britain in 1932 but left for the prairies again in 1935. The date of his final homecoming is unknown but he left Britain for Spain with a group of 10 volunteers in November 1936. So stories about Nathan being "the only Jewish officer in World War One in the Brigade of Guards" are just that, part of the legend he, obviously a man fallen on hard times, embroidered for himself and his avid listeners (he was highly admired) in 1936/37.

The record of his time with the notorious "Auxies" in Ireland is sparse in documentation. Pages were torn out of the RIC Service register in British archives, or "binned" for political reasons or shredded in order to make space for other files.[15] It seems confirmed that Nathan joined the Auxiliary Division of the RIC on 20 October 1920 and was posted as Section Leader to G Company in Killaloe, Co. Clare.[16] It also can be taken for granted that Nathan, and another officer, murdered in the night of 6-7 March 1921 George Clancy[17], the Lord Mayor of Limerick, and his predecessor Michael O'Callaghan, in front of their wives at their city homes near the Shannon river. A few hours before, a group of British agents, probably led by Nathan, had also shot Joseph O'Donoghue, the Westmeath-born manager of a meat company in Limerick who was not an active IRA member.[18] A top-secret "murder gang" of mixed Auxiliary and British Army intelligence had also assassinated Thomas Blake in late January 1921. He was a member of the local IRA and a trained chemist working in Laird's Dispensary on O'Connell Street, possibly because he was suspected of purloining chemicals for making bombs.[19] Two noted Irish historians are of the opinion that such British "murder gangs" were active in Munster from April 1920 to June 1921, an initiative of the career Army officer seconded to the RIC as a Divisional Commander, Brigadier-General Cecil Prescott-Decie.[20]

At the time of the mayoral murders, the "blood was up" with the Auxiliaries. The East Limerick Flying Column of the IRA had wiped out a RIC patrol at

---

[15] Information from Neil G. Cobbett to the author at Kew, 24.02.2010.

[16] *www.cairogang.com*, George Montague Nathan, p. 5. Accessed 18.01.2012.

[17] The friend of James Joyce who features as "Davin" and as a fellow student at UCD in "Portrait of an Artist".

[18] Thomas Toomey, The War of Independence in Limerick 1919-1921, self-publishing 2010, pp. 537-538.

[19] Ibid., pp. 508-509.

[20] Gabriel Doherty/John Borgonovo, „Smoking Gun? RIC Reprisals, summer 1920", History Ireland, March/April 2009, pp. 36-39.

Dromkeen, Co. Limerick, in early February. Nine RIC men died instantly or later succumbed to their wounds, and two others were executed after capture – an act of revenge in tit-for-tat killings and a grisly indication that both sides were ratcheting up the war. Eight of the dead RIC personnel were British-born.[21] And on the eve of the Limerick city murders, the IRA had shot dead James McGuire, a RIC sergeant monitoring anti-IRA informants, in Kilmallock.[22] In the evening of 6 March 1921, according to a fellow-officer in an interview with Richard Bennett for the *New Statesman* in 1961, Nathan came down from Dublin to the mess of the Auxiliaries at Killaloe and recruited a fellow-officer for a "job to do" in Limerick city.

Nathan and his companion, before commencing their murderous rampage, probably dined at Kidd's restaurant at 103, O'Connell Street, which for many years afterwards housed "The Brazen Head". "The Bentley Bar" now occupies the site. After their night of crime, Nathan and his assistant returned to the mess at Killaloe, where he, Nathan, "boozed up and looking like death", admitted to the six o'clock breakfast round that he had killed Clancy and O'Callaghan.[23]

It is significant that Frank Ryan and the other Irish took Nathan's contrite statement that he had served as an intelligence officer in Ireland but now saw the error of his ways, at face value. Joe Monks offered an explanation in 1961:

> I remember George Nathan telling us Irish members of the 'First Company' which he commanded in the International Brigade that he had served as an intelligence officer with the British forces in the Limerick area during the Irish War of Independence. He made this statement in the presence of Frank Ryan, who was a native of Limerick. Perhaps it is fair to say that Nathan, the volunteer for liberty, who gave such magnificent service to the anti-Fascist cause in the last year of his life, did not seem in character with the officer portrayed in Bennett's article.[24]

Frank Ryan, as we shall see, was not so forgiving of other leading figures in the British battalion. For Walter Greenhalgh, the discussion about Nathan's Irish past started when Nathan and Ryan were discussing who should command No. 1

---

[21] Toomey, The War of Independence, pp. 509-522.
[22] Ibid., pp. 535-536.
[23] New Statesman, 24.03.1961, pp. 471-472.
[24] New Statesman. 31.03.1961, p. 510, correspondence.

Company and arguing against a few left sectarians from the YCL who wanted all officers to be elected:

> *This* [Nathan's service in Ireland] *caused controversy because it was suggested that George was the only one with real military experience and should be leader, but some of the Irish did not want to serve under a Black and Tan. This was said openly in discussion ...*[25]

The version recounted by the Manchester volunteer Maurice Levine is probably exaggerated but it indicates that the matter was soon settled:

> *At Madrigueras, Nathan and the other Irishmen put Nathan on trial for his life, charging him with being a spy for the Franco forces. It was a secret trial, but one of the witnesses, Jimmy Prendergast, told me about it afterwards. Nathan was anti-Fascist. "I'm a Jew, though I never bothered with the Jewish community, and I'm against Hitler. I've come here so that I can fight back against Hitler. If you want to shoot me for what happened in Ireland, all right. But I was under orders, I was a member of the British Crown forces and I had to do what I was told. What you said I did is true." They eventually accepted his explanation and deleted all references to the past.*[26]

The engagement of the English-speaking company on the Cordoba front, the attempt to capture the village of Lopera, was an unmitigated disaster.[27] The pueblo had been abandoned but was in the hands of fascist units when the badly equipped men of the Marseillaise battalion tried to cross the ridges in front of the village. Subjected to machine-gun fire, artillery bombardments and bombing aircraft, the Internationals had to retreat. They did not have magazine clips for their antiquated Austrian Steyr rifles and were supposed to depend on the notoriously unpredictable (jamming) French Chaucat light machine-guns for covering fire. Five Dublin men (James Foley, Anthony Fox, Michael May, Michael Nolan and Thomas Wood), John Meehan from Galway and Frank

---

[25] IWM Interview Walter Greenhalgh, reel 3.

[26] Maurice Levine, Cheetham to Cordova. A Manchester Man of the Thirties, Manchester 1984, p. 39.

[27] For a description of the battle from participants, see: Levine, pp. 34-37; Monks, Reds in Andalusia, pp. 11-18; IWM Interview Greenhalgh, reel 3.

Conroy from Kildare were killed. Almost all the other Irish volunteers in the unit were wounded.

Nathan did well in the battle, displaying what would become his trade-mark: coolness under fire, armed only with his swagger stick or walking cane. But a scapegoat was found for the 300 dead and 600 wounded volunteers of the 14th Brigade. De La Salle, the French battalion commander, was executed in the aftermath, allegedly for "espionage" or so the drumhead court-martial found.[28]

Las Rozas was the next battle for No. 1 Company. That village, now a suburb of Madrid, had been taken by the fascists after Franco, having given up the hope of a breakthrough near University City, tried to encircle the capital from the north-west and his troops cut the Madrid-La Coruña road in several places. The battered remnants from No. 1 Company left central Madrid for the front on 11 January. Nathan was again in command, assisted by 'Kit' Conway and an ex-sergeant of a Highland regiment, the courageous Scot Jock Cunningham. It was a time of cold nights and swirling fogs for the 12th and 14th Brigades advancing against an unseen enemy. The Internationals had to retreat because of heavy artillery fire and tanks. Greenhalgh and Frank Edwards from Waterford were wounded. Denis Coady from Waterford Street (now demolished) in inner-city Dublin was killed by a shell blast on the second day.[29] When the remainder of the Company returned to Albacete at the end of January 1937 it numbered only 67 men out of the original strength of 145.[30]

In the meantime there had been a steady influx of Irish and British volunteers into Madrigueras which would bring the battalion up to 650 infantry men in four companies by mid-February. Indeed, over half of all Irish volunteers in Republican Spain (230) had arrived before the beginning of the Battle of Jarama on 12 February. Among the new arrivals were three men from Limerick city: Joe Ryan, Gerrard Doyle and Paddy Brady.

Joe Ryan was probably the eldest child of Joseph and Margaret Ryan, born in 1917. The family lived at 9 Mungret Street, and because Joe emigrated to England at the age of 17 or 18, his siblings have only vague memories of him. He

---

[28] Monks, Reds in Andalusia, p. 18; Levine, Cheetham, pp. 36-37.
[29] Uinseann Mac Eoin, Survivors. New and Enlarged Edition, Dublin 1987, Interview with Frank Edwards, pp. 1-20, here pp. 12-13.
[30] Bill Alexander, British Volunteers for Liberty: Spain 1936-1939, London 1982, p. 89.

attended Sexton Street CBS and learned the trade of a shoe-maker. In Ireland he had been a member of the ITGWU since 1935. He was a member of the British Labour Party and lived near Edgware Road, London. When he arrived in Spain shortly after Christmas 1936, Joe Ryan added two years to his age, stated he was a labourer with no military experience and gave his next-of-kin address that of his parents in Mungret Street.[31] From mid-1937 it was customary to send back all under 21-year-olds immediately, often at the request of their distraught parents.

Gerrard Doyle joined the British battalion on 11 February, just before the battle commenced at Jarama. He gave an address as 2, Vale Road, Forest Gate, East London, and said he had experience in the infantry, a fact which marked him out for promotion.[32] Gerrard was born on 8 October 1908 as the third child of Peter and Elizabeth Doyle. He had a brother, Frank, and a sister, Mary. His mother kept a restaurant at their home address, 36, Upper William Street, and the father worked as a cattle dealer. It cannot have been a happy family for the mother committed suicide in her bedroom in 1923.[33] Gerrard left home shortly afterwards since he did not get on with his father's new wife, finished his schooling at Sexton Street CBS and apprenticed himself to learn the trade of moulder. In 1925 he and his work-mates went on strike for over a month to avert a 24 per cent cut in wages, and the business folded. He then went to live with his mother's brother, a farmer, but tired of being exploited, signed on with Siemens & Schuckert, the German firm building the Ardnacrusha hydroelectric generation station outside the city. His employment as locomotive driver and fireman terminated in September 1929 – the Shannon Scheme was almost completed. Doyle's next employer was the tractor plant of Fordson's in Cork city, but he was soon laid-off with hundreds of others.

Out of work and with little prospect of getting any, Gerrard Doyle joined the Irish Free State Army in 1930, serving in the mechanical section of the Corps of Transport as a lorry driver. He declined to extend his period of service in 1934 and was fortunate to acquire employment with a private bus company in Dublin city. That job folded in July 1935, after the Government had "rationalized" the service, handing over the running of Dublin buses to the Dublin United

---

[31] RGASPI, f. 545, o.6, d. 91, l. 69.
[32] Ibid., l. 88.
[33] Limerick Leader,10.09.1923. I thank Mike McNamara for a copy of the newspaper article on the tragedy.

Tramway Company. After half a year on the dole, Doyle emigrated to England and worked in a series of badly paid jobs in the Midlands and London. He joined the CPGB in Birmingham before leaving for Spain.[34]

Patrick Joseph Brady, the third Limerick man arriving in Madrigueras in late 1936/early 1937, joined the British battalion on 7 January.[35] He was born on 7 March 1904. His family lived at 65, New Road, Thomondgate. At the 1911 census there were four daughters and two sons in the family. Brady may have served in the Free State Army before emigrating to Liverpool around 1930. He and his wife subsequently had five children. He probably had some form of secondary education since his Latin was good enough to give "grinds" in that language. He lived at 43, Trowbridge Street. Liverpool was still controlled by the Tories in the 1930s and the influence of the Orange order was strong.

Paddy Brady first left. Spain demonstration, Liverpool 1938

For somebody from a Catholic Irish background who was a member of the Communist Party, the prospects of employment were dim, and Paddy Brady was blacklisted for decades, even after his stint in Spain. He took part in Hunger

---

[34] RGASPI, f. 545, o. 6, d. 125, ll. 122-124, undated biography.
[35] RGASPI, f. 545, o. 6, d. 91, l. 51.

Marches organized by the National Unemployed Workers' Movement (NUWM) to London. That he was taking off on another march was the excuse to his wife when he departed Liverpool for Spain.[36]

In early January 1937, trouble was brewing in Madrigueras which eventually led to a section of the Irish volunteers joining the American battalion training in Villaneuva de La Jara, 60 kilometers north of Albacete and 30 kilometers from the British base at Madrigueras. The move to the American unit was certainly not in the interest of Frank Ryan, who in his New Year's address from Albacete to his compatriots in the International Brigades stressed that the war situation did not permit the foundation of an Irish unit, and until then "this unit [Irish] will be part of the English-speaking battalion which is to be formed. Irish, English, Scots and Welsh comrades will fight side by side, against the common enemy – Fascism. It must also be made clear that in the International Brigades in which we serve, there are no national differences … I ask for complete unity".[37]

It is difficult to establish a proper chronology for what were three separate incidents:

a) Fighting and disputes between Irish and British volunteers, fuelled by alcohol.

b) A meeting on 12 January when the Irish by a narrow majority voted to join the Americans, with the dissenters feeling they had to adhere to that decision.

c) Frank Ryan's altercation with André Marty and his temporary detention.

It should be said at the outset that the initial trouble happened in the first two weeks of January when Frank Ryan was absent at the Madrid front, as was his "core unit" of men fighting in Las Rozas. He found time to address his listeners in Ireland on Radio Madrid on the eve of that battle, speaking in Irish and English and mainly concentrating on the plight of the population under constant bombing from the air.[38] Ryan would have known only a minority of the Irish

---

[36] I am indebted to Danny Payne, Liverpool, and to Brady's grandchild Cathie Jacob, for the information on Paddy Brady.

[37] Peter O'Connor, A Soldier of Liberty. Recollections of a socialist and anti-fascist fighter, Dublin 1996, p. 16.

[38] The talk was given at 7.30pm on 10 January – Irish Press, 11.01.1937.

training with British battalion because the majority of them had travelled from England to Spain and had not been active in the Republican movement before emigrating from Ireland.

Any Irishmen creating trouble were, in all probability, no better or worse than the English, the Welsh or the Scots. A "Battalion Blacklist", the only document at our disposal on the "rows" in Madrigueras and probably compiled by battalion commissar Springhall, contains 33 names, of whom ten are Irish. They are often described as "now with American unit". The majority probably voiced their sensitivity about being treated as "Britishers", convinced Republicans like Jim O'Regan, Eamon McGrotty and Denis Holden. Charles Colman from Cork and Joe Ryan from Limerick, it was noted, had been arrested and sent to Albacete. Four others subsequently had bad disciplinary records (at least one deserted), and the man with the worst record of behaviour of all Irish volunteers, Brendan Moroney from Ennis, does not feature on the list.[39] With approximately 45-50 Irish learning to be infantrymen at the battalion base, a "bad apple" count of ten per cent does not seem a disturbing average for the collection of "odds and bods" that the British battalion was.

As regards excessive drinking, there seems to have been a temporary ban on the sale of alcohol in the village, to which the men reacted by ordering café frío, a potent mixture of cold coffee liberally laced with rum.[40] Fred Copeman, in his chortling interview with the Imperial War Museum, mentions a "punch-up between the Irish and the English late at night … sent to the guardhouse … trivial stuff", adding the erroneous comment that this was the reason that Frank Ryan took his men to the American battalion. In fact the very opposite was the case, but "old Fred", for all his affability, was never a stickler for historical detail, neither is his memoir of the war (1948) nor in the interview he gave in 1976.[41] Jason Gurney, a middle-class sculptor from South Africa and a member of the artistic Chelsea set, states in his hyper-critical memoir of the war that following a feud between the Irish and the platoon detailed for guard duties one night "practically the whole of the Irish detachment was arrested", and that the

---

[39] RGASPI, f. 545, o. 6, d. 93, ll. 23-27 (+reverse).
[40] Donald Renton Interview, p. 24, in: Ian McDougall, Voices from the Spanish Civil War. Personal Recollections of Scottish Volunteers in Republican Spain 1936-39, Edinburgh 1986.
[41] IWM Interview 794 Fred Copeman, reel 1.

aggrieved Irishmen refused to parade the next day, demanding a transfer to the Americans.[42]

This is most likely a conflation of events, perhaps excusable after the passage of forty years. The drunken escapades were a "storm in a teacup", as were the comments that one Irishman wore a green beret, some others green scarves.[43] An American historian would have us believe that the Irish conversed in Gaelic with one another and that this was banned by the Brigade staff.[44]

As the German phrase has it, the fish stinks from the head downwards. Tom Wintringham, designated to become C.O. of the embryonic MG Company, had a liberal disposition and was too busy sorting out the different calibres of bullets for his myriad of ancient weapons to bother unduly about disciplinary matters. He states in his war memoir that "Dave" Springhall and other commissars dealt with matters of insubordination, while Wilfred Macartney busied himself with the drunks and other petty offenders after morning parade.[45] Macartney, appointed battalion commander by Marty at the beginning of the year,[46] was a "ticket-of-leave man", that is he had to report to the British authorities periodically if he wanted to stay at liberty. By late January, Kerrigan and Wintringham had lost confidence in Macartney – he was "far too irritable and querulous".[47] His final departure from Madrigueras was hastened by the fact that when swopping pistols with Kerrigan on 7 February, Kerrigan's weapon went off, wounding Macartney in the upper arm. Some Brigaders believed to their dying day that Kerrigan, the absolute *apparatchik*, had wanted to get rid of the commander, permanently.[48] London's *Daily Worker* reported the tragi-comical

---

[42] Jason Gurney, Crusade in Spain, London, 1976 edition, p. 77.

[43] Tom Wintringham, English Captain, 1941 edition, p. 47.

[44] Cecil Eby, Between the Bullet and the Lie. American Volunteers in the Spanish Civil War, New York-Chicago-San Francisco 1969, p. 26.

[45] Wintringham, English Captain, pp. 47-54.

[46] National Labour History Museum, Manchester (NLHMM), CP/IND/POLL/2/6, Peter Kerrigan to Harry Pollitt, 04.01.1937.

[47] Baxell, Unlikely Warrior, p. 135.

[48] For a document in French describing the incident and Kerrigan's hysterical reaction, see: RGASPI, d. 545, o. 2, d. 68, l. 155.

accident as an injury to "a dogged fighter" who had "arrived in Madrid on sick leave ... wounded in the left forearm by enemy rifle fire."[49] He was not to return.

Macartney tried to run the battalion in the manner of a no-nonsense officer on the Western Front. His main assistant, called adjutant, was a diminutive Belfast man called William McDade who acted also as a sergeant-major and drilled the recruits.[50] An astute observer, the Clonakilty-born George Leeson, had a low opinion of battalion commander Macartney: He put men guarding an empty church, sent others to prison for seven days for drunkenness, lived in a villa with servants, rarely mixed with the men, ordered route marches and organized just one firing practice of five rounds. Leeson's estimation of his commanding officer reached rock-bottom on the occasion of a visit by a delegation from London Trades Council. The men were lined waiting in the rain and finally escorted the visitors through squelching mud to the town cinema. The delegates brought gifts of chocolate and cigarettes, were heartily cheered by the volunteers and then insulted by Macartney:

> Then Macartney got up and said that instead they should have brought us prismatic compasses for night-raids into enemy territory. He had a bee in his bonnet about night-raids ... Macartney was not a fit person to lead a battalion.[51]

The second, and most controversial, incident relating to the Irish was the meeting called by Springhall on 12 January.[52] Tension was growing between the British and the Irish not least because of reports in the *Daily Worker* about the Lopera battle which omitted any mention of the large Irish contingent there.[53] Relations with English volunteers were so bad that some Irish did not want to share the same billet with them.[54] One participant at the 12 January meeting, Peter O'Connor, states that about 45 Irishmen attended, and by a majority of five, voted to join the American battalion. It was perhaps a chaotic assembly as some

---

[49] NAUK, KV 2/68, Wilfred Macartney, press cutting Daily Worker, 13.02.1937, „Famous Author Wounded".
[50] Wintringham, English Captain, pp. 44-46.
[51] IWM Interview George Leeson, reels 1, 2.
[52] Alexander (p. 68) and Stradling (The Irish and the Spanish Civil War, p. 155) state that Springhall, and not Kerrigan, summoned the meeting. Undoubtedly he did this after consultations with Kerrigan and Marty.
[53] Baxell, Unlikely Warriors, p. 133.
[54] Ibid, p. 468.

of the men were "the worse for drink", did not follow all the arguments closely and chimed on about the wrongs done to Ireland in the past by the English. The more convinced socialists (O'Connor, Charlie Donnelly, and the Power brothers Johnny and Paddy) argued in vain that a distinction had to be made "between anti-fascist or working class comrades and British imperialism".[55] In reports to London Springhall put the vote at 23 to 11, Kerrigan 26 to 11.[56]

At my own estimation, there were 45-53 Irish-born recruits at the date of the meeting in Madrigueras, but those who joined the American battalion on 20 January numbered twenty-one, hardly many more.[57] In six or seven cases it is not clear whether the volunteer transferred or not. Training with the Americans at the time were three other Irish-born (Paddy Roe McLaughlin, Pat Hamill and Maurice Moran), part of the first American contingent of over 90 that who had left New York on the "Normandie" on St. Stephen's Day 1936.[58] Three further groups from the USA landed in France in January 1937.[59] Before the Jarama battle, some other Irish volunteers arriving after the ominous meeting joined the Americans (e.g. Colum Cox, Liam Tumilson). So a substantial number of the Irish (at least 25) stayed with the British battalion, including the "troublemakers" Joe Ryan, Charles Mitchell, William Haire, Brendan Moroney etc. If Springhall wanted to be rid of the "troublesome" Irish, why did he not "ship" them all out?

It is likely that Springhall wanted to be rid of the committed CPI-IRA contingent close to Frank Ryan in the belief that a compact Irish unit, mainly composed of ex-IRA men with their own ethos who were sensitive and critical of the battalion leadership, would undermine the authority of the unelected British leaders (Macartney, Springhall and Kerrigan). In fact, as Emmet O'Connor has amply demonstrated, British communists never understood and were wary of Irish Republicanism, the recruiting base for the CPI. After the Comintern desisted

---

[55] O'Connor, Soldier of Liberty, p. 15. See also his letter to the Irish Democrat (London), December 1978.

[56] MML, 1994 catalogue, special files, Box C, file 9/8, Springhall to Pollitt, 19.01.1937; file 9/11, Kerrigan to Pollitt, 24.01.1937.

[57] Hugh Bonner, Kevin Blake, E.J. Bourne, Charles Colman, Charlie Donnelly, Tom Hayes, Bill Henry, Denis Holden, Jackie Hunt, Michael Kelly, Eamon McGrotty, Alan McLarnon, William A. Morrison, Tom O'Brien, Peter O'Connor, Vincent O'Donnell, Michael O'Donovan, Jim O'Regan, Johnny Power, Billy Power, Paddy Stanley.

[58] I thank Ray Hoff and Alan Warren for the list of the first Americans.

[59] Arthur Landis, The Abraham Lincoln Brigade, New York 1968, p. 15.

from the practice of sending advisers to Ireland and handed over supervision of Irish communist groups to the CPGB in the late 1920s, relations between both were fraught.[60] The reasons Springhall gave for having the Irish removed were specious, for, as mentioned above, the "bad elements" he excoriated stayed in Madrigueras. On 19 January he wrote a distorted version of the split in a chauvinist spirit to Harry Pollitt:

> *They have now gone today to the Americans and we are frankly glad. We know that it can be bad politically both in Ireland and in England but they were an awful lot of ? Irish exiles from Edgware Road, petty criminals – hooligan types. So all had to go and again I will say we are glad – and knowing the Americans I am sorry for the Irish.*[61]

Equally untruthful was Kerrigan's interpretation:

> *As a result of the bad elements among them and also very many non-Party people, their decision was by 26 to 11 in favour of joining the Americans. After they took the decision some of them had doubts but it was too late to change and now their whole group is with the Americans.*[62]

At least two British volunteers present in Madrigueras were highly critical of Springhall's machinations. By the way, after he had recovered from his facial wound when fighting with the Americans on 27 February, Springhall was retained in London, hardly a sign of approbation. Following his involuntary return from Spain, George Aitken, the first Commissar of the British battalion at Jarama, wrote to Party headquarters in 1937:

> *I would remind Comrade Springhall that they do not hide removals in the Int[ernational] Brig[ade]s when they consider them necessary. They did not hide his own removal of Political Commissar of the Brigade because of his*

---

[60] Reds and the Green. Ireland, Russia and the Communist Internationals, 1919-43, Dublin 2004; "Mutiny or Sabotage? The Irish Defection to the Abraham Lincoln Battalion in the Spanish Civil War". Working Papers in Irish Studies, Winthrop University, South Carolina 2009, working paper 09-3

[61] MML, Springhall to Pollitt, 19.01.1937.

[62] MML, Kerrigan to Pollitt, 24.01.1937.

grave political mistake in helping the Irish Section of the British Bn. to transfer to the American Bn.[63]

Donald Renton of Edinburgh (Political Commissar in the MG Company) saw the "Irish affair" in the same light:

> *In the light of the struggle of the Irish people for their own national independence this* [Irish] *Company should have been, in my view, quite a separate organization, even although attached to the British battalion and part of the International Brigade. In practice, however, the Irish national struggle as a related factor to the Spanish fight was not in my opinion concretely enough recognized. So it brought about one or two ugly situations at Madrigueras during the training period. Nevertheless these were overcome and largely through the activity of Jimmy Prendergast, who had formerly been a member of what they called the Irish Republican Congress. Through his efforts and those of Frank Ryan these things were resolved in a manner that enabled the Battalion finally to go into the line at Jarama in early February 1937.*[64]

A related subject overlooked by most historians was Springhall's fear of "contagion", namely that six Glaswegians in a "cookhouse revolt" applied to Macartney to join the Irish unit, albeit shortly after the vote of 12 January. Springhall forced them, all communists from Tounhead, to write cringing letters of repentance.[65] It is possible that there had been mutterings of sympathy with the Irish for a time since the would-be transferees were either of Irish extraction or sympathized for years with the IRA. Springhall duly reported to Pollitt:

> *Glasgow or at least Tounhead so-called CP members have been a plague to me … * [They] *simultaneously put in written requests to go to the Irish section! When I called them to a section to discuss this, six of them said quite openly that they want really to go back to Glasgow! I fought them to a*

---

[63] MML, Box C special files, 17/1. I thank Emmet O'Connor and Jim Carmody for this reference.

[64] Renton Interview, pp. 24-25, McDougall, Voices from the Spanish War.

[65] RGASPI, f. 545, o. 6, d. 107 (Edwin Blood), d. 109 (George Boyle), d. 113 (Francis Casey), d. 134 (Robert Fleming), d. 162 (George Leat), d. 195 (Francis Rush).

standstill and finally got everyone to withdraw their 'requests' and to each write a statement that they understood their mistakes.[66]

That the transfer initiated by Springhall was subsequently seen as a mistake is confirmed by the fact that the remnants of No. 1 Company of Lopera fame, including the Irish, fought alongside the British at Jarama and stayed with the British battalion. Other Irish released from hospital transferred to the British, and, as mentioned earlier, all Irish arriving in Spain from mid-July 1937 onwards enlisted with the British unit. Of course, if a man wanted to be with his "mates", his wish was deferred to considering the falling number of recruits in 1937.[67] So the number of Irishmen in the Lincoln battalion dwindled over time, and there was no repeat of the transfer of 20 January.

The issue boiled up again when the unwounded survivors from Lopera and Las Rozas on the way back to Madrigueras stopped off at Albacete on 31 January. Kerrigan got an "earful" from an unnamed member of No. 1 Company, probably Kit Conway, and from Frank Ryan, and he complained to Pollitt the next day:

> *The Irish trouble cropped up again yesterday. It was raised very sharply by one of No. 1 Company who have returned from the front. He accused the military and political leadership of the battalion of being responsible for it and threatened to raise it in England and Ireland. He was supported by Ryan who was present and he demanded unity of all the Irish no matter where they were. At the same time he declared they had been driven out of the battalion and talked of chauvinism ... M. [Marty] who was present proposed a commission and it meets today to finally solve this problem. Springie [Springhall] will present the facts to the commission.*[68]

It is doubtful if the issue was solved amicably since there was the third incident, Ryan's public dispute with Marty. Peter Kerrigan argues that the shouting match

---

[66] MML, Springhall to Pollitt, 19.01.1937.

[67] As in the case of Edward Updale, formerly an electrician in the British Army, who (he was an orphan) gave an address in Kilkee, Co. Clare on joining the Brigades in October 1937. Fed up of the inefficiency of the British battalion, he transferred to the Lincolns, helped in the training and "deserted" to the front. He was severely wounded on the Ebro, losing a leg. (RGASPI, f. 545, o. 6, d. 209, ll. 3-8; f. 545, o. 6, d. 91, l. 135; f. 545, o. 6, d. 97, l. 12). I am grateful to the famous children's writer, Eleanor Updale, for sharing with me memories of, and documents about, her father.

[68] MML, Box C, special files, file 10, Kerrigan to Pollitt, 01.02.1937.

happened at the end of Scottish celebrations, on the evening before "Burns Night", i.e. 24 January.[69] The date might be wrong, the venue he gives, Chinchón, certainly is. That is where the British and Irish spent the night before the first engagement at Jarama, 11-12 February. The "Burns Supper" celebrations were held on 24 January in the 'Republican Café' in Madrigueras, an evening of poems, songs and speeches preceded by a meagre meal.[70]

Frank Ryan never put his account of the dispute with Marty in writing and the evidence for the argument is anecdotal. Fred Copeman remembers that Frank was arrested by Marty's bodyguards because he would not desist talking after the French commander of the Brigades told him to sit down.[71] Kerrigan said in an interview 40 years later that Ryan was briefly detained on Marty's orders because he vociferously demanded the transfer of the Irish to the American battalion.[72] That claim is implausible for we know that Ryan had condemned the transfer to the U.S. battalion, a decision of which Kerrigan had approved.

It is likely that the altercation between Ryan and Marty occurred in the period between the return of No. 1 Company from Las Rozas and the departure of the British battalion to the front, i.e. 1-10 February. In order to circumvent the Spanish war censorship system, Ryan waited until he was on his way home on leave to vent his anger, in a long letter to Gerald O'Reilly (New York) dated 5 March from Hotel-Picardy in Paris:

> And now for confidential news. The representatives of the British C.P. wrecked the Irish Unit. While one Irish Section was on the Cordoba front, and I was "loaned" (moryah!) to the 12th (Italian and German) Brigade in Madrid – for a week which became a month – there was another Irish Section accumulating with the Scots, English and Welsh at the Base. I had a Dubliner named Terry Flanagan (fresh from Dublin Brigade IRA) in charge of that section. Flanagan was framed as a "suspect", believe it or not, by Wilfred McCartney, Batt. Commander, ex-British officer, author of "Walls Have Mouths" and ex-Black and Tan (vide Gen. Crozier). The Irish Section was shifted off to the Americans. When I came back (end of

---

[69] IWM Interview Peter Kerrigan, reel 2.
[70] Rust, Britons in Spain, pp. 35-36. Rust states that the men had a dose of diarrhea the following day.
[71] IWM Interview Fred Copeman, reel 1.
[72] IWM Interview Peter Kerrigan, reel 3.

Jan.) I was told a pack of lies by McCartney. To cut a long story short, I discovered – as a result of my own investigation – that Flanagan was being deported as an "undesirable" and that he had reached Barcelona on his way out. I stopped the deportation and got Flanagan back ... McCartney framed another of my most important men [Domhnall O'Reilly] *for "disobeying an order", which should not have been given save through me. The man got two months imprisonment without trial.[73] I have since got him released. To the International Brigades authorities I pointed out that Ireland's nearest enemy was British Imperialism, that therefore Ireland's nearest ally must be the British working class and that therefore the Irish and British must be side by side in the International Brigades. I was able to convince the British of having made a grave political error ... Someday I will tell you the whole sordid story of the political density of some self-called British revolutionaries. For the minute here's an example. An English officer* honestly *trying to pay the Irish a tribute says to the men. "Men from England, Scotland, Wales and Ireland, all of you are representatives of the British working class"!! The tragedy is, Gerald, that the English sent out the worst officer-type. The leadership of the C.P. of Gt. Britain and the rank and file understand our (Irish) position. It just happened that we got the in-between crowd of the swelled-head adventurer type.[74]*

All differences were forgotten when the 15th Brigade was rushed to the front south-west of Madrid. Franco's forces had commenced their effort to cut the highway from Madrid to Valencia (now the seat of the Republican government) on 6 February, crossing the Jarama river in three places. In the southern sector, roughly astride the road San Martin de la Vega in the west to Morata de Tajuna in the east, the 15th Brigade was detailed to retake the central section of small hills and drive the fascists back to the river, while the Americans, still in training at Villaneuva de la Jara, were to attack the heights of Pingarron south of the British positions some days later.[75] Few of the men had military experience: Nathan had been "kicked upstairs" to the 14th Brigade, Jock Cunningham, his adjutant from

[73] O'Reilly, and his sentence, feature on an internal document of the Brigade dated 11 February – RGASPI, f. 545, o. 2, d. 46, l. 12.
[74] Frank Ryan to Gerald O'Reilly, 05.03.1937, copy in possession of the author. The letter is partially reproduced in: Cronin, Frank Ryan, pp. 90-92.
[75] The following account of the British battalion in the battle days of 12-14 February is taken from the summaries in: Wintringham, Baxell and Gurney.

Lopera, was ill and most of the other "veterans" of the original No. 1 Company were initially kept in reserve at the headquarters of the 15th Brigade at Morata. The newly formed British companies were all under-strength. Frank Ryan, assistant to George Aitken, battalion commissar, took a rifle from a dead man on the first day of the battle (12 February) and stayed in the line.[76]

On the way to the front, the men got off the trucks in Villarubia de Santiago and let off a few rounds into the hills. Most of them had never fired a rifle before, and in the MG Company, George Leeson, an ex-Royal Navy man, had to show the men in his section how to adjust the sights on the rifles. His group, and presumably the majority in the battalion, had no idea that the enemy had broken through and crossed the river or what was in store for them.[77] Brigade commander was János Gálicz ("General Gal"), a Hungarian officer of the Red Army, an ex-POW from World War One who was a graduate of Moscow's Frunze Military Academy.[78] He soon left to command a division and was recalled to the Soviet Union in 1937 where he is said to have perished.[79] Like all Russian "advisers", Galicz had no time for the "discussion culture" of the British, Irish and Americans, expected orders to be obeyed under pain of death and, to be fair, was probably overwhelmed by the task in hand.[80] Detested by some, he had a keen appreciation of his own importance and military hierarchy: when Steve Nelson, the American political commissar, visited Gal at Morata in March, he could not fail to notice the full-length painted portrait of the Hungarian (in Republican uniform) on the wall behind the General's huge desk.[81]

Vladimir Č opić was Brigade Commissar and later to lead the 15th Brigade through most of the battles until his recall to Russia in August 1938. Along with

---

[76] Cronin, Frank Ryan, p. 91.

[77] IWM Interview George Leeson, reel 2

[78] *http://forum.axishistory.com/viewtopic.php?f=47&t=81238*, accessed 30.05.2014.

[79] According to Memorial, the Russian human rights association (http://lists.memo.ru/index4.htm), one Vladimir Ivanovich Gal' was arrested in Slavgorod (southern part of West Siberia) on 18 January 1938 and shot on 19 February 1938. He was buried in Slavgorod and rehabilitated posthumously by the Military Collegium of the Supreme Court of the USSR on 30 September 1962 as there was "no evidence of a crime". As he was unemployed when arrested, a common fate of persons sacked from high office, this Gal' is probably the former general in Spain.

[80] Jason Gurney, generally very critical of all "Russians" in Spain, stated Gal had "a pleasant, easy manner" and was unfairly blamed for the Jarama failures (Gurney, Crusade, p. 93).

[81] Eby, Between the Bullet and the Lie, pp. 124-125.

ten other leaders of the Yugoslav Communist Party, Čopić was arrested in Moscow in November 1938 and executed five months later.[82] He was hardly a popular commander, and whatever his merits his inclination to subject his subordinates to opera arias left him open to ridicule.[83] Čopić was born in Senj, Croatia, in March 1891 and he worked as a child in the family's tailoring business before completing his *Gymnasium* in 1911 and entering Zagreb University to study law. His first arrest was in 1912, following an attempt on the life on a police officer in the Croatian capital. As a student Čopić was offered a commission in the Austro-Hungarian army. He served for eight months, commanding a platoon in a *Jägerbatallion*, before being captured in the Carpathians after 15 days of combat in 1915.

While a POW in revolutionary Russia Čopić joined the Communists and was a member of the Central Committee of the Yugoslav Communist Party from 1919 onwards and a parliament deputy in 1921. Following the proscription of the party, he spent five periods in prison between 1919 and 1925. After his escape in 1925 he was employed by the Executive Committee of the Communist International and worked as a teacher and party functionary at the International Lenin School. Vladimir Čopić was a model revolutionary, courageous and polyglot: He spoke Serbo-Croatian, German and Czech fluently and could read and make himself understood in English, Italian, Bulgarian and Slovenian..[84] His military capabilities are open to question, but his subordinates were no better, gifted amateurs at best. In the last resort, he was obliged to act in unison with Soviet advisers.

After a 7am breakfast at a large farmhouse near the front line on 12 February, the men of the British battalion moved forward and were in position by 10am. In reality there were in a good defensive position on a plateau; the escarpment sloped down on to open ground. In the middle distance were two small knolls, one ("Suicide Hill") capped by a white house (Casa Blanca), the other conical and devoid of cover. In the far distance one could see the cliffs on the further bank of the Jarama river. Today, the land, which was under cultivation in 1937, is covered by scrub but the main points, the two knolls and the sunken road, are

---

[82] V.Tikhanova (Ed.), Rasstrel'nye spiski. Vypusk 1. Donskoe Kladbishche 1934-1940, Moscow 1993, pp. 89-92.
[83] Gurney, Crusade in Spain, p. 96.
[84] RGASPI, f. 495, o. 277, d. 291.

discernible. Only on the morning of the attack did the scouts of battalion commander Tom Wintringham reconnoitre the ground and make crude maps.[85] Gal at Morata could not rely on modern cartography either for his maps did not contain contours for hills, just brown smudges for elevated ground.[86] Gal gave the order to advance (without aerial or artillery support) and George Nathan arrived to confirm it, pulling No. 1 Company, now led by Kit Conway, out of reserve. Shortly before 11am the companies advanced down the escarpment heading towards the two hills and passing small olive groves. Conway's No. 1 company was on the extreme right, No. 3 commanded by Bill Briskey on the left and No. 4 under Bert Overton in the middle. All companies reached the objectives without opposition, the sun was shining but the men had no entrenching tools to dig in and there was little natural cover.

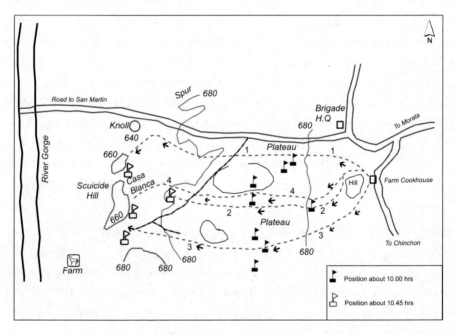

Jump-off point for British battalion on 12 February 1937

[85] For the details, see Gurney, Crusade in Spain, pp. 99-102.
[86] Wintringham, English Captain, p. 61. The state of Gal's map is confirmed by one of the brigade interpreters, the twenty-three year old Charles Picard from London – IWM Interview 18779 Charles Bede Picard, reel 4.

The Russians at the base in Morata insisted that the battalion advance further, towards the river. Gal confirmed the order on the telephone to Wintringham. But then a ferocious artillery and machine-gun barrage started. Overton's men on "Suicide Hill" were sitting ducks for the white house they occupied was a natural target for the fascist gunners. When the Franco-Belge battalion was forced back on the British right flank around mid-day, fascist machine-gunners could enfilade the valley, forcing the retreat of No. 1 Company and mortally wounding Conway. In mid-afternoon experienced Francoist Moroccan troops started their attacks and re-took the two hills. Fleeing infantrymen bunched up in the four-foot deep sunken road and were hit by machine-gun fire and snipers. Wintringham ordered a retreat but Gal countermanded it, the British had to "hold on at all costs".

For hours there was no supporting fire from Harold Fry's No. 2 (Machine-Gun) Company: the machine-gun belts for the Maxims contained the wrong ammunition and the replacement belts did not arrive quickly because the lorry driver was drunk and crashed the vehicle.[87] Fred Copeman, already wounded, and battalion commissar George Aitken, located the lorry and had the boxes of bullets retrieved. Filling the belts by hand and positioning the Maxims behind a low stone wall, Copeman directed a devastating fire on the advancing Moors around 7pm. That was the last important action of a disastrous day, the battalion was down to a third of its initial strength, 200 traumatised volunteers. When the stragglers and deserters hiding in the rear were herded together, the battalion numbered about 275, plus a Spanish company.

The fighting on 13 February, the second day, was quite confused. Wintringham, to his credit, ignored two orders issued by the Russians to advance. Aircraft and tanks were promised, but their presence could be counted in minutes. The frontline was now the sunken road, and the position to the left of the British battalion was an open space. Wintringham had placed Fry's machine-gunners rather far forward on the left flank with the argument that the position offered a splendid field of fire, and, as added security for the Maxims, had placed the survivors of Overton's company to the right of Fry's men. But when the fascist

---

[87] The man was initially condemned to death in the field but the sentence, due to Fred Copeman's plea of clemency, was reduced to a spell in the labour battalion. The culprit, a drunkard and a serial deserter, was detailed after Jarama - with other "duds" - to the battalion cookhouse. RGASPI, f. 545, o. 3, d. 450, ll. 78-81; f. 545, o. 6, d. 149, ll. 75-78.

artillery barrage recommenced, No. 4 Company, with Overton in the lead, withdrew to the sunken road. The machine gunners, expecting Spanish reinforcements on their left, were duped by Spanish Foreign Legion troops singing the "Internationale", and were overwhelmed. Over 30, including Fry, were taken prisoner. Overton retreated with his men to the rear, and Wintringham was wounded. In the evening, Jock Cunningham, returned from hospital, took over the running of the battalion.

On the third day, 14 February, the setbacks continued. Many of the volunteers were now on their third day without food. Enemy crossfire forced Cunningham to give up the sunken road. When fascist tanks appeared, the British and Irish had to retreat further. Then the left flank broke and the withdrawal became a rout. Only after a stiff talk by Gal, who emphasized that the way was now open for the Franco's troops to take the Madrid-Valencia road, did the 180 survivors of the battalion take heart and said they would return to the line. In a memorable action, later recounted in a famous passage written by Frank Ryan and included in almost all books about the British and the Irish in Republican Spain[88], Cunningham and Ryan led the men back to the front. They surprised the enemy, who retreated to the two hills, and the battalion line was re-established near the sunken road.

Frank Ryan was knocked unconscious by the blast of a tank shell which damaged a tendon in his leg. He also received a bullet wound in the upper left arm.[89] Gerrard Doyle was also wounded on 14 February.[90] Paddy Brady, a member of the machine-gun company, seems to have got through Jarama unscathed and he was soon a squad leader in the fourth platoon of Company No. 1.[91] Joe Ryan had served under Overton, which hardly did much good to his psychological state. Nine Irishmen with the British battalion died during the battle or shortly afterwards: John Campbell, Kit Conway, Pat Curley, Leslie Doran, Leo Green, Robert Hilliard, Albert McElroy, Maurice Quinlan and Richard O'Neill. Of the

---

[88] Originally reproduced in the book edited by Ryan himself, The Book of the 15th Brigade (Madrid 1938), pp. 58-61.
[89] Cronin, Frank Ryan, p. 97-98.
[90] RGASPI, f. 545, o. 6, d. 89, l. 81.
[91] RGASPI, f. 545, o. 6, d. 89, ll. 8, 10.

630-odd men of the British battalion who went into battle at Jarama on 12 February, only 80 were uninjured three days later.[92]

The Americans moved to the Jarama area on the evening of 16 February. The men clambered out of their trucks after the winding journey from Morata to be welcomed by Frank Ryan and the Brigade leadership. On the way, one truck took a wrong turning and was never seen again. Neither were the battalion records nor the 21 infantrymen on board. As with the British, the original leadership of the American battalion was badly chosen: James Harris, the military commander, had to be removed because of extremely eccentric behaviour, presumably brought on by a terror of battle.[93] He was replaced by Robert Hale Merriman, a tall Californian and a graduate of Nevada University who had been studying Soviet agronomics in Moscow. Samuel Stember, the first American battalion political commissar, dodged going over the top in the second disastrous American attack and soon returned to America. Their first rifles were antiquated Remingtons once produced for the Czar, a unfamiliar weapon because they had trained with Canadian Ross or Austrian Steyr rifles. The Irish transferees from the British battalion and the Cubans formed No. 1 Company, under the command of the Englishman Ivor Marlow ("John Scott"). The Americans were supposed to "dig in" without shovels or picks, using their helmets and bayonets.

The Americans relieved the Slav Dimitrov volunteers on 21 February, occupying their trenches. Under the supporting fire of four Maxims, the 450 Americans, with fixed bayonets, scaled the trench wall and ran towards the entrenched enemy on Pingarron Hill opposite on the afternoon of 23 February. Few got within grenade-throwing distance of the enemy positions. The Spaniards or Slavs on both flanks had not advanced as planned, and the two tanks in support were hit. The early fall of dusk on a winter evening prevented further casualties. Company commander Scott was killed and he was replaced by Bill Henry from Belfast. The engagement was broken off between 10 and 11pm, the Americans were ordered back to the take-off position and had nothing to show for their pluck except 20

---

[92] Baxell, Unlikely Warriors, p. 159.
[93] The American leadership in Spain offered Harris a chance to redeem himself: as a rank-and-file soldier in the Polish Dombrowskiy battalion.(RGASPI, f. 545, o. 6, d. 906, l. 73)

fatalities and over 40 wounded. Why the attack was launched with only 2-3 hours daylight remaining was never explained.[94]

The U.S. battalion was re-organised with Bill Henry taking over No. 1 Company, assisted by Eamon McGrotty as adjutant, while No. 2 Company was given to Martin Hourihan, a teacher of Irish extraction from the Deep South. A second attack was discussed by all involved officers with Gal and Čopić on 26 February, to take place the next morning at 7am along the whole front of the Internationals, with the Americans as the main attacking force. As with the British and Irish two weeks earlier, the promised assistance was nugatory: the tanks never arrived, and the armoured cars in their place let off a few belts of heavy caliber machine-gun fire towards Pingarron and retired; two or three aircraft appeared briefly and flew away after a strafing run; and the ancient 75 French artillery pieces on the Republican side fired shells that fell short, near Republican Spanish units. Rather stupidly, the Americans and the other Internationals had given notice of their intent by commencing to fire all weapons at the fascist lines before dawn. That brought a rain of shells and machine-gun fire down on the Republican front. Around 10am the 24th Spanish battalion on the Americans' flank advanced but soon scurried back under murderous fire. Merriman pleaded with Čopić to call off the attack since the support was not sufficient, but the Commissar was adamant. Finally, Brigade HQ sent Clifford Wattis, an ex-British Army officer, and "Dave" Springhall, to ensure that the American "boys" went "over the top" just before noon.

It was a slaughter. Merriman was wounded in the shoulder straight away, and Springhall received a bad facial injury when just out of the trench. In the next few minutes all the other officers were killed, first Bill Henry, then McGrotty. On his way to the first-aid post, Merriman insisted on being brought to HQ to see to Čopić who refused to talk to him. The attack petered out in the afternoon rain. The losses of the Americans were 127 killed and 200 wounded. In the evening, the retrieved corpses were stacked in piles like wood and set on fire.[95] Apart from Henry and McGrotty, other Irish killed on 27 February were Charlie Donnelly,

---

[94] For a succinct account of the 23 February battle, see: Marion Merriman and Warren Lerude, American Commander in Spain. Robert Hale Merriman and the Abraham Lincoln Brigade, University of Nevada Press 1986, pp.100-105; John Tisa, Recalling the Good Fight. An Autobiography of the Spanish Civil War, South Hadley Mass. 1985, pp. 41-45.
[95] Tisa, Recalling, pp. 47-53.

John Dolan and Michael Russell. The men of the British battalion also tried to advance under heavy fire on 27 February but Cunningham and Frank Ryan "called for a withdrawal immediately after seeing that no support of any kind was being given to the Lincolns and themselves."[96] There were over 30 fatalities in the British battalion, including Thomas T. O'Brien from Liverpool.[97] Many soldiers died because medical supplies were short and the journey to the hospitals over-long. A considerable number of inexperienced volunteers, like their counterparts in the early stages of the First World War, ignored warnings about snipers and thus paid the supreme sacrifice. Liam Tumilson of Belfast, the new C.O. of the MG Company with the Lincolns, was such a case in mid-March.[98]

Immediately after the 27 February fiasco, Frank Ryan took leave together with Bill Scott and Domhnall O'Reilly. Still with his arm in a sling, Ryan was handed 150 pesetas and gave an address in Dublin (176, Upper Drumcondra Road) for the duration of his visit home.[99] He flew from Valencia to Toulouse, took the train the Paris and stayed there for a week. He seems to have spent at least a week in Britain, probably visiting his physician brothers in Liverpool and Yorkshire. He was back in Dublin in mid-March.[100] Why did Frank Ryan take this well-earned break in Ireland? Originally, he had hoped to go on a propaganda tour of America, presumably for the Spanish Republican cause and, it may be surmised, to act as a kind of intermediary between warring Irish republican exiles. One reason for remaining in Ireland was a banal one: his arm wound was still giving him trouble in May. He may have been disillusioned about the Spanish struggle: the in-fighting in the Republican Zone, and the obtuseness of the Communist command of the International Brigades.[101] He may also have felt a sense of guilt because he had brought (mainly young) volunteers to Spain, only to see their lives

---

[96] Landis, Abraham Lincoln Brigade, p. 84.

[97] Baxell, Unlikely Warriors, p. 162.

[98] For a description of his death, see: Tisa, Recalling, pp. 60-61. Tisa, quoting from his diary, gives Tumilson's death as 5 April, but Moscow files (RGASPI, f. 545, o.2, d. 164, l. 94) and Sean Cronin (Frank Ryan, p. 101), referring to the eyewitness Paddy Roe McLaughlin (one of Tumilson's platoon leaders), both give the date 14 March.

[99] RGASPI, f. 4545, o. 2, d. 112, l. 28.

[100] Cronin, Frank Ryan, pp. 102-103.

[101] He said as much to Tom Barry in May, albeit after the anarchist-POUM uprising in Barcelona, a further reason for being pessimistic about the outcome of the Spanish struggle. Barry thought the war was lost and tried to persuade Ryan to stay in Ireland (Ibid., pp. 113-115).

wasted in ill-planned attacks. We may presume that he did everything in his power to discourage further recruitment in Ireland and, as we shall see later, saw it as his primary duty on return to the Spanish battlefields to "pull out" as many Irishmen as he could.

When interviewed by *The Irish Press* on 19 March, Ryan refused to disclose his further plans and preferred to express sorrow at the high Irish losses and anger because of the intervention of Italian and German troops.[102] A public appearance was the farewell party for Fr. La Borda, the Basque priest who had tried to enlighten the Irish on the true nature of the war in Spain. Ryan, and the children of James Connolly, Nora and Roddy, emphasized the international and class aspects of the struggle for freedom in Spain.[103]

Ryan was soon back "in his element", printing a new paper, the *Irish Democrat*, an initiative of left-wing and liberal figures in Dublin and Belfast that was launched in March and ceased publication in December 1937. Ryan was busy again on the typewriter and at the printing press, and he renewed old contacts from IRA days, printing six issues of *An Phoblacht*. He had trouble with distributors and printers because of the prevalent anti-Communist atmosphere. The IRA had now been an illegal organization for over a year and it was therefore no surprise when the authorities banned an Anti-Coronation (crowning of George VI, father of the present Queen) rally planned by left-wingers and Republicans for central Dublin on 11 May. It was not a purely IRA march but a joint effort by the National Association of the Old IRA, Cumann na mBan, Republican Congress and others.[104] The procession from Beresford Place was stopped in O'Connell Street by the baton-wielding police. Tom Barry, among others, ended up in hospital, and Frank Ryan had his nose put out of joint. A march the next night went off without incident. Barry, his head swathed in bandages, spoke as did Ryan and Paddy Rigney of the Old IRA, who condemned the police brutality of the evening before. All the statements were Republican mainstream: rejection of the English monarch in Irish constitutional affairs, a

---

[102] Irish Press, 20.03.1937.
[103] Irish Press, 19.04.1937.
[104] Letters to the Editor, Irish Press, 13.05.1937.

"real republican" constitution and the release of all republican prisoners North and South.[105]

Back on the Jarama, the older volunteers must have thought they were reliving the Great War: rats in the trenches, flooding of billets (the weather was exceptionally wet in March and April), talk of leave and deserters. Short leave to Madrid was granted to some, but the line had to be held and reserves were thin on the ground. Most deserters returned after a visit to "civilization". An interesting insight into the British battalion is given by Dr. Walter Fischer ("Dr. Langer"), the Viennese Communist and Chief of the Medical Services of the 15th Brigade from February to September 1937. His remarks about the English, he stresses, apply only to the early stages of the war: He found them incredibly stoical when wounded but held them *in toto* to be arrogant, believing they belonged to a superior race. He was especially critical of the British practice of not transferring the wounded by battalion ambulance from the first aid posts to the Brigade hospital near the front, but far further inland to the hospital of the 14th Brigade where they would be cared for by British staff. Fischer also writes, like a battalion doctor in the British Army in 1914-1918, of his efforts to enforce hygienic standards: the building of safe, dry toilets, clearing the passages of rubbish and explaining to the volunteers that their skin complaints were linked to lack of personal hygiene. Gradually, he adds, matters improved with the provision of a "shower-lorry" and disinfectants against the scourge of body lice.[106]

The Jarama front stayed generally quiet, apart from an unsuccessful fascist attack on 14 March and a half-hearted attempt by the Internationals to regain lost ground on 5 April. Cunningham had been wounded in a daring trench raid with grenades, so the leadership of the battalion devolved on Fred Copeman. He was a robust leader, a steel-erector in London who had gone from the workhouse straight into the Royal Navy as an orphan teenager. Copeman had gained something of a name for himself before Spain as one of instigators of the "Invergordon Mutiny" (1931) and as a boxer. One of his faults was to settle arguments with his fists.[107] For all that, Copeman was successful in bringing some

---

[105] Irish Press, 13.05.1937.
[106] Walter Fischer, Kurze Geschichten aus einem langen Leben. Mit einem Nachwort von Leopold Spira, Mannheim 1986, pp. 107-109. He titles this chapter „Die Individualisten".
[107] For a very negative portrait of Copeman, see Jason Gurney, Crusade in Spain, London 1976, pp.70-71.

kind of order after the chaos and sunken morale following the February battles. In George Aitken he had a stolid commissar. Copeman relied on his naval experience, replicating what he called "jankers", i.e. offenders reporting to the C.O. after breakfast. He implies that he sinned more on the side of leniency than severity when dealing with troublemakers, and the files of the Judicial Commission of the 15th Brigade confirm his humane attitude.[108]

The greatest enemy was boredom, but as Copeman's "Daily Orders" demonstrate, the men at least now had a structure to their day, and petty offenders had to do more digging of saps or trench reinforcements than the disciplined men.[109] The battalion stayed on the Jarama Front until mid-June, with one short break around May Day in Alcala de Henares.

Promising men were sent to what the battalion called OTS (Officer Training School), for training for the rank of sergeant upwards. Gerrard Doyle from Limerick was one of the chosen, spending two months at the school and leaving it in May as sergeant. There were 25 in the course from the British battalion, including Paddy Duff and Jack Nalty.[110] In contrast, Joe Ryan "had enough". He left his post in the line, was arrested in Madrid along with 12 others from the British battalion and sentenced in late April to one month in the labour battalion. The officers of the British battalion were "strongly opposed" to Ryan and three others rejoining the unit as they were "consistent grumblers" and because their influence was "very bad".[111] Joe Ryan probably escaped from detention for together with Joe Moran from Birkenhead, he tried to board an English ship in Valencia harbour on 7 May 1937, but they were apprehended.[112] While Joe Ryan seems to have been repatriated shortly afterwards to England, Moran passed through a series of gaols and punishment camps before being arrested once more, in May 1938, at Barcelona docks.[113]

Frank Ryan delayed his return to Spain in April because his sister Catherine, a nun at the Mercy Convent in Tralee, was dying. He visited her, and she lingered

---

[108] IWM Interview Fred Copeman, reels 3 and 4; RGASPI, f. 545, o. 3, d. 449, 450, 451.
[109] RGASPI, f. 545, o. 3, d. 495, ll. 1-29, Daily Orders British Battalion, April-May 1937.
[110] RGASPI, f. 545, o. 6, d. 125, l. 122; f. 545, o. 2, d. 48, l. 7; f. 545, o. 6, d. 89, l. 11.
[111] RGASPI, f. 545, o. 3, d. 450, ll. 95-97.
[112] RGASPI, f. 545, o. 2, d. 307, ll. 13-14.
[113] RGASPI, f. 545, o. 6, d. 175, ll. 5, 16, 18. Moran was badly wounded at the Ebro, losing a leg. He was repatriated to Britain at the end of 1938 (Information from Richard Baxell).

on for a further few months. He left Ireland in early June, spending a few days in London where he saw the playwright Sean O'Casey and the leaders of the CPGB. He pleaded for keeping the Irish in one unit but the reaction was "cool and unhelpful".[114] Arriving at Albacete on 15 June, Ryan was issued with a *passepartout*, designating him as "Responsable des Irlandais" and at the disposition of the Political Commissariat of the 15th Brigade.[115] So the altercations in Madrigueras had not diminished his status for he had shown his military worth on 14 February, been wounded and was now given the task of editing "The Book of the 15th Brigade". At the offices of the Brigades War Commissariat at Calle Velasquez 63, a mansion of four floors in central Madrid, Frank Ryan worked under Luigi Longo ("Gallo") and his closest collaborators on the book project were the Americans John Tisa and Sandor Voros. He had the rank of captain and a monthly salary of 315 pesetas.[116] Ryan would also act as a kind of one-man fire-brigade for the British battalion, visiting the men at the front and keeping track of his Irish comrades.

Just after the Republicans had lost the Basque provinces, the general staff in Madrid planned a new offensive for 6 July: to attack the village of Brunete, 15 miles west of Madrid, and destroy the fascist salient around it. It was the biggest operation of the anti-fascists to date, involving all International Brigades. Events were to show that the battle plan – the men fought in temperatures of 40 degrees centigrade – had severe flaws, not least over-stretched supplies lines on only one road: that from El Escorial, 30 kilometers as the crow flies. Franco's forces had air superiority and the trucks and ambulances of the Republican Army had to run the gauntlet of German Heinkel and Junker bombers.[117] Vincent Joseph Hunt, a Carrick-on-Suir-born writer from London who had volunteered for the British Medical Unit in Spain, was killed during such an air attack while driving an ambulance of the German 11th Brigade.

The Republican forces were led by men used to commanding battalions and brigades but now trying to direct divisions in a fluid battle. Lister made a grave

---

[114] Cronin, Frank Ryan, p. 115.
[115] RGASPI, f. 545, o. 2, d. 52, l. 45.
[116] RGASPI, f. 545, o. 1, d. 61, l. 84.
[117] For a description of an ambulance's drivers experiences at Brunete, see: James Yates, Mississippi to Madrid. Memoir of a Black American in the Abraham Lincoln Brigade, Seattle 1989, pp. 131-141.

error when he stopped after capturing Brunete for two days because a nearby village (Quijorna) was still in enemy hands. Vital time was also lost when General José Miaja insisted on overcoming the stiff resistance in Villaneuva de la Cañada instead of driving on.[118] It took two days to take the village, and the British volunteers (50 casualties) shot fascist prisoners after they had used civilians as a human shield when trying to escape. In that incident George Brown from Manchester, a political commissar, was shot by a fascist officer when on the ground already wounded. Other Irish fatalities were Bill Davis, an ex-Irish Guardsman brought down by a burst of machine-gun fire, the teenager Joe Kelly from Rathmines, Bill Beattie from Belfast (a Lopera veteran) and Bill McLaughlin (Loughran).

Losses in the two American battalions were just as heavy. Stewart O'Neill, a Belfast man who had gone to Spain from Canada, was a sergeant in the 3rd Company of the Lincolns when killed storming the village. After the capture of Villaneuva, the battalions were directed to storm "Mosquito Ridge" (the Heights of Romanillos). In this first of many fruitless attempts, the Afro-American commander of the new George Washington Battalion, Oliver Law, was killed, Johnny Power, company commissar, was shot twice in the leg, and Mick Kelly from Ballinasloe was killed by a sniper when out scouting with an American observation officer.[119] One of the most searing memories of the brigadista survivors is that of unbearable thirst during the three-week battle. The division in which they served had only one water-tank lorry, which was soon smashed up in an air-raid. A replacement tanker was found by the American doctor Sidney Robbins, but he and his assistant were killed near the front when a bomb hit the vehicle.[120]

The exhausted brigaders were withdrawn into reserve on 11 July. The British battalion was now down to 208 men, while the American losses were so heavy that the two battalions were merged into one, a decrease in effective strength

---

[118] Anthony Beevor, The Battle for Spain. The Spanish Civil War, Penguin Books 2001, pp. 278-279.
[119] O'Connor, Soldier of Liberty, pp. 26-27. For a description of Power's selfless conduct during the battle, see: Harry Fisher, Comrades. Tales of a Brigadista in the Spanish Civil War, University of Nebraska Press 1997, pp. 60-63.
[120] Landis, Abraham Lincoln Brigade, pp. 213-214; Fischer, Kurze Geschichten, pp. 114-117.

from roughly 870 to 520.[121] A week later, Franco started a crushing counter-offensive with impressive air support. His forces regained much of the ground taken by the Republicans since 6 July, but the fascist troops, too, were soon exhausted, and the battle came to an end on 26 July.

Two events in the last days had a negative effect on the already shaken morale of the British battalion. George Nathan, now a Major on the staff, was killed while organizing the final withdrawal from the Brunete salient. He was hit by a splinter from an aerial bomb just after drinking brandy in tin cups to congratulate Steve Nelson on his appointment as Brigade Commissar.[122] Shortly afterwards on the same day, there was a discussion at Brigade headquarters on receipt of the news that Republican troops were trapped in Quijorna nine miles away and needed help. Wally Tapsell was vociferously against Nelson's suggestion that the men should be asked. The ragged and exhausted remnants of the Brigade finally dragged themselves to their feet and set off, but after 500 yards the news came through that the encircled troops at Quijorna had managed to extricate themselves.[123]

Tapsell, who, like the Kilkenny-born George Brown, had grown tired of work in the political commissariat at the Albacete base and had joined the battalion as a soldier in June, was appointed battalion commissar in the last week of the Brunete offensive. His outbursts against the divisional and brigade leadership verged on mutiny, and his remarks on the "uselessness" of Spanish troops went down badly with the more politically developed British volunteers.[124] Tapsell criticized almost everybody in his immediate vicinity (Gal, Cunningham, Aitken), was detained briefly and escaped a court-martial only because of his status in the British party – former circulation manager of the *Daily Worker*, and ex-member of the Central Committee.[125]

In fact, the British leadership in Spain was hopelessly divided. Existing tensions between leading officers were exacerbated by the strains of the hellish three weeks

[121] Baxell, Unlikely Warriors, p. 232; Landis, Abraham Lincoln Brigade, p. 217.
[122] Steve Nelson, James R. Barrett and Rob Ruck, Steve Nelson. American Radical, University of Pittsburgh Press 1981, pp. 221-222.
[123] Ibid., pp. 224-225.
[124] IWM Interview Walter Greenhalgh, reel 6.
[125] RGASPI, f. 545, o. 6, d. 207, ll. 15-18; NAUK, KV 2/1192 Walter Tapsell; Baxell, Unlikely Warriors, pp. 233-237.

in the Brunete furnace. Cunningham, promoted above his ability as Major in charge of three battalions, and Copeman, seem to have suffered nervous breakdowns. In August and September, Copeman, Cunningham, Aitken (Brigade Commissar since May 1937), Tapsell and Bert Williams were recalled by Harry Pollitt. In a turbulent sitting of the Polburo, Cunningham was thrown to the wolves. Only Copeman and Tapsell were permitted to return to Spain. Meanwhile, the Welsh miners' leader Bill Paynter was trying to rebuild the battalion. He was against Tapsell being re-appointed battalion commissar, arguing that "he was bound to come to loggerheads with the leadership and react in his usual boisterous style".[126]

Frank Ryan was present at the early fighting in July, and seeing the losses, began to organize repatriations. He visited the Americans (now down from 900 to 280 volunteers)[127] on 27 July. He told Peter O'Connor (the only uninjured Irishman still with the Lincolns) that he was being sent home. In all, 38 Irishmen were repatriated during 1937, some on health and compassionate grounds. Ten were sent back at the suggestion of the British battalion, including Paddy Brady, who arrived in Liverpool with his arm still in plaster, the consequence of a shoulder injury inflicted by a sniper in Villaneuva. One Irish exile was expedited out of Spain by the Americans (the Canadian volunteer Tom "Pop" Cochrane who was 51 years of age) and the remaining twenty-six due to Ryan's lobbying. In some cases, Frank Ryan was economical with the truth, stating, for example, that Jim O'Regan was recalled for service in the IRA, and Paddy Duff for service in the army of the Irish Free State.[128]

In almost all cases Ryan could also plead chronic ill-health or wounds. Four of the men repatriated by Ryan – O'Regan, Duff, Michael Lehane and Jack Nalty – were back in the British battalion after a few months. Gerrard Doyle was also nominated for repatriation in September, but since it was not granted, he grew disillusioned and demoralized hanging around camps in the rear. He re-joined the British battalion in February 1938.[129] It says much for Frank Ryan's standing in Albacete that he could achieve this result, for most repatriations applied for by British and American volunteers were not entertained or delayed: the Republican

[126] NAUK, KV 2/1192, Walter Tapsell, Special Branch entry 03.09.1937.
[127] Landis, Abraham Lincoln Brigade, p. 233.
[128] RGASPI, f. 545, o. 6, d. 53.
[129] RGASPI, f. 545, o. 6, d. 125, l. 125.

high command needed such seasoned soldiers, and Marty was unhelpful because he had a clinching argument: The volunteers from Germany, Central, Eastern or South-Eastern Europe faced imprisonment, concentration camps or worse if they went home.

When the remainder of the British battalion was pulled back on 25 July, there were only 42 men present. At least 36 had deserted, but most of these drifted back after resting and a talk with Will Paynter, the representative of the CPGB with the Spanish party and a compassionate listener.[130] Frank Ryan was assigned to "work with the leading comrades until the [British] Battalion is once more in a strong position".[131] A few score Americans were drafted into the British unit and the leadership was now given to two Irish officers who had good records (Lopera, Las Rozas, Jarama, Chimora, Pozoblanco) – Peter Daly and Paddy O'Daire. Daly, a Wexford man, had served in the IRA and the British army and had been wounded twice, both times in the hip, at Jarama and Chimora. He was promoted captain and appointed C.O. of the British battalion on 12 August 1937. Paddy O'Daire had served seven years in infantry battalions of the Irish Free State Army and was C.O. of the British battalion for two spells in 1937.

In order to draw away Francoist troops from the northern battlefields (Santander was under siege), the Republican generals planned a new offensive in Aragon, a drive to capture Zaragoza. The area was on a dormant front and lightly held, it was said. This time the Republicans had an advantage in the number of troops, tanks and aircraft, but the military leaders again made the mistake of crushing every nest of resistance in their way instead of forging ahead towards the main objectives. The British battalion, only 400 strong and Spanish to the degree of fifty per cent, moved towards the front on 18 August. On 26 August, the other battalions of the 15th Brigade took Quinto, just south of the Ebro, after street fighting and with the help of the British anti-tank battery. To the east rose Purburell, a strongly fortified position without a water supply. Daly was told it was "lightly held" and ordered to storm it. He was fatally wounded in the stomach during the first assault and died in Benicasim hospital on 5 September.

His replacement Paddy O'Daire refused to attack Purburell Hill without artillery support. After the British anti-tank unit had knocked out the fascist machine-gun

---

[130] Baxell, Unlikely Warriors, pp. 233, 238-239.
[131] RGASPI, f. 545, o. 3, d. 441, l.87, Steve Nelson to Will Paynter, 17.08.1937.

nests on the summit the following day, the trenches at the top were cleared in an exuberant charge. Nonetheless O'Daire was "carpeted" by Čopić, but the Glenties man won the argument by quoting from his pocket edition of British Army Field Services Regulations Part III which "showed that he was correct in taking his decision."[132]

While the British lay before Mediana, the Americans, Canadians, their accompanying Spanish battalion and the Dimitrov brigade moved up to capture the village of Belchite, a veritable fortress of trenches, barricades and sniper posts, and a vital strongpoint in the fascist defensive line. Once again, the attacking forces could depend on the British anti-tank battery. Belchite was known in Spain as adjacent to the hamlet of Fuentdetodos, the birth-place of Francisco Goya in 1746, and as the town Napoleonic troops could not capture during the Peninsular War. Battle was joined on 1 September. The resistance was fierce and the main point of resistance was the church of San Augustin at the northern end of the town.

Among the Canadians with the Americans (they soon formed their own unit, the Mackenzie-Papineau battalion) was Jim Woulfe from Athea in Co. Limerick.

Athea, Bridge St., 1960s. Woulffe home corner house with plaque

---

[132] Alexander, British Volunteers, p. 149.

Born in 1899 as the fourth of seven children, four girls and three boys, Jim grew up in a prosperous household: the father had a farm and a draper's shop. He joined the IRA in 1918 and served as a signaller in 'G' company of the 2nd battalion of the West Limerick Brigade. He also took part in the Civil War, was captured in October 1922 and released fourteen months later. Like many defeated Republicans, Woulfe emigrated the following year and found work as a logger in Canada. During the Depression Woulfe, now a Communist, was blacklisted by employers. His main political task was to recruit seamen for the Canadian CP. He was one of the first Canadians to volunteer for the Brigades, arriving in Spain in March 1937.

Jim Wolfe

Killed in action on the Belchite front in Spain. Had a host of friends in Vancouver, was a soldier in the Irish Republican Army. Honored member of the Communist Party, was a loyal active trade unionist.

DON'T FORGET, HIS BUDDIES STILL NEED SMOKES.

Commemorative photo Jim Woulfe

In June he was at the Brigade's NCO training school at Pozo Rubio. So he was probably a sergeant when he took part in his first battle, at Brunete the following month as a member of No. 1 Co., Lincoln Battalion.[133]

On the morning of 2 September, most of the officers in the American unit attacking in Belchite were shot down. Their commander Hans Amlie refused to proceed further in senseless charges. His commissar Steve Nelson went scouting

---

[133] RGASPI, f. 545, o. 6, d. 575, l. 122.

and found a sheltered ditch leading into the town and continued by this route, discovering to his surprise that the olive-oil factory opposite San Augustin church was empty. The factory became Brigade HQ and groups tried to work their way into the town, fighting house to house and suffering high casualties. The attention of the Brigade staff now focused on the town, tanks were brought up, and with the British anti-tank crew, began to demolish the buildings still occupied by the fascists.

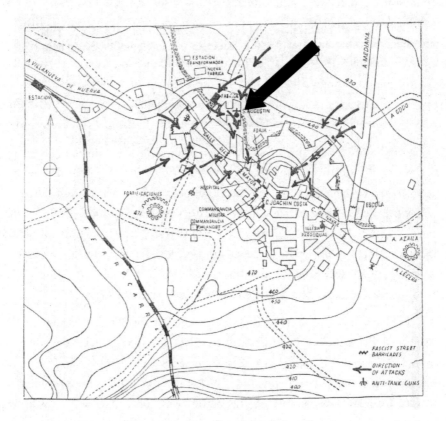

Belchite, Sept. 1937. Arrow shows where Jim Woulfe was killed at S. Augustin Church

The defenders in the church had held out for days by the expedient of rushing out of the church during a bombardment and ducking back when the shellfire ceased. Supported by heavy machine-guns and tanks, two groups from the American battalion rushed the church. One group was brought down, but the other broke in through a side door, overcame a machine-gun crew and hoisted a light MG up to the gallery. Using picks and hand-grenades the men broke through the gallery wall, and firing from above, killed the remainder of the fascist garrison. That was 5 September. Jim Woulfe was badly wounded in the face and neck by a hand-grenade and he collapsed in the church courtyard. He could neither speak nor smoke, so he gave his cigarettes to his friend Peter Nielson. Woulfe died that evening in hospital, probably in Hijar. The fighting now entered its most vicious phase, when the Internationals had to move forward by breaking down the walls from house to house to escape the snipers and street barricades of the defenders. The tide began slowly to turn, the first fascist troops surrendered. Captured snipers were executed on the spot. Then Brigade Commissar Dave Doran "borrowed" a Republican propaganda truck and let the defenders know over the loud-hailer that their only hope was to give up. The last act in the bloody drama, played out in the evening of 5 September, was an attempt by the most fanatical officers and Falange officials to escape using fleeing inhabitants as a human shield. The 24th Spanish battalion attached to the 15th Brigade finished that sortie, killing every fascist officer.[134]

The news of the death of Jim Woulfe in the *The Irish Press* of 29 November shocked Athea village. His mother Maryanne, now in her early sixties, called on Fr. Chawke, the Catholic curate, and he in turn contacted Dublin where Walter Gilligan, an official in the Department of Local Government, asked his colleagues in External Affairs to ascertain if the report were true. The Spanish Legation in Shrewsbury Road was able to furnish the death certificate, in Spanish and English, on 10 February. Mrs Woulfe received the document in April.[135]

The Republican drive to Zaragoza ended in one of the worst debâcles of the International Brigades during the whole war: the attempt to take the town of Fuentes del Ebro with tanks in the second week of October. It was over-ambitious, badly planned and ended in disaster: the British battalion, numbering only 150 Irish and British before the battle, was further reduced, losing its commander, Harold Fry; the Americans had 70 casualties and the new Canadian

---

[134] Victor Howard with Mac Reynolds, The Mackenzie-Papineau Battalion. The Canadian Contingent in the Spanish Civil War, Carleton University Press 1986, pp.135-139; Landis, Abraham Lincoln Brigade, pp. 287-303.
[135] NAI, DFA, 4/339/84.

battalion of 605 men suffered 170 killed and wounded; the attached Spanish 24th battalion was virtually annihilated.[136]

Frank Ryan was busy collecting material for the Brigade book, using couriers like Walter Greenhalgh to collect manuscripts from the units and have them typeset in Madrid.[137] Initially, the American leadership, intent on getting maximum space in Ryan's publication for their leading comrades, believed the book would be finished by November 1937, after which Ryan should go on a propaganda tour of America.[138] The wounding of Steve Nelson at Belchite, however, prevented Ryan from leaving the 15th Brigade to concentrate on the typescript. Then he fell ill and there were probably production problems with the printers because of the heavy aerial bombing of Madrid in early winter 1937/38. Ryan had to defer his departure planned for Christmas week, hoping to be in Ireland for St. Patrick's Day after he had sent the typescript to the printers in February.[139]

When the Republican front broke in Aragon in early March, there could be no more talk of an imminent homecoming. Ryan hurried to the Brigade at the front and had to argue with the American Brigade Commissar Dave Doran (Nelson's successor) to gain access to Čopić whose only fault with the proofs was that they did not "state the correct I.B. line". In a more conciliatory tone he intimated he would talk to Luigi Longo in order to have the book published as soon as possible. Doran, too, promised his support and suggested that Ryan should work for him in the British battalion. Ryan was glad to be back with the British, as he wrote to Madrid on 28 March:

> *They're feeding me and giving me little jobs to keep me going. They're a very good bunch, better than at any previous stage, I'd say.*[140]

---

[136] Landis, Abraham Lincoln Brigade, pp. 314-323; Howard, Mackenzie-Papineau, pp. 141-150.
[137] IWM Interview Walter Greenhalgh, reel 5.
[138] RGASPI, f. 545, o. 3, d. 441, ll. 95-96.
[139] Cronin, Frank Ryan, pp. 124-132.
[140] RGASPI, f. 545, o. 6, d. 129, l. 18.

3

Prisoner: Frank Ryan
1938-1940

In the early spring of 1938, Franco's troops and his Italian allies smashed through the Republican lines in Aragon, in two main thrusts, beginning on 9 March and resuming the offensive three weeks later. His men finally reached the Mediterranean on 15 April, cutting the Republic in two. The superiority of Franco's insurgent forces during the "March retreats" was so overwhelming as regards air-power (Messerschmitt 109s and Stukas), artillery (German 88 anti-aircraft pieces) and tanks (mainly Italian) and the losses in the 15th Brigade so grave, that desertions were commonplace. The English-speaking battalions had been chased around Aragon by a superior enemy, repeatedly finding that the next town on the line of retreat was already occupied by the fascists. It was like the story collected by the Grimm brothers about the race between the hedgehog and the hare, the hedgehog (fascists) was always at the finishing line before the hare (republicans), who finally drops dead from exhaustion – the hare could not distinguish the male from the female hedgehog. At the beginning of March the British battalion was at the full strength of 650 due to partially trained recruits being rushed from the training base at Tarazona, or men discharged from hospitals and punishment companies.

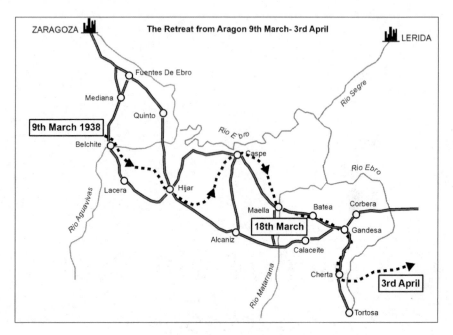

Map of retreats

Numbers had fallen to about 300 when the worst in a series of debilitating disasters occurred at dawn on 31 March. The other IB units were positioned on a defensive line behind a river, but the British Battalion was pushed south and west on the road from Gandesa to Alcaniz in order to link up with Spanish Republicans. What the battalion did not know was that the 11th Division led by Enrique Lister on their flank had already retreated. The front was open and there was no sign of retreating Republican soldiers. Moving gingerly forward, the unit camped outside Calaceite late on 30 March and resumed the advance before dawn. The men proceeded through the village and were supposed to take up defensive positions a kilometer beyond. Rounding a bend in the half-light, the main group of the British battalion ran into Italian tanks, while other tanks and charging infantry emerged from the trees on the side of the road.[1] There was a bloodbath on the highway, many Internationals running for their lives; the men had no hand-grenades, it was every man for himself. Major Frank Ryan, now in the ranks as a simple soldier, initially thought the tanks were friendly ones. So did Wally Tapsell, Battalion Commissar, who was shot dead by one of the drivers.

---

[1] Baxell, Unlikely Warriors, pp. 314-316.

About 140 Internationals were captured (including at least 25 Irishmen) and 150 killed or wounded.[2]

Three Irishmen, Bob Doyle, Eddie Vallely ("Peter Brady") and Jackie Lemon were carrying their Degtyaryov light MG, ammunition and spare parts in the column beside Frank Ryan. They were surrounded and captured with Ryan, who had neither pistol nor rifle. In his tunic, with his Sam Browne belt, breeches and leggings, he was obviously an officer. Marching off into captivity, Ryan said to Doyle, "My book comes out today." Lined up against a barn, the captives were asked who their officer was. Despite the protests of his comrades, Ryan stood up and gave his name and rank. An execution squad of the Guardia Civil drove up and intended to shoot the prisoners against a wall, but Italian officers argued with the dreaded police who left. It was now late morning and the prisoners were kept in a wired compound. Ryan was again questioned by an Italian officer, and refusing to give further information, was struck in the face. Lemon and Doyle had to restrain Frank from retaliating.[3] The British and Irish prisoners were fortunate that their captors were Italians, eager to exchange these "Reds" for Italian aviators, or soldiers taken prisoner in one of the few Republican successes of the war – the battle of Guadalajara a year previously. So the Calaceite prisoners were spared summary execution, unlike 140 Americans captured by Spanish units.[4]

Max Parker from New York was Ryan's interpreter as they marched against the flow of hostile troops and their transport. Ryan tried to keep spirits up, shouting encouragement and insisting to the Italian officers that the prisoners be given food and water. While the parched men were drinking, a German officer approached. He asked why Frank Ryan was fighting in Spain and not in Ireland. He received the answer that it was the same fight in both places. The men were loaded on to trucks and driven to Alcaniz.[5] The next day the prisoners were taken to San Gregorio Military Academy in Zaragoza and, two days later, placed under heavy guard on the train for Burgos. Their destination was the Benedictine

---

[2] Alexander, British Volunteers, p. 179.
[3] Doyle, Brigadista, pp. 62-65.
[4] Carl Geiser, Prisoners of the Good Fight. The Spanish Civil War 1936-1939, Westport Conn. 1986, pp. 263-266.
[5] Ibid., pp. 62-63.

Monastery San Pedro de Cardeña, a decrepit building near the city and the burial place of El Cid.

The captives, including Ryan, had been interrogated at Zaragoza, and some were allowed to talk to journalists on 2 April. Ryan's name was mentioned and that he, as an officer, was in immediate danger of death.[6] Back in Dublin, his sister Eilís heard on the radio that night that an Irish newspaper editor had been captured by Franco's troops. On the advice of Peadar O'Donnell, she and her parents visited Eamon de Valera at his home. The Irish Prime Minister immediately telephoned the Irish representative in Spain, Leopold Kerney. The Ryan family also approached Alfie Byrne, the Lord Mayor of Dublin, Cardinal McRory, the Papal Nuncio and Eoin O'Duffy. All signed a petition to Franco asking for clemency.[7] When news of his capture was printed in Irish newspapers from 4 April,[8] public bodies such as Limerick County Council,[9] the students of UCD[10] or the executive of the Gaelic League[11] followed suit. There were few instances of open, as distinct from clandestine, protests against this campaign of humanity. Timothy Linehan, a Fine Gael T.D. from North Cork, argued for the closure of the Irish Legation to Republican Spain, adding:

> I say that if there are Irish nationals who have chosen to go out and take the part of the Red Government of Spain and find themselves in trouble...the money of the taxpayers of this country should not be used to get these people out of their trouble.[12]

The second open protest came from Fr. James O'Dea, Chairman of the Galway County Board of the GAA, who attacked the endorsement of the Frank Ryan clemency appeal by the Gaelic League as "an example of abject cowardice", with the grotesque comment that he knew "many people in the Gaelic League who

---

[6] Ibid., p. 97.
[7] Saothar 1996, pp. 137-138.
[8] Irish Press. 04.04.1938.
[9] Irish Press, 09.05.1938.
[10] Irish Press, 03.05.1938.
[11] Irish Press, 02.05.1938. Other bodies seeking clemency for Ryan were: The Irish Academy of Art, NUJ, and INTO (Geiser, Prisoners, p. 118).
[12] http://debates.oireachts.ie/dail/1938/07/14/00030.asp. Accessed 21.11.2013.

have always been against the GAA and whose sole object was to revive Rugby in this country".[13]

Relations between the Irish Free State and Republican Spain were correct, but sporadic. Dublin refused the request of the Valencia government to appoint a new legate to Dublin in June 1937 (the earlier one had gone over to Franco), obviously fearful of the reaction of the Catholic Church.[14] Leopold Kerney was the official Irish representative to the Republican authorities since August 1935, but in May 1936 he took seriously ill, and on orders from Dublin, the Madrid Legation was closed in mid-August 1936. Again on instructions from home he did not return to the Spanish capital on resuming office in February 1937. Instead he set up office in a hotel in the French resort of St. Jean-de-Luz just across from the Spanish border town of Irun. It was extremely fortunate for Ryan that Kerney was not in the Republican Zone, in Valencia or Barcelona, whence visits to fascist territory would have been virtually impossible, but near Spain's northern border, 240 kilometers away from Franco's headquarters in Burgos.[15] Kerney was considered somewhat of an outsider by his colleagues in the Department of External Affairs in St. Stephen's Green because, having taken the Republican side in the Irish Civil War, he had been sacked in 1922, only to be reinstated by de Valera ten years later.[16]

On 4 April, the day that the telegram from de Valera reached Franco's office, Frank Ryan was having an altercation in Zaragoza with William Carney of *The New York Times* who was in the company of Colonel Jusset, Franco's military judicial assessor. Carney was dubbed "General Bill" by the American brigaders because of his pro-fascist sympathies. The row between him and Ryan started, according to Kerney who met Carney eight days later, on the question of the American's journalistic impartiality. Carney did everything to blacken the man from Limerick in the eyes of the Irish diplomat: Ryan was a glowering gorilla, an atheist, anti-religious and a separatist like the Basques and the Catalans. He then added tit-bits from Jusset, that Ryan had shot nationalist officers at Brunete the

---

[13] Irish Press, Readers' View, letter from Liam O Buachalla, Vice-President of the Gaelic League, 01.07.1938.
[14] Michael Kennedy et al. (eds), Documents on Irish Foreign Policy (DIFP), 5, 1937-1939, Dublin 2006, p. 78.
[15] Ibid., p. 288. Kerney to Dublin, 02.05.1938.
[16] Ibid., p. xxvi.

previous July and had looted their property; another murky source consisted of statements of American prisoners trying to curry favour with their gaolers, that "Ryan was a 'tough guy' and that anybody might not be very safe in his company and that he frequently killed prisoners". Kerney duly reported, in diplomatic terms, that he considered Carney a hostile witness, and should no progress be made in attempts to release Ryan, he suggested that the British representative to Franco, Sir Robert Hodgson, might enquire in Burgos.[17]

One factor that hampered Leopold Kerney in his tireless endeavours over the next two years was the campaign of deceit, disinformation and denunciations against Frank Ryan, Franco's most highly ranked prisoner from the ranks of the International Brigades. Whether putting Ryan on the list of British nationals on whose behalf Hodgson was negotiating a prisoner exchange would have expedited his release or not is open to question. On the occasion of visit by Col. C.C. Martin, British military attaché at Burgos, whose main concern was to find out who recruited the men in Britain, Frank Ryan refused to be put on his list, saying he would never "hide behind the Union Jack". Neither did Doyle, Lemon or Maurice Levitas, a plumber who grew up in the Jewish community on Dublin's South Circular Road. All three declared their Irish nationality and were not released until February 1939.[18] Furthermore, Hodgson turned out to be another pedlar of unfounded rumours about Ryan, while at the beginning eager to believe what the fascist officers told him about that "very bad case" Frank Ryan – he had looted prisoners.[19] In any case, Ryan was an "official Irish" prisoner, and questions posed in the House of Commons by the left-wing Labour M.P. George Strauss on numerous occasions were answered in that vein.[20]

Meanwhile, back in the San Pedro concentration camp, on the upper stories of the monastery, the prisoners were trying to organize themselves into some form of unit discipline. Ryan, although often so ill as to spend most of the day lying down,[21] was seen as a leading figure. The men were held in appalling conditions in the dormitories: there was only one water tap for over 600 Internationals, a

---

[17] Ibid., Kerney to Dublin, 13.04.1938.
[18] Doyle, Brigadista, pp. 80, 90-91.
[19] DIFP, 5, pp. 270-271, Kerney to Dublin, 16.04.1938.
[20] http://hansard.millbanksystems.com/commons/1939/may/17/spain; ibid. 21.06.1939, 14.12.1939,24.04.1939, 29.01.1941. All accessed 06.11.2013.
[21] Doyle, Brigadista, p. 80.

handful of toilets and starvation rations; many men were still suffering from wounds, and were further tormented by lice and fleas because there were no washing facilities, soap or towels. Diarrhoea and boils caused by lack of vitamins were common complaints. The hospital was run by kind Basque nuns who were imprisoned because they had refused to sign a statement that Guernica had been bombed by the "Reds". Going down to the courtyard for meals or the count parade was the opportunity for a trio of sadistic sergeants to flog the men with canes – one wielded a weighted bull's penis sheathed in leather. And there was a separate *sala de tortura* where a prisoner for the slightest of transgressions was subjected to prolonged beatings by the military warders. Prisoners slow on their feet down the stairs were easy targets, like Jack O'Beirne from Balbriggan who suffered badly from arthritis.[22]

Frank Ryan was the unanimous choice to chair a kangaroo court to try an International who had been caught red-handed stealing a bread roll (*chusco*) from a comrade, and he said:

> *Our circumstances here make it necessary for us to take a different attitude towards stealing. We are in the hands of the fascists and what they have in store for us we do not know. But we do know that it is important that we stand together, fully united. And to be united, we must be able to trust each other. It is because stealing a small piece of bread threatens this all-important unity we treasure so highly that this court has been convened. The object is not so much to punish the guilty as it is to preserve and strengthen our unity as we face our fascist jailers.*

The defendant admitted his guilt and the matter was considered settled when he agreed to share his *chusco* over some days with his aggrieved comrade.[23]

As the Irish Free State (it was called Éire after December 1937) did not recognize Franco's junta until 10 February 1939,[24] Leopold Kerney could not contact the fascist authorities himself in 1938 and was reliant on what others told him in respect of the effect, if any, that Irish clemency appeals were making in Burgos.

---

[22] Geiser, Prisoners, p. 156-157; Doyle, Brigadista, p. 224-225.
[23] Geiser, Prisoners, p. 113-114.
[24] De Valera wanted to do so earlier but felt he had to follow the example of other Commonwealth countries. See: McGarry, Irish Politics and the Spanish Civil War, pp. 228-233.

In late May Kerney had a long discussion with Carney on the Ryan case, when he learned that the American journalist had been led to believe that Ryan would be handed over to Hodgson, even though the latter, complaining about pleas from Ireland sent to him from the Foreign Office, felt "that this Ryan case was a nuisance because he had many other serious matters to attend to". Carney had also been told by his fascist contacts that Ryan "was supposed to have commanded firing squads and to have executed prisoners with his own hands".[25]

More disturbing was news about the machinations of Thomas Gunning, a sinister informer and intriguer, a convinced fascist who had studied as a seminarian in Heidelberg and was later editor of the Catholic *Standard* in Dublin. He was a close associate of Eoin O'Duffy since 1933 and his aide-de-camp in Spain with the "Irish Brigade" in 1936/37.[26] Robert Stradling's pithy portrait of the man is all warts:

> *From the moment that O'Duffy agreed to the appointment of Tom Gunning as his personal assistant, he and his men were bought and sold. Gunning was a failed priest and failed journalist, who turned into an arrogant adventurer, out for a good time at others' expense. Heavy drinking, indiscreet and anti-Semitic, he ended up working for the German Ministry of Propaganda in 1940. In the interim, after the disbandment of the Brigade, he added personal defamation to his betrayal of O'Duffy, and (moved by little more than gratuitous spite) intrigued with various nationalist contacts to procure the execution of Frank Ryan, captured leader of the Irish Internationals.*[27]

Evidence about Gunning indicates that he was an alcoholic in the last throes of TB – he was spitting blood. Perhaps he was, temporarily at least, mentally unstable. William Carney told Kerney that he knew Gunning as a minor correspondent for Reuters and Associated Press with close contacts to Franco's inner circle, including foreign minister General Gomez Jordana. The terminally-ill Gunning, Carney added, was in favour of Ryan being shot, and failing that, he should be extradited by Hodgson. Since Gunning was criticizing Ireland's non-

---

[25] NAI, DFA 244/8, Kerney to Dublin 24.05.1938.
[26] McGarry, Irish Politics, pp. 23, 38, 267.
[27] Stradling, The Irish and the Spanish Civil War, p. 118. As he censored the mail of the Irish Blueshirt volunteers in Spain, Gunning, Stadling believes, had links to the Francoist secret service (Ibid.).

accreditation to Burgos and saw Frank Ryan as a left-wing ally of de Valera, Kerney believed him to be agitating actively against official Irish foreign policy, not only as regards Ryan's fate.[28] Gunning was a traitor of sorts, for on 1 June he wrote to the Francoist authorities that Ryan should be shot because he had assassinated seven people in Ireland.[29] On the same day Kerney sent his secretary Mary ('Maisie') Donnelly to dine with journalists from New York, and the group was witness to a drunken rant of Gunning's in a restaurant in St. Jean-de-Luz. To the astounded listeners, including the world-famous journalist Walter Duranty of *The New York Times*, Gunning expounded on Franco's treatment of enemies ("too damn soft") before giving details of a case close to his heart:

> *There's one man, an International, that was captured at Gandesa; he had seven murders to his name outside the country and he was a scoundrel; for two months I have been trying to get him shot; I've gone to them with tears in my eyes to get them to shoot him and they <u>won't</u> shoot him.*

Asked by Duranty if these murders had taken place in Spain, Gunning answered, "No, Ireland", and if he "had his way no time would be wasted court-martialling prisoners; they should be shot right away".[30]

Two days later, Gunning went to the confessional – to Leopold Kerney's office at the Golf Hotel. He tried to unburden his conscience to the Minister in a partial "confession", refraining from mentioning that he had alleged that Frank Ryan had carried out seven assassinations in Ireland and giving his opinion that it was now unlikely that the Limerick man would be executed: at Zaragoza, he emphasized, Ryan was badly beaten because he refused to give the fascist salute but had not been killed on the spot, as Internationals usually were, because a Spanish journalist had mentioned his presence to his colleagues. Gunning now believed that the charge that Ryan had shot Francoist prisoners had no basis in fact.[31]

On Sunday, 12 June, one hundred British prisoners were released from San Pedro and transferred to a prison in San Sebastian. They finally arrived home in

---

[28] NAI, DFA 244/8, Kerney to Dublin 24.05.1938
[29] Geiser, Prisoners, p. 125.
[30] NAI, DFA 244/8, Kerney to Dublin, 02.06.1938. Emphasis in the original.
[31] Ibid., Kerney to Dublin, 07.06.1938.

late October 1938.[32] Among them was Gerrard Doyle from Upper William Street, Limerick, who stayed in Britain.[33] Ryan was also led away on 12 June from San Pedro, by three armed guards in a jeep. He believed his liberation was at hand and carried notes from Bob Doyle and Jackie Lemon to post in Ireland.[34] But it was not to be, for Ryan was taken to the Central Prison in Burgos, a modern gaol with a capacity for 1,000 inmates and now holding four times that number. The prisoners spent their day in the courtyard and executions were frequent. Ryan was interrogated on 13 June for nine hours. Two days later the "trial" took place. Ryan could speak to his "defender" for a precious few minutes beforehand. He and the interpreter, Ryan sensed, were sympathetic to his plight. It was obvious that the tribunal had no case, only denunciations from Ireland. Ryan, resigned to being shot, the fate of thousands of POW officers in Franco captivity, objected to a conviction based on anonymous letters and demanded that the representative of the Irish Government in Spain be called to vouch for his character. This was dismissed out of hand since Kerney was still accredited to Valencia. Ryan was probably amazed to hear that he was charged with involvement in the murder of the father-in-law of Robert Hodgson, whose presence at the farcical proceedings Ryan now requested.[35]

The murder victim was Vice-Admiral Henry Boyle Townshend Somerville who had been assassinated by the IRA at his home in West Cork in March 1936 because he had written letters of recommendation for local boys wishing to join the Royal Navy. The killing was probably a botched operation: the order "get him" was taken literally by the killers, while it seems that IRA leader Tom Barry wanted the old man kidnapped.[36] Ryan, who had left the IRA two years previously, had nothing to do with the murder – it was a "local job".

---

[32] Baxell, Unlikely Warriors, pp. 369-370.
[33] Limerick Chronicle, 27.10.1938, cited in: Barrie Wharton/Des Ryan, „The Last Crusade: Limerick's role in the Spanish Civil War", Old Limerick Journal, Summer Edition 2001 (online), p. 14.
[34] Doyle, Brigadista, pp. 81-82.
[35] DIFP, 5, pp. 470-475, Kerney to Dublin, 17.06.1939.
[36] Bell, Secret Army, p. 126; Meda Ryan, Tom Barry, IRA Freedom Fighter, Cork 2003, p. 218. The IRA squad leader Jim O'Neill who carried out the attack was never charged. His grandchild Joseph O'Neill wrote a book about the incident. See: http://www.theguardian.com/books/2001/feb/10/books.guardianreview, accessed 26.04.2014.

Frank Ryan was also surprised how his defending officer at the tribunal on 15 June had the information to plead that he had three sisters nuns in Ireland. When asked to speak himself, he did not ask for mercy and said his "only crime" was to have fought in the Republican ranks. When Ryan left the court he was saluted by all present and kept in handcuffs for nine hours after his return to prison. At the trial he noticed the prosecuting officers leafing through press-cuttings and believed that the long letter from Ireland on his "crimes" (the murders of Kevin O'Higgins in 1927 and Somerville nine years later, for example) read out in translation to the court was largely a transcription of Professor James Hogan's *Could Ireland Become Communist?: The Facts of the Case*, published in Cork in 1936. Ryan surmised that the letter had been sent by Miss Aileen O'Brien, a lobbyist for Franco in the USA.[37]

O'Brien, born in 1913, was the daughter of an American ambassador and, like Gunning, had been educated in Germany. She was international secretary of the Pro-Deo Movement, a kind of ultra-Catholic "Black International" based in Switzerland, had come to Ireland in 1936 and was briefly international secretary of Belton's ICF. She helped Belton receive the bulk of the monies collected in Irish churches for Franco, but was dismissed from his inner circle at the end of 1936 because she was more "Spanish fascist" than "Irish Catholic" in her outlook.[38] Later Ryan believed that his comrade Vincent O'Donnell from Dun Laoghaire, a prisoner in San Pedro, perhaps knew the identity of the anonymous letter-writer.[39]

Ryan was under sentence of death, which could be executed at any time. He shared a cell with 17 others, of whom nine were taken out for execution each day and their places filled by nine others.[40] He learned only eighteen months later that the capital verdict had been commuted to thirty years in prison.[41] Under this tremendous psychological strain and in poor health, he wrote in French to Eilís on 29 June, thanking her for the money sent via Mr. Kerney, asking for clothes

---

[37] DIFP, 5, pp. 473-474, Kerney to Dublin, 17.06.1939.
[38] McGarry, Irish Politics, pp. 110, 126, 128, 174, 282, 286.
[39] NAI, DFA, A 20/4, Frank Ryan, Part 2, undated letter from Ryan to Kerney, handed in at the Irish Legation in Madrid on 4 January 1940.
[40] Irish Times, 10.04.1975, Frank Ryan Profile 4 by Michael McInerney.
[41] DIFP, 6, pp. 122-123, Kerney to Dublin, 23.12.1939. The commutation was dated 12.11.1939.

and shoes and, as was his wont, saying he was physically well. The last line was a plea in Gaelic code:

> Best Regards to all my friends, and especially Deireadh le [end of], Baolbáis [danger of death] and Sílim [I think].[42]

In July-August 1938 Frank Ryan was visited in Burgos prison on several occasions by a Franco officer, Antonio Vallejo Nájera, in civilian life professor of psychology at Madrid University. He did not make any promises to Ryan, saying the interviews would be used "neither in favour nor against". With death peering over his shoulder, Ryan felt he had nothing to lose in describing the motivation for his Spanish involvement, arguments he had not wished to present to the tribunal. There is no documentary evidence to contradict the essence, if not the detail, of Ryan's succinct summary:

1) *I didn't bring a battn. To Spain. I could have done so. In fact, I prevented many from coming. I was satisfied just enough to offset the O'Duffy propaganda.*

2) *I came back to Spain [mid-June 1937] just when the return of O'Duffy was foreshadowed (in letters from his disgruntled men). I considered my mission to Spain ended when he was leaving Spain; I came back to pull out men, and so to save lives. The number of my men who returned to Ireland June to October 1937, is evidence. After October the Irish unit existed only in name.*

3) *Why did I remain in Spain? (i) It was slow and difficult work repatriating men. (ii) When I was getting men home, I was getting the responsibility of their lives off my shoulders, and becoming more of a free agent, i.e. more of an individual than a representative. (iii) Then pride kept me here; after the fall of Asturias and then after Teruel I couldn't pull out and be considered "a rat who left the sinking ship". (Contradictory reasons perhaps, but taken in sequence, related to the events of the war, you will see there is some coherence).*[43]

---

[42] Cronin, Frank Ryan, p. 146.
[43] NAI, DFA, A 20/4, Frank Ryan, Part 2, undated letter from Ryan to Kerney, handed in at the Irish Legation in Madrid on 4 January 1940. Underlined passage in the original.

Ryan would not have been so forthcoming had he known that Vallejo was to Franco what Alfred Rosenberg was to Hitler: a specialist on "race", who before the war had argued for the castration of psychopaths, and now as head of psychiatric services in Franco's army, had just carried out medical investigations of the Internationals in San Pedro, presumptive carriers of the "Red criminal gene". Vallejo provided the justification for the widespread policy of stealing 12,000 children from "Red" parents for "catholic" adoption.[44] His joint Spanish-German team in San Pedro asked Bob Doyle to interpret photographs and wanted to know if he had slept with a prostitute, before having him photographed naked.[45]

Not knowing if Ryan was still alive, de Valera offered to act as a go-between to end the Spanish war. He discussed the proposal, to be put to Franco by the Vatican, with the Papal Nuncio Pascal Robinson. De Valera rightly believed that one of the reasons the Republicans, who had obviously lost the war by August 1938, continued fighting was a lack of an amnesty, for they knew more than enough about Franco's ferocious policy of retaliation. Nothing came of the initiative.[46] Minister Kerney's attempts for an equitable prisoner exchange for Frank Ryan looked promising, but it transpired that there were no Italian POWs in the Republican Zone of similar rank; and the proposal to exchange Ryan for the son of one of Franco's generals was not answered by Barcelona.[47] At least Kerney learned in October that Frank Ryan was still alive, from Viscount de Mamblas, Franco's agent in Biarritz.[48]

Following Franco's victory and the recognition of his regime by Dublin, Kerney paid his first visit to General Jordana, the dictator's foreign minister, on 11 April 1939. Learning that Ryan's death sentence had been commuted to one of penal servitude, Kerney pressed for his release, stressing the man's popularity in Ireland and that his liberation would put Hispano-Irish relations on a firm footing. He then, perhaps, made a tactical mistake, stating that it would be a "fatal blunder to

---

[44] Preston, Spanish Holocaust, pp. 513-515.
[45] Doyle, Brigadista, p. 81. Other prisoners had their skulls 'calibrated' (Geiser, Prisoners, pp. 145-147).
[46] DIFP, 5, pp. 328-329, Walshe, Dublin, to Macaulay, Rome, 20.08.1938.
[47] Ibid., pp. 338-339, memorandum by Joseph Walshe, Dublin, 16.09.1938.
[48] Ibid., p. 357, Kerney to Dublin, 10.10.1938.

hand him [Ryan] over to the British rather than to myself."[49] Kerney was referring to the replies of R.A.B. Butler (Under-Secretary to the Foreign Office) to questions in the House of Commons on 15 February and 13 March which implied that HM Government was intervening on behalf of Ryan and 54 other Internationals still in captivity.[50] It is striking that all further replies in the House this question (1939-41) refer to Ryan as an Irish national, for whom the Irish Legation in Madrid was responsible. Did Kerney lose an opportunity to "tag on" to the British prisoner release scheme which had been underwritten by a trade agreement between Britain and Spain? Did Kerney's Republican convictions play a part? The available evidence would suggest that he felt that Hodgson had only desultory interest in the Ryan case which had changed to inaction, or worse, because of the Somerville murder. Were Franco and his cohort waiting for a trade deal from Ireland for their starving population, or a large monetary reward?[51] But, as mentioned earlier, Ryan had refused to be repatriated by H.M. Government.

Frank Ryan, who was now, after the cessation of hostilities, in regular receipt of clothes and money from his sister in Ireland, met Minister Kerney for the first time on 17 June 1939. Ireland is a small place and it transpired that not only did Leopold Kerney know Elizabeth (Budge) Mulcahy, Clissmann's wife, from her stay as a student at the Sorbonne when he was posted to the Irish Legation in the early 1930s, but that he had also briefly met Frank Ryan at the Mulcahy Sligo home, possibly in May 1935.[52]

The Irish Minister brought Ryan cigarettes, a parcel of clothes and insecticide powder. Kerney, who was told by the director he could visit Ryan any time, spoke to the prisoner for 30 minutes. He found Ryan thin and complaining of heart palpitations which were relieved by spells in the infirmary. Frank needed money for a set of false teeth and recounted his "trial" in great detail. Kerney, pleased with the visit, was convinced that there was no charge against Ryan except "evidence of character" and expressed the hope that he would find out

---

[49] Ibid., pp. 434-435, Kerney to Dublin, 11.04.1939.
[50] *www.hansard.millbanksystems.com/commons*, debates of 15.02.1939, 13.03.1939. Accessed 26.04.2014.
[51] Tom Jones, a close friend of Ryan in Burgos, later stated that the Anglo-Spanish trade agreement had cost the British taxpayer £2 million and "Ireland had nothing to offer". (Cronin, Frank Ryan, p.154)
[52] *www.leopoldkerney.com/page4.html*, accessed 19.12.2013.

why Hodgson had used influence against the prominent prisoner's release.[53] Ryan had two other new friends. Blanca O'Donnell, 5th Duchess of Tetuan, had sympathy for men from the land of her forbears, earlier acting as intermediary between the feuding officers of Franco and O'Duffy and visiting the sick Irish *bandera* volunteers in hospital.[54] Visiting Ryan in Burgos nine days after the outbreak of World War 2, the aristocrat was favorably impressed and she promised Kerney that she would seek an audience with Franco who was reputedly reluctant to make any decision in the Ryan affair.[55] According to Tom Jones, a fellow-prisoner, Ryan had helped the Duchess and her children flee Madrid to France, and she finally settled in San Sebastian in the Franco zone.[56]

The second person to support Ryan was to spend one year sharing a cell with him – Tom Jones, a miner from Wrexham, a former member of the British anti-tank battery of the 15th Brigade taken prisoner in September 1938. With multiple wounds, Jones was first incarcerated in Bilbao and later transferred to Zaragoza where a tribunal sentenced him to death in January 1939.[57] Two months later the sentence was commuted to 30 years' confinement and Jones was delivered to Burgos Central Prison. Interviewed forty years later, Tom Jones, who had met Ryan briefly in the company of Ernest Hemingway in Madrid in late 1937, spoke movingly of his friendship with the Irish officer:

> [He] *was the bravest and most honourable man I have ever known. We were more like brothers than friends … We used to work out the year we would be released, but then we had to find something to laugh at in that terrible place. We had only 18 inches of space to sleep in and were protected from the concrete floor by a thin blanket. Many of the prisoners were physical wrecks from TB and skin disease. Frank's own health was bad. He suffered from chest pains, rheumatism and heart trouble. Though he received food parcels, cigarettes and money from the Irish Ambassador, he would share them with the other prisoners, including myself … When the news of the IRA bombing and loss of lives in London and Coventry came through Frank was outraged. I have never seen him so angry. He described*

[53] DIFP, 5, pp. 470-475, Kerney to Dublin, 17.06.1939.
[54] Ibid., pp. 64-65, Kerney to Dublin, 12.05.1937.
[55] DIFP, 6, pp. 26-27, Kerney to Dublin, 14.09.1939.
[56] *www.irelandscw.org*, manuscript of Tom Jones, February 1975.
[57] For details of his service in Spain and capture, see Geiser, Prisoners, pp. 233-234.

the IRA as irresponsible political lunatics, utterly destroying the hopes of
support of the British workers for Ireland's progress towards socialism ... He
later said that Ireland could not now be united by physical force, but by
friendship between Catholic and Protestant workers in the North, and with
the support of the TUC ... and revolutionary movements ... It was
surprising that I never heard Frank condemning de Valera, though I know
he was opposed to him in Ireland. On the contrary, he clearly had respect
and admiration for him. 'But Dev was no socialist', he would say, 'and that
held us back' ... The Hitler-Stalin Pact of August 1939 shocked Frank
Ryan. He feared a mighty empire stretching from Europe to the Far East ...
the anti-fascist cause for which so many had died and suffered, had been
betrayed.[58]

On 25 September Kerney met a cheery and philosophically-minded Ryan in Burgos, who was more worried about his parents' health than his own.[59] Ryan had probably heard that he was not forgotten by his ex-comrades either. In London, the Frank Ryan Release Committee, organized a public march in June 1939, and a few days later an open-air meeting was held in Dublin.[60] Ryan was kept reasonably well informed of international affairs by a prominent fellow-prisoner, and of Irish affairs because Leopold Kerney used the diplomatic bag to receive and answer, in Frank's name, letters from friends like Gerald O'Reilly (New York) and Rosamund Jacob (Dublin). The Minister also wrote regularly to Eilís Ryan. However, as nothing substantial was happening as regards his release, Ryan's hopes were waning, but he was distracted by his English lessons to Spanish cell-mates, and now proficient at Spanish, was refreshing his knowledge of Irish and Welsh (to talk to Tom Jones, a native speaker). He had also started to learn German, as his request for books demonstrates.[61]

Minister Kerney had problems in interpreting remarks from Franco's entourage regarding the further imprisonment of Ryan. In November he met the new Foreign Minister, Ramón Serrano Suñer, Franco's brother-in-law, who claimed he had raised the question with the dictator on several occasions. Suñer intimated

---

[58] Irish Times, 10.04.1975, Frank Ryan Profile, 4, by Michael McInerney.
[59] DIFP, 6, pp. 63-64, Kerney to Dublin, 05.10.1939.
[60] Irish Times, 19.06.1939, 03.07.1939.
[61] *www.irelandscw.org*, manuscript of Tom Jones, February 1975; NAI, DFA , A20/4 Frank Ryan, Part 2, letter to Kerney, 15.10.1939.

that the release of 400 foreign prisoners hinged on a proposed trade agreement, and when asked specifically about Ryan, he said that Franco's hesitancy in the matter was motivated by "a great many letters from Ireland on this question, saying that Ryan was a dangerous man and begging Franco not to release him". If that was so, Kerney countered, de Valera should be his gaoler and not Franco.[62]

By now Leopold Kerney had engaged the services of Antonio Michels Baron de Champourcin, a lawyer who had been in Franco's secret service, and as the Irish Minister was to learn subsequently, a confidante of German Military Intelligence (Abwehr) in Spain. De Champourcin used his contacts to obtain a copy of the commutation of Ryan's death sentence dated 12 November 1939. The paper mentioned the name of at least one Irish informer – Jane Brown from Enfield, Co. Kildare, a trained nurse with a noble Spanish family who had to leave Spain, losing all her belongings, in early winter 1937. De Champourcin's remarks to Kerney suggest that the Spaniards were being deliberately obstructive: while it was clear that Ryan had committed no crimes in Spain, he may have agitated against the Spanish military junta while home on leave between March and June 1937 and this, if proven, would rule out a pardon. Kerney deposited a copy of the commutation with the foreign minister and awaited events.[63]

On Christmas Eve 1939, Kerney undertook the long car journey from Madrid to Burgos. By now, Ryan was highly respected in the prison, because of the large number of cards arriving; the sub-warder said he was a *caballero* (gentleman). Kerney translated the commutation sentence to Ryan, who said he had been charged at his "trial" in June 1938 with carrying out propaganda work for the Spanish Republic during his period of convalescence in 1937, in Dublin, London, Liverpool and Glasgow. He had denied the charge, and now stated to the Irish Minister that the only political meeting he had attended in Ireland was the anti-Coronation protest in May, when he had his nose broken by a Garda baton.[64] Another route was also explored when de Valera's officials impressed on the Spanish Ambassador the importance the Government attached to the imprisonment of Frank Ryan, primarily, it seems, because Franco's officials queried if Kerney's indefatigable lobbying was a personal matter or part of official

---

[62] DIFP, 6, pp. 98-99, Kerney to Dublin, 21.11.1939.
[63] Ibid., pp. 122-123, Kerney to Dublin, 23.12.1939.
[64] Ibid., pp. 123-125, Kerney to Dublin, 27.12.1939.

Irish policy.[65] In Dublin, Señor Ontiveros "bristled" when Frank Ryan was mentioned, so he could not be depended upon.[66]

With the *drôle de guerre* soon to turn into *Blitzkrieg* in Western Europe, the situation was grim for Frank Ryan in two main respects. First, his state of his health, while precarious for years, was bound to get worse since he was still forced to sleep on a concrete floor of a crowded cell with diseased and lice-ridden comrades barely surviving on inadequate prison rations. Photographs or drawings of him from that time show a haggard man with a haunted gaze, looking ten to twenty years older than his 37 years. Second, there were hardly any foreigners left – the last eight Americans were released in February and March 1940, including three from Burgos, of whom two had been originally sentenced to death.[67] Ryan informed Kerney in a hand-written note of their release, repeating the rumour (true) that Franco had only relented when the U.S. Government "threatened to withhold promised cotton supplies."[68] Then Tom Jones was liberated on 20 March, and Ryan, with tears rolling down his cheeks, said farewell and reminded the Welshman of the tasks he had promised to carry out for him in Ireland. Jones, despite wartime travel restrictions between Britain and Ireland, spent a week with the Ryan family in Dublin and met some IRA leaders at a cloak-and-dagger meeting. They promised to do their best to expedite Frank's release.[69]

Leopold Kerney now felt more than ever that he was up against a brick wall: he attributed Ryan's incarceration to "occult forces", i.e. not only opposition from Ireland but also from another country he did not wish to name. He mentioned the only obvious solution, one expressly ruled out by Joseph Walshe,[70] the Secretary of the Department of External Affairs, two weeks earlier:

> *I am afraid we must agree to differ about that suggestion of mine which strikes you as being so thoroughly bad; I think I know the Spaniards better than you do; the Americans mentioned cotton and the Spaniards gave way; the English would not sign a trade treaty without a promise of immediate*

---

[65] Ibid., p. 141, Kerney to Dublin, 26.01.1940; ibid., p 157, Joseph P. Walshe to Juan Garcia Ontiveros, 23.02.1940.
[66] Ibid., pp. 178-179, Walshe to Kerney, 12.04.1940.
[67] Geiser, Prisoners, pp. 223, 260-263.
[68] NAI, DFA A/20, Frank Ryan, Part 2, Extract from report Kerney, 11.03.1940.
[69] *www.irelandscw.org*, manuscript of Tom Jones, February 1975; Irish Times, 10.04.1975.
[70] DIFP, 6 , pp. 178-179, Walshe to Kerney, 12.04.1940.

release of Englishmen; forceful arguments are necessary at times, at least in Spain; I know my suggestion to be thoroughly good, but I defer of course to your view. Can you imagine a Government claiming a ransom of £5,000 in a case which is fresh in your memory? You cannot always compare one Government with another.[71]

What could the Irish have offered shattered Spain in way of foodstuffs? Ireland had no ships until the founding of Irish Shipping in March 1941, and any goods would have to be transported through waters infested by German submarines. What grain Ireland was forcing reluctant farmers to grow was for the home market. We can at least be sure that de Valera, who knew Frank Ryan, did not want him in the country when Ireland's neutrality was under attack in Britain. Dev wanted his fellow County Limerick patriot safe and in good health, but preferably somewhere else rather than in Ireland where he had many extremist Republican friends in internment camps and gaols. The Taoiseach ruled out Ryan's repatriation as long as the war lasted.[72] In October 1941 when on leave in Dublin, Kerney told Irish Military Intelligence "that 'he had no means of getting a decision on that matter from the department of External Affairs so he took it upon himself the responsibility' of agreeing to Ryan's release".[73]

In June 1940 William Norton of the Labour Party and James Dillon of Fine Gael queried de Valera in the Dáil about Frank Ryan's imprisonment. He refused to disclose on what charges Ryan was being held but stated "representations continue to be made".[74] A last resort could have been a major bribe, which even today governments are reluctant to pay to terrorist kidnappers; if money does change hands, it is usually denied. Such a suggestion was unthinkable for a sovereign state three-quarters of a century ago, and it was probably never considered seriously in Dublin. Finally, Franco was somewhat of a pariah in the eyes of the democracies in 1940, at the very least an "unfriendly neutral".

If Frank Ryan was not to die in a Spanish prison, a solution to free him had to be found outside the normal diplomatic channels. Ryan's departure from Burgos prison in July 1940, staged as a "prison escape", is still a controversial subject,

---

[71] Ibid., pp. 186-187, Kerney to Walshe, 23.04.1940.
[72] McGarry, *Frank Ryan*, p. 70.
[73] Ibid., p. 63.
[74] *http://debates.oireachtas.ie/dail/1940/06/0600003.asp.* Accessed 06.11.2013.

mainly because it was due to the cooperation between the secret services of two fascist states, Spain and Germany, and because of the involvement of the Irish legate in Spain, Leopold Kerney. Neither he, nor indeed Frank Ryan, was a free agent in the matter.

There seems to have been three separate approaches which dovetailed – from Ireland, Germany and within Spain. First, when Stephen Held, a contact man between the IRA and the Nazis (arrested in Dublin, 25 May 1940), spoke to German Abwehr officer in Berlin in April, he brought a request from his Republican friends that Frank Ryan should be released from Spanish captivity.[75] Sean Russell, head of the IRA Army Council since April 1938, had gone to America a year later to raise funds for the IRA but could not return home once the Second World War broke out because he would have been arrested and interned. Russell was the disputed head of the IRA when the "bombing campaign" was launched against Britain from January 1939. Mastermind of "S-Plan" was the ESB engineer Jim O'Donovan who visited Germany three times in 1939 to negotiate with Abwehr officers. Both were strict "physical force" Republicans, not Nazi sympathizers: they wanted to "milk" the Germans for money and equipment, as they had attempted with the Soviets in the mid-1920s, with mixed success.[76]

Russell managed to reach Genoa as a fire-stoker on an American ship in May 1940, where he was met by Abwehr agents and taken to Germany.[77] His "minder" was the interpreter Professor Fritz Fromme, and the duo arrived in Berlin on 3 May. Russell was given accommodation in a comfortable villa in the bourgeois suburb of Grünewald and had a bodyguard/general factotum at his disposal.[78] Soon afterwards Russell asked the Germans if they could arrange the release of Frank Ryan.[79] The Irish Government knew in early June that Russell

---

[75] Cronin, Frank Ryan, p. 184.
[76] Stealing British passports and procuring weapon blueprints from Britain for Soviet military intelligence was the main source of income for the IRA in the mid-1920s. See: Tom Mahon/James J. Gillogly, Decoding the IRA, Cork 2008.
[77] Cronin, Frank Ryan, pp. 184-185.
[78] Enno Stephan, Spies in Ireland, Four Square Paperback Edition, London 1965, pp. 98-99.
[79] Carolle J. Carter, The Shamrock and the Swastika. German Espionage in Ireland in World War II, Palo Alto, California 1977, p. 114.

was in Germany and surmised that he was proposing "to lead a Fifth Column in Ireland during possible parachute attack".[80]

Second, an initiative from Jupp Hoven, who, like Helmut Clissmann, was a friend of Ryan's and other IRA leaders since the early 1930s and had accompanied the IRA Chief-of Staff Tom Barry to Germany in 1937.[81] While Clissmann does not seem to have been involved in spying for the Nazis while in Ireland during 1936-39,[82] Hoven carried out espionage there for the German army while posing as a student of anthropology in 1937/38, or at least he handed over his "travel notes" (*Reisenotizen*) to the Oberkommando der Wehrmacht (OKW).[83] He even enrolled at Queen's University Belfast to write a sociological thesis on the "Ulster Problem" in early 1939.[84] Hoven, posted after some difficulty because of his left-wing past to the Brandenburg Regiment, a commando unit attached to the Abwehr, pointed out to his superiors in 1940 that the liberation of Ryan would make a good impression in Ireland and that the man might be used in some capacity to the advantage of Germany.[85]

Third, as documented by Minister Kerney in cryptic hand-written notes in the last days of April 1940, the final strand emanated from the Legation's lawyer de Champourcin and indicates that

a) The "Spanish" initiative had come from de Champourcin and his German "friends" were awaiting an interview with their Spanish counterparts.

b) Franco's intelligence service agreed to the German proposal.

c) Neither de Champourcin nor Kerney could impose any conditions.

d) Kerney held the transfer of Frank Ryan to Germany to be "inadvisable and out of the question, but USA, perhaps".

[80] NAI, DFA, A20/4, Frank Ryan Part 3, decoded telegram from Geneva, 04.06.1940.
[81] Horst Dickel, Die Deutsche Aussenpolitik und die Irische Frage von 1932 bis 1944, Wiesbaden 1983, pp. 77-78.
[82] This was the view of G2, Irish Army Intelligence – Joachim Lerchenmüller, Keltischer Sprengstoff. Eine Wissenschaftliche Studie über die deutsche Keltologie von 1900 bis 1945, Tübingen 1997, p. 364-365.
[83] Dickel, Deutsche Aussenpolitik, p. 232.
[84] Robert Fisk, In Time of War. Ireland, Ulster and the Price of Neutrality, 1939-1945, Paladin Books London 1987, p. 89.
[85] Stephan, Spies in Ireland, pp. 143-144.

e) De Champourcin planned to visit Ryan in Burgos with a German "colleague", using Kerney's car.[86]

Kerney was not kept up to date of developments on a regular basis, which is understandable, seeing that all sides were aware that no suspicion should arise about the Irish Legation being "an accessory after the fact". The German negotiator with Franco, with his chief of police and with the head of Spanish Intelligence was probably Wolfgang Blaum, Abwehr chief in Madrid.[87] The Irish Minister visited Ryan on 12 July, his last round trip of over 400km from Madrid to the penitentiary at Burgos. Kerney got Ryan to agree that neither had any choice in the matter – "sometimes a remedy can be more annihilating than the disease". They discussed IRA leaders (the prisoner knew from Gerald O'Reilly, that Russell was already in Germany)[88], and Kerney warned him about getting involved in violent politics once more in Ireland. Ryan replied that if he got to Ireland he would thank de Valera personally for all he had done on his behalf, while retaining his right to oppose Government policy.[89]

Matters seem to going well until the inscrutable Franco dithered, and he did not say definitely "Yes" until 3 July, then changed his mind and said he could not issue a pardon (*indulto*), but finally relented to the plan of Ryan's "escape". The Legation paid for the hire of car by de Champourcin and for petrol for the journey from Madrid to Burgos because the lawyer, and not the Irish Minister, was to be witness to the "handover". At 2am on 25 July two cars parked outside the prison. The first contained Franco's chief of police and a German (Blaum), the second two armed *Falangistas* from Serrano Suñer's personal bodyguard. They emerged with Ryan 20 minutes later and passed de Champourcin's Packard. Kerney's lawyer reached the border at Irun at 7.30am before the others. He parked the car in the town and went by foot to the international bridge. At 8.30am the two cars crossed the barrier into France. Ryan gave de Champourcin a quick glance showing that he recognized him – they had met once in prison, probably in the presence of a German agent.

---

[86] DIFP, 6, p. 190, handwritten minutes of Kerney, 29., 30.04.1940.
[87] Stephan, Spies in Ireland, p. 144.
[88] O'Reilly had arranged Russell's transatlantic voyage (Cronin, Frank Ryan, p. 185).
[89] DIFP, 6, 312-314, Kerney to Dublin, 29.07.1940.

Later that day in San Sebastian, de Champourcin was handed a note by a German "friend". It was from Ryan who wrote to Kerney that everything had gone off without a hitch, but he was not returning immediately to Ireland but "going on a journey that would take some weeks".[90]

De Champourcin gave his opinion that his destination might be the USA via Siberia. Kerney heard nothing more until 22 August, when de Champourcin said the "friends" allowed him to say that Ryan had escaped with American help. Kerney rightly saw the operation as a concession to Germany and not to Ireland. Only then did he send Dublin a blow-by-blow account of Frank Ryan's "escape".[91] Minister Kerney was soon to learn that he had been duped: Germany, and not the USA, was to be Ryan's final, and fatal, destination.

Lieutenant (*Sonderführer*) Kurt Haller of the Abwehr drove Frank Ryan from the border to Paris.[92] He was shocked by his appearance – an "emaciated figure in the loose-fitting civilian suit who reeked of prison disinfectant".[93] Ryan was accommodated in a country house and given new clothes. He was obviously disorientated, for when he dined out with Haller and another Abwehr officer in the famous *Tour d'Argent* restaurant in the French capital, Ryan, as Haller remembered, was "completely flabbergasted by the whole thing and thought he was dreaming!"[94] Helmut Clissmann (now an Abwehr officer) arrived in Paris in late July and with Jupp Hoven spent the next two weeks mainly in the company of Frank Ryan. The Irishman was suspicious, but his German friends argued that anything "that hurt Britain was good for Germany", further that when Ryan "reached America he could make up his own mind what he wanted to do."[95] Ryan left Paris for Berlin in the company of Clissmann on 4 August, so he had

---

[90] According to Eamon C. Kerney, the son of the Irish Minister, his father, not trusting anyone involved in the handover, followed de Champourcin's car in his own vehicle and witnessed, from a distance, how Ryan was driven across the frontier bridge. See: *www.leopoldkerny.com/page 3.html.* Accessed 19.12.2013.

[91] DIFP, 6, pp. 339-343, Kerney to Dublin, 26.08.1940.

[92] The National Archives, Kew (TNAK), KV2/769, Part II of Interrogation of SdF (Z) Kurt Haller, 07.08.1946.

[93] Stephan, Spies in Ireland, p. 144.

[94] Ibid., p. 145.

[95] Cronin, Frank Ryan, pp. 162-163.

not enjoyed anything like an adequate period of rest and recuperation. He was to meet Sean Russell in the German capital, but nobody told him that.[96]

Helmut Clissman in Wehrmacht uniform

On reflection, the last sentence might not be true. Why would Kerney or Frank Ryan believe (rather than harbouring the hope) that the Abwehr would go to such great lengths to facilitate the journey of one of the best-known officers in the International Brigades to the United States? After all, people with this political background were sent to German concentration camps. Once Ryan was in New York he was outside German control and would undoubtedly have drawn attention to the barbarities of Franco's rule – the prison conditions and the mass executions. That was certainly not in the interests of the Third Reich who was busy wooing the Spanish dictator. Hitler travelled to Hendaye to meet Franco in

[96] Ibid., p. 188.

October 1940. The German leader had little to offer, and Franco had a long list of demands. The meeting was not a success and Hitler later confided to Mussolini that he "would 'prefer to have three or four teeth taken out' than go through another nine hours' discussion with Franco".[97] So Ryan's "escape to America" was perhaps a code-word which served to hide an unpleasant dilemma, a stratagem chosen because nobody lost face – neither the Abwehr, Kerney nor Frank Ryan.

---

[97] Ian Kershaw, Hitler. 1936-1945: Nemesis, Penguin Books 2000, pp. 328-330.

4

Frank Ryan in Germany

German strategy for Ireland in the Second World War is an over-written subject, a playground for all kind of conspiracy-theorists, enemies of Irish sovereignty, and attention-seekers in the British and Irish media. They all are inclined to make mountains out of molehills.

On the one hand, Irish neutrality was advantageous to the Third Reich because the southern part of Ireland was free of British military and naval forces so that British Atlantic convoys had to take a longer route, from Scotland, or Liverpool through the Irish Sea, and around Northern Ireland westwards. This interpretation was shared by Eduard Hempel, Hitler's representative in Dublin, an old-school diplomat who argued against any espionage operations of Nazi organisations in Ireland.[1] On the other, de Valera's neutral stance favoured the Allies as the war progressed because security and meteorological information was shared with the British, German combatants were interned and Nazi spies soon arrested (with one exception). British and American fliers were, in almost all

---

[1] John P. Duggan, Neutral Ireland and the Third Reich, Dublin 1989; Sunday Press, Interviews with Eduard Hempel by John Murdoch, 17.11.1963, 24.11.1963, 01.12.1963, 15.12.1963, 22.12.1963, 29.12.1963, 05.01.1964, 12.01.1964.

cases, released immediately after crash-landing, and, finally, links of the German Legation with Berlin were more or less capped when its radio transmitter was seized in December 1943. These facts are well-known and uncontested.

Probably the most-levelled headed of the German intelligence-gatherers in Ireland were military men, though their engagement was sporadic. The photographs of the Irish infrastructure were supplied by members of the German community in Ireland before the war, committed Nazis with good jobs in Government organisations (National Museum), semi-state bodies (Turf Development Board), multinationals (Siemens-Schuckert, Osram) and exchange academics at Irish universities.[2]

General-Major Leo Geyr von Schweppenburg, Military Attaché at Germany's London Embassy, who had jumped in 1934 at the Dublin Horse Show, carried out two motor-tours of Ireland in 1937. He was struck by the preparations for transatlantic air-traffic, especially the development at Rineanna, Co. Clare, which was built in 1936-42 and later known as Shannon Airport. For him it was a sign that the Americans would never see Britain defeated and he reported to his superiors in that sense, repeating his warnings after the conclusion of the Anglo-Irish Agreement in April 1938. His expertise was of no interest to the Hitler loyalists in the OKW.[3]

Only after the Fall of France did the German Army seriously begin to plan an invasion of Ireland from Brest, which would be coupled with a major landing on the east coast of England by troops stationed in Norway and Denmark. German strategists had never planned a major water-borne expeditionary force, nor had Wehrmacht units trained for such an enterprise. The operational goal, worked out by General Kaupisch of the 7th Army, was a landing on a wide-front between Dungarvan and Wexford in late September, early October. Building a bridgehead along the line Gorey-Mount Leinster-Thomastown-Clonmel-Dungarvan, the Germans would advance towards Kildare and Dublin. Speed, avoiding the Royal Navy and favorable weather were key elements. The Wehrmacht could not commandeer enough ships for the 50,000 "Grün" force, maps were scarce and a moonless night was vital for the element of surprise. Following the defeat of the Luftwaffe in the Battle of Britain, "Operation Grün" was put on hold, but re-

---

[2] Lerchenmüller, ,Keltischer Sprengstoff', pp.358-381.
[3] Sunday Press, 06.12.1964.

animated by Hitler on 27 November on the foot of reports that a British invasion of Ireland was imminent. On 3 December, Admiral Erich Raeder convinced Hitler that a major attack on Ireland had no prospects of success: the numerical superiority of the Royal Navy, the rugged Irish coast, the difficulty of delivering heavy supplies after landing, the inability to guarantee an element of surprise etc. That month Hitler decided to order plans for the invasion of the USSR so Ireland disappeared from German offensive considerations.[4] Perhaps better known is that de Valera rejected in late 1940 the German offer of British arms captured at Dunkirk.[5]

As regards perceived threats of invasion, the most critical moment came just before Christmas 1940, when the Germans tried to fly in replacement staff for their Legation to Ireland. Two German officers, a captain and a major, and a radio-operator were seconded for intelligence duties in Dublin.[6] De Valera, sick in hospital, and several of his ministers, had adamantly refused Hempel permission. On the morning of Christmas Eve, a German plane flew over Rineanna, and seeing the obstacles on the runway, banked and flew out of sight. The soldiers below were under orders to arrest anyone who landed.[7] A British invasion, or an Anglo-U.S. incursion into the South, could never be discounted. We have the benefit of hindsight, the Irish Army of 1939-45 had to be prepared for all eventualities, not knowing, that, despite the blustering of Churchill eager to re-possess the Irish Treaty Ports in 1940/41, the British Chiefs of Staff as early as January 1938 had argued: "the retention or capture of the ports in the face of a hostile attitude on the part of Ireland would at best involve a most formidable military commitment and might, even so, be impossible".[8] This diagnosis had

---

[4] Charles Burdick, „'Gruen' German Military Plans – Ireland 1940", An Cosantóir, Vol. XXXIV. No. 3, March 1974. See the statements of German generals post-war on the subject, which concur with Burdick's exposition: An Cosantóir, Vol. IX, No. 1, January 1949 (General Blumentritt); An Cosantóir, Vol. XXXIV, No. 7, July 1974 (Letters from the Irish historian Dermot Bradley about his interviews with Generaloberst Halder, General der Infanterie Blumentritt and Panzer General Geyr von Schweppenburg).

[5] Robert Fisk, In Time of War. Ireland, Ulster and the Price of Neutrality 1939-45, Paladin Books London 1987, pp. 254, 366.

[6] F.M. McLoughlin, Irish Neutrality During World War II, with Special References to German Sources, M.A. thesis, UCD 1979/80, p. 74.

[7] Joseph T. Carroll, Ireland in the War Years, New York 1975, pp. 76-77. See also Irish Times, 18.09.1979, Letters to the Editor from Dan Bryan (former head of G2, Irish Army intelligence).

[8] Carroll, Ireland in the War Years, p. 26.

even more force once Ireland had mobilized according to its meagre resources. In any case, Britain, practically bankrupt at the end of 1940, was desperately dependent on the USA for loans and equipment; she would have encountered strong opposition from the Irish lobby in America if British Army units had violated Irish neutrality.

Why then, since de Valera's neutrality policy was not inimical to Germany's military or strategic interests, did German intelligence dabble in hare-brained schemes that would endanger Ireland's isolationist position? This has to do with ideology, National Socialist ideology, and the rivalling bureaucracies that characterize totalitarian states. The Party "swallows" the State and there is no ministerial responsibility as in a functioning democracy. In the Germany Army, the Aussenamt (Foreign Office) and the Abwehr, the Nazi ideologues had to contend with (underground) opposition from traditional Prussian patriots, largely men who wanted to revise the results of the 1919 Versailles Treaty but abhorred the racial beliefs of Hitler and his entourage. All secret operations in connection with Ireland were in the hands of Dr. Edmund Veesenmayer. He possessed a doctorate in political science from Munich University, was a member of the NSDAP since 1927 and joined the SS in 1933.[9] The Bavarian Veesenmayer was a roving diplomat for Foreign Minister Ribbentrop, and made responsible for missions to Ireland from 28 March 1940.[10]

It cannot be emphasized enough that Aussenamt/Abwehr interpretations of information about Ireland were extreme examples of wishful thinking. When it suited him, Woermann, head of the political department at the foreign office, ignored the balanced reports sent from Dublin by Minister Hempel, and agreed to cock-eyed schemes based on two highly unlikely scenarios: a British invasion of southern Ireland was probable; German agents could somehow facilitate joint operations between de Valera's administration and the IRA in the case of British military incursions, or indeed in military attacks on British installations north of the border.

Such German plans were being hatched at a time when political prisoners were dying on hunger-strike in Ireland and the Irish police were under attack by bomb

---

[9] Igor-Philip Matič, Edmund Veesenmayer. Agent und Diplomat der nationalsozialistischen Expansionspolitik, München 2002, pp.19-25.
[10] Ibid., p. 99.

and bullet from IRA men still at large. While it can be assumed that Colonel Erwin Lahousen, Head of Abwehr II (sabotage), Ribbentrop and Veesenmayer knew next to nothing about the distant island west of Britain, this was not true of some key Abwehr staff – Helmut Clissmann, who had lived in Ireland for about five years in the 1930s and had married the Sligo woman Budge Mulcahy in 1938; or his friend, the spy-scholar Jupp Hoven. The reasons for their motivation and participation in Nazi Germany's secret sorties to the Green Isle deserves further investigation and cannot be dealt with in this study. Whatever future historians may uncover about their wartime activities or evolving political beliefs, it is indisputable that they proved to be Frank Ryan's best friends in his German exile.

As regards Sean Russell, a top level conference with the IRA leader in Berlin at the end of May 1940 agreed that he would be sent as soon as possible with radio-operators to Ireland. Two events delayed his departure: the arrest of the Nazi agent Stephen Held in Dublin, which led to diplomatic tensions between Dublin and Berlin, and the unexpected arrival of Frank Ryan in the German capital. The Germans gave Russell a free hand in what steps he might decide to take once landed, and he asked that Ryan accompany him. Immediately on his arrival in Berlin, Ryan met Russell, and although they stood at opposite ends of the Irish Republican spectrum, they had always been good friends, as was now apparent to the Germans who witnessed their joyful re-union. The second surprise sprung on the man from Limerick, who was far from healthy and still disorientated from his unexpected release from the hell-hole of Burgos Central Prison, was that he (Richard II) was to travel as the subordinate of Russell (Richard I) on a German submarine to Ireland. On 5 August, Russell's mission was discussed when he met Ribbentrop, Admiral Canaris (Abwehr supreme commander), Veesenmayer and Lahousen. All was ready, Russell and Ryan were driven to Wilhelmshaven the following day and the submarine left for Ireland on 8 August. The two men were to be landed in Smerwick Bay on 15 August (Feast of the Assumption), an area often visited by Ryan when looking up friends in the Gaeltacht. But they had no radio-operators to assist them because the cramped space on the U-Boot (U-65) allowed for only two passengers.

Russell began almost immediately to complain of severe stomach cramps and he died at sea on 14 August. Because of the danger of Russell's corpse rapidly decomposing in the humid air of the submarine, he was buried at sea. When the submarine, which was supposed to continue out into the Atlantic to hunt merchantmen, developed engine trouble, it returned prematurely to Lorient in Brittany. Frank Ryan and all crew members were interrogated in order to rule out the possibility of Russell having been poisoned. The diagnosis of two independent medical experts was a burst gastric ulcer. German officers in Berlin had noticed that Russell had struck to a strict diet when happily experimenting in Abwehr's bomb laboratory in Berlin.[11]

Russell, who died in Ryan's arms 100 miles west of Galway, had not confided in his companion, partly because the crew might have heard the details of a top secret mission, partly because the constant noise of the engines in a confined space made an intelligible conversation with Ryan, who was hard of hearing, impossible. And of course, Sean Russell was in excruciating pain. So Ryan was in a dilemma when Russell's corpse slid beneath the waves: even if he did land, he had no knowledge of the dead man's plans, no radio code, and would have been at a loss to explain the absence or demise of Russell to the Irish authorities or to his ex-comrades of the underground IRA. Since he had opposed the Dublin man (Russell was from Fairview) in the debates about the direction the IRA should take in the early 1930s, Ryan would have had to face the accusation that he murdered his erstwhile rival with the assistance of the Germans. He had no evidence to discount it, only his word of honour. Captain Gerrit von Stockhausen would have landed Ryan in Kerry, but he declined, staying on the submarine, a decision he regretted to his dying day.[12]

At the end of August Eilís learned officially from the Department of External Affairs that her brother had been "unofficially" released and was now in the United States. She was requested to treat the news as strictly confidential.[13] In order to keep the fiction alive that Ryan was in or on his way to the USA, German agents on 20 August posted an airmail letter from him to Kerney, from Estoril in Portugal. In the brief note, which took a month to reach the Irish Legation in Madrid, Ryan apologized for his "unceremonious departure", saying his "American friends" left him no time for leave-taking, and he asked Kerney to inform his parents that he was safe and sound. Kerney probably deduced that Ryan was in Germany from the following passage:

---

[11] Matič, Veesenmayer, pp. 103-107.
[12] Stephan, Spies in Ireland, pp. 147-150.
[13] DIFP, 6, pp. 346-347, Joseph P. Walshe to Eilís Ryan, 27.08.1940.

Although it's liberty, although I can at last do what I like and only what I like, it is unfortunately impossible for me to get home until the war is over.[14]

In late November 1940, Kerney knew for sure, after he had received a letter from Budge Clissmann from Copenhagen, whose family (the Mulcahys) he had visited years before in Sligo. She wrote, "I have seen someone who has many reasons to be thankful to you and who asked to be remembered to you."[15] Shortly afterwards Ryan sent the Irish diplomat Christmas greetings, the first of six long letters. It was in code ("Gerald's" was the USA, "Mr Mulcahy Jnr." was Helmut Clissmann) and Ryan called himself a "gentleman at large" without news from Ireland or his family. He described his status:

... nobody can make me do anything I don't want to do. (Incidentally no one has even (or ever) tried here – a thing that surprised me at first, but no longer does. I have met only gentlemen. Let that be on record as coming from Me! [16]

One German initiative in which Ryan was involved concerned the recruiting of Irish or Anglo-Irish POWS captured in France in 1940 for operations in Ireland, either as part of a unit to assist the Irish in case of a British invasion or as saboteurs and radio-operators. It was to be as ill-starred as its predecessor, Casement's Irish Brigade of 1915/16. Clissmann and Ryan, in civilian clothes, visited the camp at Altdamm, near Freisack in Brandenburg, in 1941, where they assisted Jupp Hoven in the process of weeding-out suitable candidates from about 80 prisoners. Ryan, it is said, was immediately recognized and greeted by his first name, and he afterwards regretted his participation in the affair.[17] Ten Irishmen were finally chosen and brought to Berlin. Some of them misbehaved (womanising, breaking security rules), and Frank Ryan, much to his embarrassment, had to intervene with Abwehr officers to have one notorious offender rescued from the Gestapo in Düsseldorf. The man survived the concentration camp, and two of the group managed to escape from Germany before the end of the war. The experiment was discontinued, at least in its

---

[14] Cronin, Frank Ryan, p. 237.
[15] DIFP, 6, p. 411, Kerney to Dublin, 05.12.1940.
[16] Cronin, Frank Ryan, pp.237-238.
[17] Carter, The Shamrock, pp. 124-135, here p. 135.

original concept, when Hoven transferred to a parachute regiment in May 1942.[18]

Thereafter Ryan was a prisoner in a gilded cage, rarely called upon to do anything or offer advice, living on an Aussenamt allowance in a large apartment under a false identity ("Johannes Richard"). He had no links to the Gestapo and avoided visiting the Irish Legation in the Tiergartenstrasse. In the first few months in Berlin he visited the apartment of Francis Stuart, a propagandist in the foreign section of German radio, in the Westfälische Strasse near the Kurfürstendamm. Frank was generous with his food coupons, the British air-raids on Berlin were as yet sporadic and he shared nostalgic memories with Stuart, who, too, had been interned in the Curragh in 1922/23. Sometimes there were bundles of old Irish newspapers to read. Stuart remembers these meetings:

> *These months in the latter half of 1940 when I saw Frank nearly every day had one atmosphere, and after this, all my memories of him had another ... Strangely enough I do not recall us ever discussing these things* [progressive politics]. *Partly it may have been that Frank was by no means glibly articulate when it came to talking of world problems, partly, too, it may have been because our deepest contact was on the personal and limited ground of Ireland.[19]*

Reading between the lines, one can speculate that Ryan did not trust Stuart, the contrarian publicist in the pay of the Nazis, yet was glad of his company like many Irishmen thrown on their resources and with few friends in a foreign land. He would have been reluctant to air his innermost thoughts about the regime to somebody who was part of its propaganda machine. One reason why Ryan had little to do for about a year was because Vessenmayer and his advisers were hoping that de Valera would accept a large shipment of German arms. When it became apparent that this tactic had failed, plans to land Ryan in Ireland were revived. One variant was that Ryan, Clissmann and a radio-operator could be dropped from a Heinkel seaplane in Brandon Bay, and put ashore in rubber dinghies. The location for this risky adventure was then transferred to a Roscommon lake, studded with islands, a natural hazard for any pilot flying

---

[18] Ibid., p. 135; Stephan, Spies in Ireland, pp. 215-220.
[19] Francis Stuart, „Frank Ryan in Germany", The Bell, November 1950, pp. 37-42, here p. 39. Stuart also mentions his friendship with Ryan in The Sunday Press, 23.07.1978.

through air space monitored by the vigilant Irish Coast Watching Service.[20] Clissmann was to liaise with the IRA, and give them £40,000, while Ryan was supposed to act as a peacemaker between the IRA and de Valera. Hitler vetoed the operation in September 1941, possibly because he preferred to negotiate with the governments of neutral countries and not with their internal enemies. Another cause may have been the split in the IRA during the so-called "Stephen Hayes Affair".[21]

Veesenmayer then changed gear, and using Clissmann's contacts, visited the Irish Minister Leopold Kerney in Madrid in August 1942, and in Biarritz thirteen months later. His liaison officer Helmut Clissmann met Kerney five times (November 1941, January 1942, May 1942, August 1942 and July 1943). It is not clear if Kerney was aware that Clissmann, at least at the early meetings, was no longer an official of the German Cultural Institute (a post he had filled in Dublin in 1936-39 and in Copenhagen after the outbreak of WW2) but an Abwehr officer and a subordinate of Veesenmayer.[22] Clissmann acted as a courier for the Kerney-Frank Ryan correspondence. Nothing came of the soundings between Veesenmayer and the Irish Minister, and the reverberations of these contacts in Dublin need not detain us here. Veesenmayer gave nothing away, except to say that Germany respected Irish neutrality, and that Ryan was a "fighting man". He denied having ever heard of Sean Russell.[23]

In his letter dated 6 November 1941 and handed over to Kerney by Clissmann, Ryan gave an outline of his status in Berlin:

> *My status – that of a non-party neutral – is established. I act merely in a 'consultative' capacity – my views are asked when there are situations and news that require interpretation (I flatter myself that my efforts are surprisingly often correct). I am not working for – not even in communication with – any organization at home. (I do not even know if such an organization is aware of my whereabouts). I am, as I have already*

---

[20] See Michael Kennedy, Guarding Neutral Ireland. The Coast Watching Service and Military Intelligence, 1939-1945, Dublin 2008.

[21] Matič, Vessenmayer, pp. 110-112; Carter, The Shamrock, pp. 120-121. See the personal account of Stephen Hayes: "My Strange Story", The Bell, July 1951, pp. 11-16; August 1951, pp. 42-51.

[22] Stephan, Spies in Ireland, pp. 222-227.

[23] DIFP, 7, pp. 231-236, Kerney to Dublin, 24.08.1942.

said, an individual claiming to represent myself, and only myself. That attitude I shall maintain, and (I feel sure) without difficulty.[24]

In January 1942, the occasion of Clissmann's second visit to Kerney, a note from Ryan to the Irish Minister gave details and the date of Russell's death, without mentioning that it had occurred on a German submarine.[25] In the covering letter to the note, Ryan argued (he was now receiving Irish newspapers, albeit a month old) that "country comes before party" and that "Dev should get 100% support". He added that he was at a loss to understand why leading IRA men of the 1919-21 struggle were not now holding top posts in the Irish Army. His tone was somewhat resigned in that he assumed – this *was* really theoretical – that he would not be allowed to voice opposition to Fianna Fáil's economic and social policies if he were in Ireland even though he would make his unequivocal support of Irish neutrality public knowledge. Further comments indicated that Ryan was very homesick, but, as always, he ended on a positive note:

I want for nothing. Food and clothes I have in plenty. Coffee and tea are not lacking. Neither are cigs. I'm specially privileged. Who'd have forecasted this for me a few years ago?[26]

In May 1942, Helmut Clissmann ferried the next letter from Frank to Mr. Kerney. It is worth quoting at length because it describes the exile's life in some detail, information that readers, not conversant with the three biographies of Frank Ryan, would need in assessing Ryan's role in Germany:

I still exist. Eating and sleeping are my main occupations…So far as comforts go, I lack nothing. I have special privileges with regard to food and clothes. Time hangs heavily on my hands; that is the only drawback. Partly from the necessity of maintaining an incognito, and partly from choice, my range of friends is very small. For instance, I avoid most people who have ever been in my country, as well as most who hail from it. I get everything I ask for – except for a deportation ticket! … Life is pretty monotonous for a

---

[24] Cronin, Frank Ryan, p. 239-241. Kerney learnt of Russell's death "somewhere in France from ulcerated stomach causing green vomiting following constipation" from Clissmann as well. (NAI, DFA 20/A/4/Frank Ryan, Part III, telegram from Madrid received 25.11.1941)
[25] Cronin, Frank Ryan, p. 244, Note to Kerney, 14.01.1942. Kerney telegrammed this news to Dublin on 19.01.1942 (NAI, DFA 20/A/4/Frank Ryan, Part III, Madrid telegram 19.01.1942).
[26] Cronin, Frank Ryan, pp. 241-243, letter of 14.01.1942.

person like me; I always have the fear of coming home in a beard and on crutches.[27]

In August 1942, just before Veesenmayer arrived in Madrid, Frank wrote Kerney that the German was insistent "that the status quo of the little island is not to be interfered with" and that he, Ryan, had voiced criticism of German bomb attacks on Ireland (Dublin's North Strand, Belfast) and Irish vessels ("City of Bremen") to the Bavarian trouble-shooter of Ribbentrop. Ryan was obviously cautious, emphasizing that "He [Veesenmayer] must know *nothing* of correspondence between you and me".[28] Earlier, according to Francis Stuart, Ryan, on the occasion of the German attack on the Soviet Union (22 June 1941), had said to Veesenmayer: "Your war is lost."[29]

Living in a large gloomy flat, Ryan was slowly building up a circle of German friends. Unfortunately for him, his closest ones, the Clissmanns, lived in Copenhagen and he visited them on several occasions.

Frank Ryan and Maeve Clissmann, Christmas 1942

[27] Ibid., p. 244, letter of 14.05.1942.
[28] DIFP, 7, pp. 228-229, Ryan to Kerney, Berlin, 13.08.1942.
[29] Carter, The Shamrock, p. 122.

Ryan suffered his first stroke on 14 January 1943. His heart was malfunctioning because arteritis prevented the aorta valves from closing fully, thus leading to minor haemorrhages and insufficient blood circulation in the respective inner organs.[30] As Francis Stuart, one of his frequent visitors, relates, Ryan spent months in the Berlin Charité Hospital, partially paralysed, but determined to get well.

He was released around May 1943 and moved to a new abode, a house where he met a pharmacist, Hilda Lübbert, who became a true friend in need. In September Frank was again hospitalized because of an ulcer and subjected to a severe diet. The cure was successful but drastic – he lost 12 kilos and now weighed only 61. Following this sojourn in hospital Ryan had trouble with his ration cards and learned for the first time about German wartime bureaucracy – his supporters Veesenmayer, Clissmann and Hoven were not around to help.

Just before Christmas 1943 Ryan moved again, acquiring a room in a house ("digs" in his parlance) in Johannesbergerstrasse in the south-west suburb of Friedenau. Fräulein Hübbert also had a room there. This was shortly after the commencement of mass-bomber raids of the RAF on the German capital. Frank disdained bomb shelters, calling them "funk-holes" – he had had enough air-raids to last a normal lifetime when working at the Political Commissariat of the International Brigades in Central Madrid in the years 1937/38.

During one horrendous bombing night in Berlin at the end of January 1944, Ryan stayed in his unheated flat and contracted pneumonia.[31] Budge Clissmann and his own inventiveness (he falsified his temperature) ensured his escape from a wartime temporary hospital and transfer to the clinic of Dr. Weidner in the Löschwitz suburb of Dresden.[32] Francis Stuart and another friend visited him there on St. Patrick's Day 1944:

> He had a warm room high over the Elbe. There was a library, sitting rooms, comparatively good food, medical care. I had never seen him so miserable. They had kept his papers in Berlin. Even if he had become well enough to leave he was a prisoner ... Let it be said that up to the time of his death he

---

[30] Cronin, Frank Ryan, p. 254.
[31] For details of the RAF's 'Battle for Berlin', see: Max Hastings, Bomber Command, Pan Books 2007 Edition, pp. 257-269.
[32] Cronin, Frank Ryan, pp. 224-230.

was treated in a manner, which in all the circumstances, was, from the German point of view, one of tact and consideration … At the end of May he returned to Berlin.[33]

Ryan planned to leave Berlin for Luxembourg, where the Irish section of German radio was located from September 1943 to August 1944. He had earlier refused to speak on air for the Germans, something he had willingly done at least twice on Radio Madrid seven years earlier. Furthermore, Ryan had written a memorandum arguing against the establishment of a Nazi "black propaganda" transmitter in occupied Holland for Irish listeners. He envisaged working in Luxembourg as a translator, nothing else.[34] If Francis Stuart's account is to be believed, Ryan was so desperate as this stage that he agreed that Stuart should sound out the Irish Legation on his case.[35] Nothing came of it because the Legation building was completely destroyed in an air-raid on 22 November 1943.[36]

On the basis of enquiries from Jim Larkin Junior T.D., the Irish diplomats still in Berlin afterwards tried to find out about Ryan, but as he lived in Germany under a pseudonym, the Aussenamt denied any knowledge of such a person.[37]

After his return to Berlin Frank Ryan had a relapse and found it difficult to breathe. Francis Stuart, his wife Gertrud and Fräulein Lübbert cared for him and organized his return to the clinic in Dresden:

A car was sent for him. A compartment booked on the train. He asked me to shave him and as I did so I remember him telling me to keep the rest of the razor-blades which were almost unprocurable. I and a soldier who was driving the car helped him down the stairs and into it and, accompanied by the German girl who had been his friend [Hilda Lübbert], he was driven away. This was the last time I saw him. The next day I had a phone call from her from Dresden that he was dying and before I could get the permit to travel another phone call came to say he was dead. In a diary I noted

[33] Francis Stuart, Frank Ryan Story. Part II, The Bell, December 1950, pp. 38-39.
[34] Cronin, Frank Ryan, pp. 228-229; David O'Donoghue, Hitler's Irish Voices. The Story of German Radio's Wartime Irish Service, Belfast 1998, pp. 143-155.
[35] Stuart, The Bell, November 1950, p. 42.
[36] DIFP, 7, pp. 366-369, William Warnock to Dublin, 16.12.1943.
[37] NAI, DFA 20/A/4, Frank Ryan Part III, telegram Dublin-Berlin 06.04.1944; telegram Berlin via Berne-Dublin, 15.04.1944; telegram Dublin-Madrid 16.05.1944.

under the date, June 15, 1944: 'Went to Dresden yesterday with S. and L. for Frank's funeral. A formal little ceremony, in the neat Löschwitz cemetery on the banks of the Elbe ... Mrs Clissmann had come from Copenhagen and took charge of it ... An intense sense of loneliness leaving F's body there in that place, far from everyone. A feeling of final and utter loneliness. And yet that is not the last word. I do not think that it is the last word'.[38]

Frank Ryan died, as the journalist Johannes Richard, born in Boston on 3 April 1900 and a resident of Berlin-Charlottenburg, at 1700hrs on 10 June 1944 in the clinic at Malerstrasse 31, Dresden.[39] Because of chaotic wartime conditions in Germany, Irish authorities learned only months later about Ryan's final days. In July 1944, three weeks after Frank's death, Kerney informed Dublin that Mrs. Clissmann (the letter was probably written six months earlier) was seriously concerned about his state of health and that she urged his repatriation on humanitarian grounds.[40] Immediately after her return to Copenhagen following Ryan's funeral, Budge Clissmann sent a detailed report on the demise of her friend to Mr. Kerney, but her letter did not arrive in Madrid until 11 December 1944. It was a precise account:

His last illness was very brief. He caught a cold which by Monday the 5th of June had developed into pleurisy. As on the 7th his condition was if anything worse. His Berlin doctor recommended that he should be got back to Dresden ... On the 9th he left for Dresden, very pleased to be going there and in the care of Miss Lübbert, a good friend who had been looking after him for over a year. On admission to the sanatorium, the doctor realized immediately that that which in Frank's case was most to be feared, had happened. His circulation system, handicapped by his fairly advanced arteritis, which prevented one heart valve from closing properly, was unable to bear the strain put upon it by the inflammation of the lungs and he passed away on the Saturday afternoon during a period of unconsciousness. At the end he had no pain and was not aware of the seriousness of his illness ... The funeral at Löschwitz on Wednesday, 14th June, was preceded by a Mass for the dead and was held in full accordance with the rites of the Catholic Church. Francis Stuart and some friend were there but

---

[38] Stuart, The Bell, December 1950, pp. 39-40.
[39] NAI, DFA20/A/4, Frank Ryan, Part II, Sterbeurkunde dated 15.06.1944.
[40] Ibid., Part III, F.H. Boland to Col. Dan Bryan, 08.07.1944.

unfortunately Helmut and several old friends were prevented by the war for attending. The grave lies in a beautiful quiet cemetery in the country on the banks of the Elbe and the ceremony was simple and sincere and for us Irish, very lonely.[41]

Kerney informed Dublin on 23 December, and de Valera's officials waited until after the festive season to impart the news to the Ryan family.[42]

Frank Ryan's grave, Dresden 1945

A Government statement, issued on 23 February, was immediately taken up by the dailies.[43] The memorial meeting planned for the Mansion House on 28

[41] Cronin, Frank Ryan, pp. 255-256.
[42] NAI, DFA 20/A/4, Frank Ryan, Part III, telegram Berlin-Dublin, 27.01.1945.
[43] Manchester Guardian, 24.02.1945; Irish Press, 24.02.1945.

February was refused by the City Manager, a decision which was not explained. That was the occasion for that old warhorse Jim Larkin to excoriate the authorities in the Council Chamber on 2 March 1945:

> *Whatever faults Frank Ryan might have had, his record during the years he lived in this country was second to none, and no man, despite his political views, could challenge Ryan's bona fides. There was no more courageous or upright man than this great Irishman. Any dog or devil can get the Mansion House, owned by the citizens, but the men and women who served their country could not.*[44]

A memorial meeting attended by about 80 people in the Dublin Trades Council Hall one week later constituted a committee to have Ryan's remains brought back to Ireland.[45] More detailed news of Frank Ryan's German exile were provided by Budge Clissmann (her husband was in British detention in Germany at the time), when she returned to Ireland with her children in January 1946.[46] Some months later she gave a long interview to Frederick Boland, Secretary of the Department of External Affairs, repeating what Ryan had told her about Sean Russell's death.[47] Finally, after much preparations and set-backs, Ryan's remains were released by the GDR authorities. His funeral to Glasnevin took place on a cloudy summer day, 21 June 1979.[48]

Most of the historians who have written about Frank Ryan take cognizance of his dilemma when trying to appraise his role after release from Burgos in 1940. To use a modern phrase, they "contextualise" his situation: he was a prisoner of circumstances in Germany, trying his best not to compromise his political views, while at the same time supporting Irish neutrality; and his hurried departure from Spain saved his life, as he saw it. In Germany he had to perform a delicate balancing act. If he refused outright to co-operate with the Germans, he could fear the worst. Fortunately, such a confrontation between Ryan and his "minders" never arose. Frank Ryan could reason that opposition was unwarranted: he could influence German policy towards Ireland, and important

---

[44] Irish Times, 06.03.1945.
[45] All Irish dailies 09.03.1945.
[46] Irish Times, Irish Press, 19.01.1946.
[47] DIFP, 8, pp. 152-153, Memorandum by F.H. Boland, 06.06.1946
[48] See Saothar 21, 1996, Interview with Eilís Ryan, for the controversies involving Ryan's re-interment.

advisers in the Abwehr were the friends (Clissmann, Hoven) who saved him from a slow death in fascist Spain. Through them he had a conduit to Dublin via Leopold Kerney that would ensure that the Irish Government would know that he had not become a traitor or a fascist collaborator. Moreover, he realized that he was a privileged "guest" of the Third Reich, had no cause for complaint and, with one exception (the Freisack experiment), could fend off some of the more, for him, unacceptable demands on his services.

Fearghal McGarry, an expert on Ireland and the Spanish Civil War and on Frank Ryan's life, writes of "Ryan's decision to go to Germany", and that he was a collaborator of the Germans.[49] A careful reading of the sources, I believe, would suggest that such statements are too unequivocal. The alternative for Ryan in 1940 was to refuse to be part of the Abwehr "escape-plan" and die slowly in his Burgos prison cell. He survived for four years in Germany, it is doubtful if he would have lived that long as a Franco captive.

Frank Ryan packed many lives into one. He was only 41 when he died from multiple ailments which, considering the state of medical science at the time, would have proved lethal in Ireland or anywhere else. He was, medically if not politically, "ein Toter auf Urlaub", a dead man on holiday. But he knew that and never gave up.

---

[49] McGarry, Frank Ryan, p. 68. Chapter Four of his book is titled "Collaborator".

5

The Killing of Maurice Emmet Ryan

Maurice Emmett Ryan, known to his family as Emmet and inevitably dubbed "Paddy" in the British battalion of the 15th International Brigade, was without doubt the most colourful and controversial of all Irish volunteers fighting for the Spanish Republic. Details of his family are fragmentary. Emmet's mother was Mary Cusack, the only child of Hanora (Norah) and John Cusack, who had a farm at Coolyhena, Ballysimon, near the Limerick-Tipperary town road.

Mary married Edward Ryan, a clerk, in June 1910 in St. Patrick's Catholic Church, in Limerick city. His address was George Street (now O'Connell St.) and he may have worked in Cannock's, the department store. Edward Ryan – the name is very common – may have been a farmer's son from Annagh, Clonkeen, in East Limerick. Six sons were born to the couple. John in 1911, Thomas in 1912, Edward (Eamon) in 1913, and Maurice Emmett (as on his birth certificate) in May 1915. Michael Kevin followed in 1916, and Oliver Plunkett Desmond (Des), the youngest, in 1919. The last three boys were born overhead "The 41 Bar" in Upper Catherine, Street, Limerick city. By the time of

Desmond's birth his father's occupation had changed from draper to furniture buyer. The building had previously housed Pope's spirit and grocery store.[1]

Ryan family, 1923
Back row: Edward Ryan and Mary Cusack Ryan
Middle row: Emmet, Tom and John
Front Row: Desmond, Eamon and Kevin

Further documentation on the Ryan family is scanty. Mary Ryan applied for a license extension for "The 41 Bar" in October 1924.[2] Shortly afterwards, and certainly before the end of 1926, Mary Ryan acquired the building next-door (No. 40), probably on a 99-year lease, and converted it into "The Desmond Hotel". When the lease went up for sale in 1929 the hotel comprised 15 bedrooms and a dining-room seating 27 persons.[3] The auction took place in

[1] For information on the family of Emmet Ryan I thank Ger McCloskey, Mike McNamara, Eamon Ryan and Mary Davis Ryan.
[2] Limerick Leader, 14.10.1924.
[3] Limerick Leader, 06.04.1929.

134

April 1929 at the Sales Yard, Mulgrave Street.[4] The buyer was Christina O'Grady who applied officially for a transfer of the liquor license in September 1929.[5] She lived at the hotel address until at least 1942/43 (electoral list).

Tracing the Ryan family afterwards was very difficult. Mainly because the electoral lists for Limerick City are missing for the years 1924-1931. Even if the records survived, the parents' names are very common and the boys would not have surfaced because they were under the voting age of 21. The only other piece of evidence for Maurice Emmett is from the 1959 Centenary Yearbook of Crescent College, namely that Emmet Ryan of the Desmond Hotel attended the school in the academic year 1928/1929.

To judge from the dissembling, exaggerated and inaccurate accounts Maurice gave to his comrades and superiors in Spain, he was the "black sheep" of a very religious and conservative family; one brother, he said, was in the O'Duffy *bandera* in Spain, and that he, Maurice, wanted to settle scores with him. We know that a "J. Ryan" was the organizer of the volunteers for O'Duffy's expedition in Limerick.[6] And that a "Teddy Ryan" was a Blueshirt volunteer in Spain.[7] However, Fearghal McGarry in his study mentioned two Ryans with O'Duffy, both from Tipperary.[8] Bob Stradling states that the two Ryans in the bandera were from Dundrum, Co. Dublin (Teddy) and Cashel (J. Ryan).[9] There are two references to an "E. Ryan" in local papers in 1932/33: as county organizer for Cumann na nGaedheal in early 1932[10] and to a man of the same name who attended an UIP (forerunner of Fine Gael) meeting in the Town Hall as a delegate from the Limerick South Rural ward in December 1933.[11] Evidence acquired to date would suggest that "my fascist family" was the product of Emmet Ryan's fertile imagination.

---

[4] Ibid.
[5] Limerick Leader, 31.08.1929.
[6] Barrie Wharton/Des Ryan, „The Last Crusade: Limerick's role in the Spanish Civil War", Old Limerick Journal, Summer Edition 2001, p. 15 (online).
[7] http://www2.ul.ie/web/WWW/Services/Library/Special_Collections/Stradling
[8] Fearghal McGarry, Irish Politics and the Spanish Civil War, Cork 1999, p. 257.
[9] Robert A. Stradling, The Irish and the Spanish Civil War. Crusades in Conflict, Manchester 1999, p. 262.
[10] Limerick Chronicle, 19.01.1932.
[11] Limerick Chronicle, 07.12.1933.

All the Ryan boys left Ireland. John, Tom and Edward Junior (Eamon) migrated to the United States in the early 1930s. Kevin left for to Canada after WW2, and Desmond, a medical doctor who had held a series of hospital appointments in Ireland, pulled up roots and started a new life in Australia in 1958. The family may have been in straitened circumstances after the sale of their hotel 1929 and probably moved to Dublin. Still, money could not have been that scarce for they sent their youngest son, Desmond, to a boarding school in Tipperary at a very early age and then moved him as a boarder to Mungret, the Jesuit school outside Limerick.

Des Ryan and his dandy brother Emmet ca. 1933

Maurice seems to have left Ireland under a cloud, and his parents paid his expenses when he lived in Spain, France and Portugal in 1933-37. He got into trouble when living at the Hotel Aviz in Lisbon. He was arrested, finger-printed and fined 60 Escudos (11 shillings sterling) in July 1935 for the offence of "not obeying the order of the police guard". He gave his age as 20 years, the names of his parents and their home place (no address) as Limerick. His occupation was given as "capitalista", surely a joke on Maurice's part. The Portuguese Consul in Dublin sent a copy from the Lisbon police register and an incomplete translation of same to Taoiseach de Valera in August 1935. The Assistant Secretary of the

Department of External Affairs initialed the file and someone else scribbled P/A on the cover – "put away". So the parents Mary and Edward in Limerick were not officially informed.[12] Seeing that Maurice later had a record of heavy drinking, it was probably some public order offence.

Seaman's papers of Maurice Ryan, Empress of Australia

About a year later it seems that his parents cut off his allowance. In the summer of 1937 Maurice (6 feet 2 inches, hazel-eyes, fresh complexion) worked as an assistant steward on the "Empress of Australia", a luxurious vessel that plied the Southampton-Quebec route but also featured as a world-cruise ship. He signed

---

[12] National Archives of Ireland (NAI), DFA/4/44/79, Maurice Emmett Ryan. I thank Dr Michael Kennedy of the Royal Irish Academy for locating the file and explaining the hieroglyphics on its cover.

on board in Southampton on 24 June 1937 and was discharged at the same port a month later. He seems to have immediately re-engaged, this time on the "RMS Arlanza" (built at Harland and Wolff in 1911), which may have been somewhat of a come-down because the vessel was scrapped in 1938. His seafaring career did not exceed two months.[13]

Maurice arrived on 5 November 1937 in Spain, at the assembly point in the fortress of Figueras, having crossed the border (presumably he climbed over the Pyrenees) at Massanet.[14] He entrained for the IB base at Albacete four days later.[15] The journey generally involved stop-overs in Barcelona and Valencia. Ryan was unfortunate in that the man who interviewed him at Figueras was a sinister figure, Lieut. Antonio de Maio, a Communist boiler-maker from New York. De Maio was an agent of SIM (*Servicio Investigacion Militar*), the Republican military counter-intelligence branch. His first posting within the SIM was to the notorious re-education unit in "Camp Lukacs", where the demoralized and the deserters were held pending further deployment.[16] De Maio afterwards got into trouble in the USA because of alleged involvement in the execution of volunteers.[17] One veteran remembers him as a bully wont to wave his pistol about when fellow-Americans spoke back to him.[18]

De Maio was bored stiff in November 1937 because there were so few arrivals to interrogate.[19] His "Bolshevik vigilance" (Russia, not to mention Spain, was in the convulsions of a spy mania in 1937/38) was immediately aroused when Maurice stated that he was sent over on his own from London. In Britain prospective volunteers were interviewed by R.W. ("Robby") Robson of the Central Committee of the CPGB and, if deemed suitable, sent to Paris in a group with weekend-tickets for the ferry and train. No passports were needed. De Maio learned subsequently that Ryan had been "picked up" in Paris, i.e. Maurice,

---

[13] Merchant seamen's papers acquired from *cityarchives@southampton.gov.uk*, 2013. See also the BT index at www.nationalarchives.co.uk.

[14] RGASPI, f. 545, o. 6, d. 35, l. 169.

[15] RGASPI, f. 545, o. 2, d. 303, l. 108.

[16] RGASPI, f. 545, o. 6, d. 880, l. 6f.

[17] Peter N. Carroll, The Odyssey of the Abraham Lincoln Brigade. Americans in the Spanish Civil War, Stanford 1994, p. 186, 233. De Maio was cited before the House Committee of Un-American Activities chaired by the Texan congressman Martin Dies in 1940.

[18] Harry Fisher, Comrades. Tales of a Brigadista in the Spanish Civil War, University of Nebraska Press 1999, p. 135f.

[19] RGASPI, f. 545, o. 6, d. 880, l. 14f.

living now in France, had probably gone straight to the assembly centre at Place du Combat for incoming volunteers. A second point of suspicion was the statement that Maurice had served as officer in the Irish Free State Army but had been "thrown out".[20] He then said he was an officer in the IRA, a claim de Maio dismissed because Maurice said that he had never heard of Frank Ryan, the leader of the Irish in Spain and a famous IRA man. Having established that Maurice Ryan had "no working class affiliation", de Maio sent a report on the same day to his SIM superior "Camarade Leppo" with the request, "Please notify me further on what is done with this person".[21]

Maurice Emmett Ryan was an unusual Irish volunteer in other respects. First, his middle class origin and education, for archival evidence suggests that only a handful of the Irish volunteers had gone to secondary school (Frank Edwards, Frank Ryan, Charlie Donnelly, Robert Hilliard, Eamonn McGrotty, Liam McGregor, Jack Nalty); most were from poor backgrounds with a predominance of unskilled or semi-skilled labourers, seamen and ex-soldiers (Irish Free State Army, British Army). A second point is Maurice's knowledge of Europe and his proficiency in foreign languages (Spanish, Portuguese, French) and the self-confidence that comes from fending for oneself in foreign environments. Thirdly, his height and manly appearance would have boosted his self-confidence. Finally, however deep his sympathies for the Spanish Republic were, he was a constant "piss-taker" about conditions in the 15th Brigade (insufficient and bad equipment, woeful logistics and food shortages, leaders with little or no military expertise etc.) and by all accounts felt that he could do a better job of leading the men himself.

He won the men's affection because of his wit, courage and efficiency – even his enemies cited him as the best machine-gunner in the British battalion. He was the born "slagger", had no respect for authority but seems to have gone out of his way to antagonize "the powers that be". His ridiculing of Party slogans, and their disseminators the political commissars ("comic stars"), was not unusual but he brought unnecessary and additional suspicion on himself by loose talk about his allegedly rich and fascist family, and especially, that he had a brother fighting in Spain with O'Duffy's *bandera*. Obviously, Maurice would have behaved

---

[20] There is no record of a Maurice Emmett Ryan having served in the Irish Army as an officer cadet in the 1930s. Information from Michael Keane, Irish Military Archives, 10.03.2014.
[21] RGASPI, f. 545, o. 6, d. 195, l. 58.

differently in a regular army: six months of a "glasshouse" regime would have taught him a lesson.

But in the International Brigades there was a haphazard system for punishing recidivist offenders: on a minor charge a soldier would be held in the battalion jail and forced to dig latrines or trenches; his destination on another misdemeanour was Camp Lukacs and Villa Maruja, detention centres in Chincilla six miles south-west of Albacete. There the British battalion culprits (usually deserters, malingerers, "front-dodgers", hopeless drunks, petty thieves and the demoralized pleading for repatriation) were detained in the hope that they would "see the error of their ways" and ask to be re-admitted to the battalion. More serious transgressors could end up in a labour battalion and be posted to the front to carry out dangerous work, e.g. building fortifications on the front line under enemy fire or being posted for similar tasks in no-man's-land.[22] Incarceration in Spain was probably worse when the offenders were arrested outside the remit of the International Brigades and had been caught without papers, especially the *salvo conducto*, i.e. permission to leave Spain. These deserters were often picked up in the vicinity of British ships docked in Barcelona, Valencia or Alicante. The next address of these men who were often totally demoralized, if not shell-shocked, was often a city prison – there seems to have been no proper psychological treatment facilities within the *sanidad* of the International Brigades. The most feared of prisons was the fortress of Castelldefels near Barcelona, a "hard regime" gaol run by a mafia of French communists, who were removed after a major scandal in 1938.[23] The last IB prisoners there, including some Irish, were not released and repatriated until February 1939.

In retrospect, this fortress by the sea south-west of Barcelona could have been Maurice Ryan's final destination in Spain, but he was not the usual "hard-case" playing "the old soldier" and pleading for repatriation but an excellent infantryman and machine-gunner when sober, albeit with the black mark that he was politically highly suspicious because of his origins, statements and lack of any links to the labour movement, in a word, a "suspicious element".

---

[22] Julius Ruiz, „'Work and Don't lose Hope': Republican forced Labour Camps during the Spanish Civil War", Contemporary European History, Vol. 18, no. 4, 2009, pp. 419-441.
[23] Rob Stradling, „English-speaking Units of the International Brigades. War, Politics and Discipline", Journal of Contemporary History, Vol. 45, no. 4, 2010, pp. 744-767.

Maurice Ryan's military career had an unusual beginning: his stay at the training battalion at Tarazona de la Mancha (at this stage in the war about 3-4 months instruction) was short. He joined the 2nd recruits company on 12 November[24] but arrived at the British battalion six days later.[25] The reason for his speedy integration into the British unit, which was in a process of reformation after the hard battles in Aragon in September-October (Belchite, Quinto, Fuentes des Elbro), could be that the cadre specialists believed that Maurice was an experienced or very promising soldier. On an index-card typed at this time, Ryan is described as "Guardsman", an obvious reference to his height or previous service in the British Army which does not occur again in his documents. His next-of-kin address on the buff paper is probably that of a seafaring colleague (E.R. Radcliffe, The Old White House, Shefford, Bedfordshire).[26]

In November 1937 the British battalion, now severely under strength at 165 British and Irish, was situated in Mondejar and Albite, in a wine-growing area on the Valencia road south-east of Madrid. Maurice was posted to No. 2 Company, the machine-gunners with their Russian 1910 Maxims, a cumbersome heavy weapon replete with metal wheels and a steel shield.[27] A Maxim crew consisted ideally of 12 members – a sergeant commander, the corporal, No. 1, who fired the weapon, the No. 2 who fed the belts into the feed block, a third man carrying the spare parts box and the shield, with the remaining eight doubling as ammunition carriers and riflemen-defenders of the gun emplacement.[28] In November 1937 the battalion command consisted of Fred Copeman, commander, and Wally Tapsell, political commissar. Both had been withdrawn to Britain by the CPGB but had returned to former prominence by October with the sanction of the CPGB Polbureau; the squabbling continued, fuelled by the predominance of the Americans on the brigade staff and the interference of Bill Rust, the representative of the CPGB at the Central Committee of the Spanish

---

[24] RGASPI, f. 545, o. 2, d. 258, l. 296.

[25] RGASPI, f. 545, o. 6, d. 195, l. 62.

[26] Ibid., l. 60. I sent a letter to the mayor of Shefford in November 2013 enquiring about Mr Radcliffe but did not receive a reply.

[27] For details of the training in Mondejar, see Bob Clark, No Boots to My Feet. With a Foreword by Jack Jones, Stoke-on-Trent 1984, p. 31. Clark was with Maurice Ryan in the MG Company.

[28] M.E. Ryan, „The Heavy Machine Gun", The Volunteer for Liberty, 06.08.1938, p. 5. (RGASPI, f. 545, o. 2, d. 363, l. 27)

Communist Party.[29] Copeman, as previously stated, tended to settle arguments by brute force. John Dunlop, a trainee accountant from Edinburgh and a Communist, remembers the explosive encounter between Maurice Ryan and Copeman:

> *As for Ryan, he was a bull of a man, a huge fellow. I'm pretty tall myself but he was as tall as me and about twice as wide. A hugely amusing character, a big curly haired fellow, a tremendous drinker – his main aim in life seemed to be to make fun of everything we were doing … He disliked Copeman, the commander of the battalion of that time – not only disliked him but hated him. And Copeman thoroughly reciprocated. One time when Ryan was up on a charge for being drunk and disorderly he annoyed Copeman so much that Copeman jumped over the Orderly Room table and felled him with a blow to the jaw. I was on guard on the small cell where Ryan was incarcerated for a while, and all he could do was to nurse his jaw and spit oaths at Copeman … And yet the man, although he was such a rogue, was an extremely likeable rogue. He could be extremely amusing, highly diverting at times.[30]*

Maurice was gaoled for ten days, with ten days' loss of pay for "insulting the commanding officer when drunk".[31] On 10 December 1937 the battalion entrained for the north, to southern Aragon in anticipation of the Republican offensive against the ancient city of Teruel set in a fastnesss of high peaks and deep gorges. On the train ride to Alcaniz Maurice had a dispute with Tapsell because the voluble Irishman got off for a chat with the "Lincoln boys". Ryan was arrested but no charges were proffered –"the whole thing blew off".[32] After a long march from the railhead the battalion reached the village of Mas de la Matas in the province of Teruel. It was here that Bob Clark from Liverpool, another machine-gunner, got to know Maurice ("Paddy") Ryan better:

> *Among the volunteers in the village was a huge Irishman, altogether a rather amazing character and fond of claiming his aristocratic lineage. Most*

[29] Richard Baxell, Unlikely Warriors. The British in the Spanish Civil War and the Struggle against Fascism, London 2012, pp. 275-276.
[30] Ian McDougall, Voices from the Spanish Civil war. Personal Recollections of Scottish Volunteers in Republican Spain 1936-39, Edinburgh 1986, pp. 145-146.
[31] RGASPI, f. 545, o. 6, d. 195, l. 59 (reverse).
[32] Ibid.

of the lads believed him as he was well educated and spoke three or four languages fluently. He was very popular, but too fond of the booze. In half a joking way he was fond of saying that his brother was a major in Franco's army and the only real reason why he had joined the Republicans was (he being the black sheep of the family) was to shock his aristocratic relations. Of course we paid very little attention to these statements of his and put it down to drink, but events many months later unfortunately proved that there was a certain amount of truth in his statements. If any man had the makings of an excellent officer, he had. His humour was irresistible and when he was sober he was a very likeable chap. Even during the few weeks of training [in Mondejar] he had already seen the inside of the local Calaboose. But he was forgiven because he had expressed regret and for a while was a model soldier and about the best machine-gunner in the whole Fifteenth Brigade.[33]

The 15th Brigade took no part in the capture of Teruel and the British battalion was enjoying unusually good fare at Christmas, a visit from Harry Pollitt, the British communist leader carrying sacks of post, and the timely arrival of food parcels (and scarce cigarettes) from well-wishers in the United Kingdom. Two days before Christmas, Copeman, a non-drinker, who had been complaining of stomach pains for months, was whisked off to hospital. His life was in danger (acute appendicitis) but he survived and was later invalided home. On New Year's Eve, the 15th Brigade was rushed to the front to beat off the fascist counter-attacks on Teruel.

The battle for the next five weeks was in Artic cold, with units clinging to mountain tops or ridges and under constant bombardment from artillery and planes. More Internationals died of cold than in battle, 21 in the British battalion were killed (one third of the effective strength) before the city fell to Franco's troops on 21 January.[34] Frank O'Brien (Dundalk) and David Walsh (Ballina) were among the fatalities, while Maurice was wounded on 23 January in somewhat unusual circumstances, as John Dunlop relates:

---

[33] Working Class Movement Library (WCML), Salford, Interview script 946.081 CLA, p. 29. I am indebted to John Halstead (Sheffield) for making the journey to Salford and taking copious notes at my unashamed bidding. It is noteworthy that Clark does not mention Maurice Ryan or his subsequent fate in his published memoir "No Boots to My Feet".
[34] Baxell, Unlikely Warriors, pp. 281-285.

He himself told me that before he came to Spain he was a gigolo in the South of France. He was in our machine gun team that I was detailed to, on the Teruel front. He was sitting up on the wall of the trench one day delousing his shirt. A sniper's bullet from the other side passed through his chest and tore a big flap of flesh away from his shoulder blade. He was extremely annoyed about this because it left a huge scar on his shoulder and spoiled his beauty for the ladies on the beaches of the Mediterranean.[35]

The British units did well at Teruel, earning a commendation from Corps commander Juan Modesto. The fire of the British machine-gunners was devastating, either in providing covering fire when their riflemen changed positions or near the end, when the MG Company wiped out a fascist battalion advancing across the floor of a valley.[36] It was here that Maurice Ryan showed his proficiency with the Maxim and gained his reputation as an expert MG crew member, No. 1 on the gun. Despite his valour in the field, Ryan was still a suspect, according to the English Section of the Cadres Department at the headquarters in Albacete:

Ryan Maurice. English. Aged 22. No occupation, secondary education. No Party. From England 11.11.1937. Bourgeois extraction. Says has brother Officer on Fascist side. Family Fascists. Had fascist leanings himself once. Went to British battalion 18.11.1937. Jailed for disruption. Present whereabouts unclear, probably in jail.[37]

This list contains 14 names of persons who were politically "unreliable", not run-of-the-mill malcontents or "barrack room lawyers" but non-Communists, and primarily members of the anti-Stalinist Independent Labour Party and now collectively slandered as "Trotskyists". Unfortunately, Maurice Ryan did nothing to allay suspicion, quite the contrary.

While recuperating from his flesh wound in the hospital of the Internationals beside the sea in Benicasim on 24 February, the Limerick man strolled into one of the cafés in the resort frequented by trainee policemen (Guardia de Asalto),

---

[35] McDougall, Voices, p. 145.
[36] Bill Alexander, British Volunteers for Liberty. Spain 1936-1939, London 1982, pp. 164-168; Clark, No Boots, pp. 50-52.
[37] RGASPI, f. 545, o. 6, d. 99, l. 3.

whose school was nearby.[38] A row developed with a police officer and Ryan was felled with a blow from a rifle-butt. He was placed under arrest and sent in disgrace to Vladimir Čopić, the Croatian Commander of the 15th Brigade. Ryan was transferred to the Tarazona training base for English-speaking volunteers where he soon earned the displeasure of the base commandant, Major Allan Johnson. His real name was McNeil, a Scottish veteran of WWI who had served as paymaster in an infantry battalion of the U.S. Army on the Philippines.[39] He was an efficient commander, if somewhat of a martinet, and often the butt of derision from the more hard-boiled of the American recruits. Especially his insistence that the men not only salute him but also the Spanish republican flag on the village square was a source of ridicule.[40] Johnson had joined the CPUSA in 1932 so he was not at all amused when Maurice Ryan parodied a song of the Young Communist League of America, a sacrilegious version that soon became a favourite:

> *YCLers are we*
> *Brave members of the I.B.*
> *Machine guns they rattle*
> *And cannons they roar.*
> *We rush at the Fascists*
> *Just screaming for more.*
> *YCLers are we etc.*[41]

Ryan probably resented being posted to a company of recruits, and was disinclined to go on parade, so Johnson put him in the lock-up. He was then interviewed by an unknown IB officer, whom he told some unlikely tales, spiced with accurate details of his bad disciplinary record since enlistment. The "facts" stated did not add up in a chronological sense: From Blackrock [Co. Dublin], law student of law at Oxford, joined the Free State Army at 17, spent two years as a 2nd Lieutenant and left the army for religious reasons, then adding he had been "thrown out"; October 1934 in Barcelona, 1933 in Portugal, again in 1935, Cote d'Azur, gentleman of leisure 1933-35, allowance from parents stopped when he came to Spain; never interested in politics; five brothers, one fascist, O'Duffy

---

[38] I thank my friend Guillem Casan for information on Benicasim.
[39] Eby, Between the Bullet and the Lie, p. 116.
[40] Fisher, Comrades, p. 88.
[41] McDougall, Voices, p. 146 (John Dunlop)

captain, officer in Ireland already; religious question in family; "trying to help the weaker side", came to Spain because "he dislikes Fascism for unnecessary slaughter".[42]

This rough summary in pencil was on the back of a letter by Johnson's adjutant dated 22 March 1938 to SIM at Albacete, outlining Ryan's disruptive record. The letter included the damning addendum that Ryan, since coming to Tarazona, "has continued in a similar manner". Howard Goddard, acting for Johnson, recommended "that he be thoroughly investigated by your Service [SIM]."[43] After arrival under guard in Albacete, Ryan was supposed to be sent to a forced labour battalion but soon took ill and was in the hospital in the central barracks (Albacete) two days later.[44] "Should be very closed watched" was the entry in his cadre file, which included new incriminations, obviously untrue: that he had never worked for a living and that his father owned 20 hotels in Ireland.[45] There is no record of Ryan's deployment between April and June, but it is likely he was soon re-integrated into the British unit.

After the disastrous retreats in March-April 1938, the British battalion commenced a long period of re-adjustment and morale-building which was facilitated by the longest rest and training period the volunteers ever experienced, from May to late July 1938. The re-opening of the border to France between March and May meant new equipment (some Bren guns and mortars, for example) and the arrival of the last volunteers, including 16 Irishmen.[46]

In June the 15th Brigade settled in a secluded dale between the villages of Marçà and La Torre de Fontaubella on the northern bank of the Ebro near Falset. The idyllic site was soon dubbed "chabola valley", named after the Spanish word for the roofed shacks the men built. Food, tobacco and clothing were in short supply. The relentless diet of *garbanzos* (chick-peas) and lentils caused havoc with digestive systems so that diarrhoea was common, with periodic outbreaks of

---

[42] RGASPI, f. 545, o. 6, d. 195, l. 59 reverse.

[43] Ibid., l. 59.

[44] RGASPI, f. 545, o. 6, d. 39, l. 35.

[45] RGASPI, f. 545, o. 6, d. 195, l. 62.

[46] The new men who travelled from Ireland: Eugene Downing, Hugh Hunter, Alec Digges, Tom O'Brien, Bill McGregor, Michael O'Riordan, James F. O'Regan and Liam Burgess. Paddy Duff, Michael Lehane and Jack Nalty were on their second tour. George Gorman, James Lord, Jim Haughey and James Domegan travelled from Britain, Albert Fulton from Australia.

dysentery. Due to the shortage of water, the men were plagued with lice and scabies. However, the good weather, prominent visitors, fiestas and rigorous training raised spirits. The Irish scrounged enough food and wine to hold a "Bodenstown" celebration in honour of Wolfe Tone.[47] When Jawaharlal Nehru, the future first Prime Minister of India, visited the British battalion on 15 May, Maurice Ryan put on a machine-gun display, knocking chunks out of a tree across the valley.[48] Eugene Downing from Dublin, new to the battalion, says of the incident that when the first crew, over-awed by the occasion, failed to impress, "the gun was taken over by Maurice Ryan of Limerick, the best-machine-gunner in the battalion, and a very difficult person to over-awe, I may say. His display certainly made an impression, especially on the trees on the other side of the valley".[49]

Downing, a member of the CPI, had a soft spot for Maurice, and 60 years later he offered a plausible interpretation of the Limerick man's personality:

> *Actually he was too bright, too independent-minded and too outspoken, he could see that things weren't well organized and would say so, point out what should be done, so the left-wing working class British running it [battalion] resented him. He got up their noses, and didn't care if he did. He could run it better than they were doing. He was the best machine-gunner, but as he said himself, it didn't take much brains to work a machine-gun.[50]*

In his Irish-language memoir of the war, Downing recounts in his typical wry style Maurice's battle with his two worst enemies – *vino* and the battalion command. One night Eugene was on sentry duty at battalion HQ when he saw Maurice Ryan and two comrades returning to their *chabolas*, dancing on the road and singing "Nellie Deane". They must have woken Jack Nalty, who as C.O. of Ryan's MG Company (No. 2) had the Limerick man brought under guard to

---

[47] Michael O'Riordan, Connolly Column. The Story of the Irishmen who fought in the Ranks of the International Brigades in the national-revolutionary war of the Spanish People 1936-1939, New Books Dublin 1979, pp.124-125.
[48] *www.irelandscw.com/ibvol-EDinterview1.htm*. Accessed 01.09.2013.
[49] Angela Jackson, At the Margins of Mayhem. Prologue and Epilogue to the Last Great Battle of the Spanish Civil War, Pontypool 2008, p. 90.
[50] Notes of talks between Harry Owens and Eugene Downing, n.d. I am grateful to Harry Owens for this material.

Downing. Such was the charm of the prisoner that he wheedled Downing next morning to get him his mess tin near Nalty's billet so that he could have his breakfast. Maurice also had at least one confrontation with battalion C.O. Sam Wild, who asked the large Irishman menacingly if he was calling him a liar. Ryan denied the accusation, but won the outstaring contest.[51]

Wild was a 30-year Mancunian with a Mayo mother and grew up in a household steeped in Irish nationalist lore. Like Copeman, he had been in the Royal Navy, but he jumped ship in South Africa in 1932, served his punishment and returned home. His had a distinguished record in the Spanish war, being wounded several times before taking over the British battalion in February 1938.[52] Wild's insouciant style of leadership, unmilitary ways and "laddish" attitude (settling scores with his fists, for example), together with his fearlessness and sang-froid under pressure, made him arguably the most popular leader in the history of the British battalion of the 15th Brigade. On the other hand, his conduct was erratic and his superiors had their doubts about his leadership qualities: "Not very good attitude towards Spanish comrades. Needs political development, drinks too much".[53] Fred Thomas, who wrote one of the best memoirs of the war, held Wild to be "a bit of a roughneck, elemental in his nature."[54]

There was a slide in discipline and Wild's leadership was put in question when he banned drinking in the battalion because of drunken antics of the volunteers in a nearby village. The Spaniards in the battalion, and most of the English-speakers, considered *vino* (they were stationed in an area where wine was cheap and plentiful) as part of their rations and rebelled. At a meeting of Party members Wild was accused of "getting drunk most nights and being brought home in a lorry" and persuaded to rescind the order, a sign that the political commissars were getting the upper hand.[55]

---

[51] Eoghan Ó Duinnín, La Niña Bonita agus An Róisín Dubh, Baile Atha Cliath 1986, p. 46.
[52] Greater Manchester International Brigade Memorial Committee (Ed.), Greater Manchester Men Who Fought in Spain, Manchester 1983, pp. 55-68.
[53] RGASPI, f. 545, o. 6, d. 215, l. 30.
[54] Fred Thomas, Tilting at Windmills. A Memoir of the Spanish Civil War, Michigan State University Press 1996, p. 177.
[55] Hopkins into the Fire, pp. 304-305; Jackson, At the Margins, p. 37.

Considering that Wild had "virtually no knowledge of military tactics",[56] Paddy O'Daire might have been a good replacement. But the Donegal man had been in conflict with Čopić in Aragon in 1937 (see above) and was considered "inclined to be lax as a result of having had little political training"[57] and retaining "a sort of 'rank and file' complex", i.e. having a good way with the men, an easy-going Irishman, and certainly not a political zealot.[58] He was therefore not battalion commander in May 1938, but the leader of No. 1 Company from April until his repatriation (long sought for by Frank Ryan) in mid September, ten days before the general withdrawal of the Brigades.[59] In the coming and last battle, O'Daire won the admiration of Jack Jones (in later life head of the TUC) by reading a French military manual under heavy fire.[60]

One method used to raise morale in the brigades around Marçà was the "activist movement", which suggested, in typical Stalinist error-analysis, that not bad leadership or lack of modern equipment had led to innumerable military setbacks but the soldiers' performance: they were not sufficiently "politicised". The ensuing propaganda went hand in hand with the establishment of a Party organisation in the British battalion. The prime organizer was W.J. ("Billy") Griffiths, a fanatical Welsh Communist, whose ceaseless proselytizing won him few friends. Even George Murray, SIM agent in the battalion, felt that Williams was "inclined to be doctrinaire" and repelled "some people by his lack of adaptability or consideration of the human element".[61] Wild was initially skeptical about Party cells, while Jack Nalty was scornful ("The Party is a waste of time."), ordering Griffiths to dig gun emplacements.[62]

Griffiths, however, recovered his freedom to agitate full-time, and in a sinister ploy which foreshadowed Maurice Ryan's execution, he advocated draconian punishments for dissidents and the demoralized. The best documented case was that of another Welshman, Alec Cummings, a former company commander who had served with distinction at Jarama and Brunete. By June 1938 his nerve had broken and he threatened to desert if sent into action again. Cummings confided

---

[56] Hopkins, Into the Fire, p. 248.
[57] RGASPI, f. 545, o. 6, d. 444, l. 10.
[58] Ibid., l. 29.
[59] RGASPI, f. 545, o. 6, d. 89. ll. 37-39.
[60] Baxell, Unlikely Warriors, p. 337.
[61] RGASPI, f. 545, o. 6, d. 143, l. 13.
[62] Hopkins, Into the Fire, p. 300.

his sorry state to Griffiths, a fellow-Rhondda man. Billy Griffiths had arrived in Spain in March 1938 and therefore had no personal experience of what the men had gone through earlier. The Party leadership deliberated about what to do with Cummings. Since Army Headquarters was insisting on severe punishment for deserters (or potential deserters), Griffiths and Harry Dobson (International Lenin School graduate, Brigade staff) argued for a court-martial and the death penalty. Battalion adjutant George Fletcher (Wild was away at the time) and battalion commissar Bob Cooney disagreed. Cummings disappeared or "was disappeared" in the last days of fighting in late September.[63] There are uncorroborated rumours about one or two further possible assassinations in the British battalion. In one case, a company adjutant had complained about a trouble-maker in the ranks and demanded a pistol at headquarters. Wild loaned the sergeant his own weapon, saying, "No more complaints about X!"[64] There was at least one "unofficial" execution in the American battalion, after a political commissar finally found somebody to "bump off" an undesirable.[65]

While these affairs were known to a small, conspiratorial circle, there were public incidents that distressed the men of the British battalion. The first was the official fiesta of the battalion held for the soldiers and the villagers on 14 July – the Americans had staged their celebrations on Independence Day (4 July), the Canadians on Dominion Day (1 July). After speeches, a sports contest and an unusually ample meal, the men sat down to watch the main attraction of the fiesta: a contest between the machine-gunners. It went horribly wrong and resulted in the death of a Spanish recruit.[66]

According to the Battalion Party secretary Billy Griffiths, the heats in the heavy MG contest were ending in a final between Maurice Ryan and his No. 2 against

---

[63] The case of Cummings had been treated in detail by Hopkins and Baxell, but the most exhaustive account of the sinister affair is by a fellow Welshman. See Robert Stradling, Wales and the Spanish Civil War. The Dragon's Dearest Cause, Cardiff 2004, pp. 143-150.
[64] Baxell, Unlikely Warriors, p. 260.
[65] Fisher, Comrades, pp. 140-141. Stradling ("English speaking Units", p. 763, his FN 101) believes Milton Wolff was the assassin. Wolff admits as much in his strongly autobiographical novel Another Hill.
[66] George Wheeler, To Make the People Smile Again. A Memoir of the Spanish Civil War, Newcastle upon Tyne 2003, pp. 59-60; Baxell, Unlikely Warriors, pp. 322-323.

Gordon ("Dusty") Bennett from Walsall, probably assisted by his brother Don.[67] Fletcher was betting on Ryan's team, Wild on Bennett's. The contestants had to run to the gun, assemble and load it, then sight the target and pretend to pull the trigger. Before the winners were announced and while a crowd was assembling around the guns, one weapon went off (it is not clear which one). Two Spanish soldiers were wounded, one of them fatally. Somebody had omitted to pull back the Maxim lock to clear the chamber and one or two bullets were ignited either by pressure on the trigger or because rounds "cooked up" in the hot barrel. The Spanish troops in the battalion were so incensed that "they refused to let any English attend the funeral".[68]

The second event of 14 July that throws a negative light on Wild's leadership had occurred immediately beforehand. Lieut. John Leith ("Hooky") Walker, the popular quarter-master in the British battalion, had spent days preparing for the dinner on the big day but had got into a hopeless alcoholic state in the morning. He was arrested and brought back to battalion headquarters. After the meal Wild returned there and subjected "Hooky" to an unmerciful beating.[69]

A week later the assembled men were told of their immediate transport by boats across the Ebro, to take part in what was to be the longest and bloodiest battle of the war. Quite apart from the fact that the equipment of the 15th Brigade (rifles, light and heavy machine-guns and a few mortars) was hopelessly inadequate to prevail in a modern, all-arms battle, the strategy and tactics were flawed. Prime Minister Negrin pressed for a new offensive because he hoped that the crisis brewing over Czechoslovakia would spill over into a major European conflict that would finally persuade France and Britain to side with republican Spain, the active enemy of Hitler and Mussolini. On the tactical level, too, the Ebro offensive south across the Ebro was a huge gamble: attacking the enemy at his strongest point and with a river to re-cross if retreating, without adequate air

---

[67] See the portrait of the Bennett brothers by Peter Rhodes: www.expressandstar.com/news/2011/07/18/ black-country-brothers, accessed 03.12.2013.
[68] Jackson, At the Margins, p. 102 (from the manuscript by W.J. Griffiths held in the South Wales Miners' Library, Swansea).
[69] Ibid.

cover or armour, and advancing in rocky terrain where digging deep defensive positions was impossible.[70]

The 15th Brigade was ferried across the Ebro in rowing boats early on 25 July. The Republican forces advanced rapidly, capturing world headlines, as had been the case with the capture of Teruel seven months before. The thrust south soon came to grief. Republican logistics were held up by the continual aerial bombardment of the pontoon bridges so that the British battalion went without food and water supplies for four days; for the same reason equipment and ammunition were running short. Corbera, which is today a ruin like Belchite in Aragon, was captured by Spanish units, but Gandesa, 5 km to the south and the main objective of the 15th Brigade, proved impregnable. One of the smaller heights on its outskirts, known to IB survivors as "Hill 481" or "The Pimple" and flanking approaches to the town, was topped by concrete pill boxes and barbed wire fortifications. And the British battalion was supposed to capture it, despite enfilading fire from the surrounding hills and Gandesa, artillery barrages and constant attacks from the air.

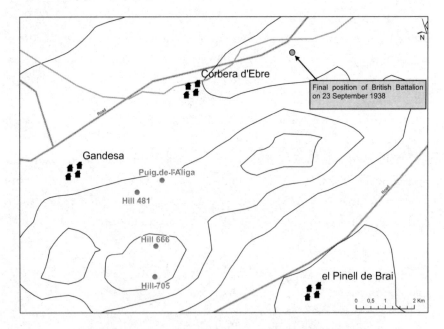

Positions of British battalion during the Battle of the Ebro

---

[70] Anthony Beevor, The Battle for Spain. The Spanish Civil War 1936-1939. Penguin Edition London 2006, pp. 349-359.

From the Republican forces in the early stages of the battle there were no aircraft or heavy artillery available to crack this nut. For five days the riflemen stormed across the valley and up the slopes of Hill 481, getting quite close to the summit once, even attacking unwisely at night, but the result was always defeat and appalling losses. The last attack was broken off at 10pm on 1 August, the bank holiday Monday in Britain and Ireland.[71]

In this atmosphere of frustration, fear, exhaustion, hunger and thirst the decision was taken to kill Maurice Ryan. At this time Ryan was still viewed by SIM as a "very bad and suspicious individual".[72] There are no documents about the execution, only oral evidence which is inconsistent. It is not entirely clear when the shooting happened. Even the reason for the killing is disputed. Most witnesses or instigators were either killed shortly afterwards or chose to remain silent, for reasons of loyalty to an "unsullied cause" or a bad conscience. Others felt that "Paddy" Ryan did not deserve a bullet in the head and a lonely grave on a Spanish wayside. Only the most fanatical held to the belief that Ryan, if eccentric and unpredictable, was some kind of enemy or "anti-Soviet agent".

The story entered the public sphere, albeit that of specialists or history buffs, when Ian McDougall published his "Voices from the Spanish Civil" in 1986 and included the reminiscences of John Dunlop. The Scot thought there was something suspicious ("not the clean tattie") about Maurice Ryan when he and Harold Horne, a dedicated Communist and graduate of the International Lenin School, watched Ryan "capering about" and disturbing the drill of a Spanish unit in Tembleque, a rail junction in Toledo province. Both were on their way back to the battalion from a training course and concurred that the silly intrusion was the work of a "fascist".[73] Dunlop's version of the cause of Ryan's final and fatal arrest has been accepted by historians:

> *But later on, in the attack across the Ebro in the summer of 1938, he was in*
> *charge of one of the machine guns and he was found guilty of firing on our*

---

[71] William Rust, Britons in Spain. The History of the British Battalion of the XVth International Brigade, 2nd edition, London 1939, pp. 177-182. Rust's somewhat chauvinistic text was based on the battle diary of the British battalion, an invaluable source which disappeared soon after his book was published.

[72] Harvey Klehr et al (eds.), The Secret World of American Communism, New Haven and London 1995, list on pp. 164-184, here p. 173. The list is from: RGASPI, f. 545, o. 3, d. 451.

[73] McDougall, Voices, pp. 146-147.

own men as they were advancing down a valley and up towards the crest
that the enemy was occupying. I myself was under that fire and we knew
that a gun from our side but we did not know which one it was.[74]

Dunlop reported to Sam Wild who had Maurice Ryan arrested:

He was flaying drunk – I don't know how many of our blokes had been hit
and wounded by this gun, but he was overpowered and arrested.[75]

Ted Smallbone's memory of "one bloke who definitely was a fascist", a planted
"informer", refers to Maurice Ryan without naming him. The passage has the
ring of information from second or third hand:

What happened exactly I am not sure… The story went that this 'Fascist' lost
the rest of his team – I don't know whether part of his team had been hit or
whether he had deliberately lost them – and when our lads caught up with
him he was well in advance of our lines and had mounted his machine gun
and pointed it in the opposite direction – against us. Anyway, he forthwith
disappeared. Whether he was taken out and shot I don't know …[76]

This version can be discounted because of its vagueness and the impossibility of a
heavy machine-gun team, not to mind a group of riflemen, advancing ahead of
the main body of men across the Gandesa killing zone. A theory worthy of
further analysis is that the bullets, instead of flying over the heads of the
advancing British companies in bursts from the Maxim and forcing the Franco
soldiers on the opposite ridge to keep their heads down, were falling short, i.e.
landing near to, and endangering the British and Irish riflemen struggling
forward. This could happen if the barrels of the Maxims were either not being
maintained or not replaced regularly: the heat caused by long bursts damaged the
bore, chipping particles off the side, so that the bullets did not exit like an arrow
but rather like a lozenge, rotating in the air and missing the target by falling
short. Both conditions (the lack of replaceable barrels, overheating due to

---

[74] Ibid., p. 146. See Baxell, Unlikely Warriors, pp. 258-260 and also Stradling, The Irish and
the Spanish Civil War, p. 190-193. Stradling calls Ryan a "mad Irishman" and a possible
"fascist saboteur".

[75] IWM, Interview 11355 John Dunlop, reel 10. This script is not yet online and I am
indebted to Richard Baxell for his notes of the recording.

[76] Howard Williamson, Toolmaking and Politics. The Life of Ted Smallbone – an Oral
History, Birmingham 1987, p. 51.

constant use) could have applied during the assaults on Hill 481 if we are mindful that the supply lines were overstretched and totally capped at times. There is strong evidence that one American machine-gunner (Nick Pappas) ceased firing in support of his advancing comrades because the bullets were falling short:

> [Nick Pappas] *I am not going to be responsible for shooting our guys in the back ... Close your mouth, Castle* [Milton Wolff, commander of the American battalion], *I know what I am talking about. I've seen too many of them get it that way. Cover fire, my ass. You know what the cone of fire is on these old guns? I'm not killing any of our guys.*[77]

So the incident to which John Dunlop drew Wild's attention could have been one of inadvertent "friendly fire" and not "sabotage". A second point, and this is of greater import, is the strong likelihood that Ryan was not firing the gun at all but enjoying a siesta with a bottle of wine. Jim Brewer from the Rhondda was a member of Ryan's MG team. The two long interviews he gave have to be read with caution, because apart from obviously incorrect information, the accounts do not contain one shred of self-doubt but disparaging and unjustified attacks against fellow brigaders.[78] Finally, there are strong contradictions between what Brewer tells about his politics and battle record and the documents in his file in Moscow.[79] Brewer obviously disliked Ryan and resented the Irish predominance (three company commanders and one company commissar) in the battalion:

> He [Ryan] *always had a bottle of wine. I wondered where he got it from. And he was always wandering about at night. And he had a brother who was with O'Duffy's crowd fighting for Franco, and his main idea, he told me in one conversation, that he hoped to meet his brother on the field of battle and wipe him out. So there was a lot of personal animus there, altogether a very mysterious fellow!*[80]

---

[77] Milton Wolff, Another Hill. An Autobiographical Novel, University of Illinois Press, 1994, p. 340. I thank Alan Warren and Ger McCloskey for drawing my attention to this reference.
[78] IWM, Interview 9963 Jim Brewer, reel 6 (Bert Williams), reel 8 (Tom Jones, Jack Nalty).
[79] RGASPI, f. 545, o. 6, d. 110, ll. 76-79.
[80] IWM, Interview Jim Brewer, reel 5.

Notwithstanding these reservations, Brewer's account of the Ryan affair as given to a researcher from the South Wales Miners' Library in 1969 deserves to be quoted at length:

> In the last battle, of the Ebro when our [anti-tank] guns were taken from us, some of us went into the machine gun company and I was No. 3 on the machine gun, I think. Well, George Fletcher was the machine gun company commander [incorrect, it was Jack Nalty, Fletcher was battalion adjutant] and there was an Irishman [Maurice Ryan], No. 1 sergeant on this gun, and he was a bit of an odd character. George [Fletcher] had taken a dislike to him and didn't trust him very much … We were engaged in a battle one afternoon and this chap was, deliberately I think, trying to sabotage his gun. With these Maxims, if you kept your finger on the trigger then you just – they were so old – very shortly got the thing jambing [sic] and you would get it running too hot and it would seize up, you see. Well, the thing to do was in any case you'd always fire in short bursts. The only time you would really open up and keep your finger on the buzzer would be if you saw a battalion ahead and the enemy coming towards you and you'd just go all out sort of thing. Well, this fool was just doing this and so Fletcher ordered him off the gun and said "You are no good there" … he got him off it and this chap subsequently was shot, he was one of the very few people who was actually shot there for an offense. Well, he was put No. 2 and another bloke was moved up to No. 1. We continued with this action and the following day the enemy were attacking us and we were giving covering fire to our troops. This fellow goes away … he been put back in charge of the gun now, he just walks away. He'd got a full bottle of wine and presumably went off and found a quiet spot and drank it, you see. In the meantime this chap Thompson took over as No. 1 and a shell landed nearby. I think it blinded him, it definitely blinded him temporarily … So when he was gone [for medical attention], I took over on this gun. Fletcher came along and he said, "Where is so and so?" I said, "We haven't seen him all the afternoon. And he said, "And this battle going on". "He just wandered off", I said. So Fletcher went in search of him and he found him in a drunken sleep under a nice little boulder. [81]

---

[81] SWML, James Brewer Interview, p. 22.

156

In his second interview, given in 1987 to the Imperial War Museum and now available online, Brewer stays closely to his earlier statement, adding the (false) piece of information that Maurice Ryan afterwards received "a proper court martial".[82]

The last evidence found to date from an eye-witness is from Tom Murray, a Labour councillor in Edinburgh and a clandestine member of the CPGB.[83] Born in 1900, Murray was originally an agricultural labourer, later a temperance organizer and a long-term labour activist when he led 12 fellow Scottish volunteers to Spain in mid-March 1938. He had very little military experience, having served three weeks in the British Army at the end of the First World War. His brother George was SIM agent in the British battalion[84] and his sister Annie was a very popular nurse in IB hospitals who served in Spain from September 1936 until she accompanied the invalid volunteers to France in 1939.[85] Tom Murray was posted as political commissar to Jack Nalty's machine-gunners, so he must have known Maurice Ryan fairly well. For some inexplicable reason his description of Ryan's demise does not mention the charge of "firing on his own" or of being drunk during the battle. The "final straw" for Murray, a hardline Communist, was a furious row about the siting of a machine-gun in the heat of battle, possibly an incident on 26 July mentioned by Steve Fullarton in an interview in the 1980s:

> There were two boys called Bennett in the machine gunners, two brothers. The machine guns they had were those heavy Maxim things where you had to carry a heavy cast iron tripod that one carried on his shoulder and the other one carried the gun mounting. Anyway it happened that in trying to deal with this sniper or snipers the machine gunners had to be called on to provide a machine gun because we couldn't see who was doing it. So the best

---

[82] IWM, Interview Jim Brewer, reels 5 and 6. There are passages where the listener does not know if Brewer is talking about Jack Nalty, whom he professes to have detested, George Fletcher or Alec Cummings.
He also intimates that while Ryan had been protected for a long time by his commander Nalty, Irish officers were "very stern with their own fellows…and [felt] superior to the rest of us" (Ibid., reel 5).
[83] The following account is taken from two interviews given by Murray to Ian McDougall –"Tom Murray: Veteran of Spain", Pencrastus (Edinburgh), no. 18, 1984, pp. 16-19; McDougall, Voices from the Spanish Civil War, pp. 306-330.
[84] Interview with George Murray in: McDougall, Voices, pp. 100-104.
[85] Interview with Annie Murray in: Ibid., pp. 68-75.

thing was to rake the area with a machine gun. Anyway this big fellow, a big Irishman again by the way, Ryan, I think his name was, he got on top of this knoll and wandered about there. Now we had been getting shot at right, left and centre and he stood about there and said, "Right, then, we'll have the gun over there", and he came back down again. And I marvelled at this. "How the hell? The snipers must be away." Well the boy Bennett started to climb over this sort of banking but only got probably up to chest height and he got shot – killed outright, like that. And as I say, big Ryan had got away with wandering about. Whether the snipers were reloading their gun or whatever happened I don't know. But there was Bennett killed right in front of me, and his brother too, because his brother was carrying the gun.[86]

Tom Murray's version, given fifty years later, of the killing of Maurice Ryan suggests that time was running out for the Limerick man in a contest of wills:

Well, there was one bad character. When we were up at the front there was a member in my Company. I won't mention his name. He was Irish, he came from the Free State, he came from the South. And he was quite a capable bloke, too. It was an unsavoury business. But we decided on a certain move, and he resisted it. He was in charge of one of the machine gun crews, and he resisted it. And we could not understand why on earth he was resisting it. And he wanted to place the machine and his crew in a situation which we thought was extremely vulnerable. I said to him, "Look here now, you are going to do what you are told … "We are at the blooming front, we are not playing around in the rear. We are at the front. The enemy is over the dyke more or less." And he said, "To hell with you. I'll so-and-so so-and-so." He picked up a hand grenade and was about to throw it at me. I jumped out of the way and we took him to the rear. However, we were sure that there was something radically wrong before he was taken back and quizzed. And of course he was boiling with hostility by this time because we had dragged him back from the front, from the front line and demoted him, as it were. He would be a cabo [corporal] or sargento [sergeant] or something like that, you see, in rank. And we dragged him back and of

---

[86] McDougall, *Voices*, p. 297. I thank Richard Baxell for confirmation of the date of "Dusty" Bennett's death. His brother Don survived the Spanish war.

course he was very angry with us. There wasn't much of a court martial but there was established information, and his conduct of course was reprehensible at the front, his carry-on, you see. You couldn't stand for that sort of thing … I won't tell you who did it. I didn't do it and I won't tell you who did it. But there was a decision taken to get rid of him because of what we had discovered about him. We were suspicious of this customer. Just as we had of course infiltrators on the other side they had infiltrators on our side. Well, at any rate, it was decided to let him have it, as we had discovered that he had a brother in the Fascist ranks. He had a very strong anti-Soviet background and anti-socialist background. At any rate he was got rid of, just shot in the back of the neck.[87]

There had been one official execution six months earlier, after a proper court martial by military tribunal of two deserters from the British battalion at Teruel. Both had tried to cross over to the fascist lines on 4 January 1938 but had been intercepted by a cavalry patrol of the 224th battalion. "Alan Kemp" (he had enlisted under that pseudonym) and his younger confederate Paddy Glacken (from Greenock but born in Donegal) were found guilty. Kemp was shot by his comrades on 10 January, but Glacken's sentence was commuted to an unspecified spell in the labour battalion. He was killed at the front ten days later. The tribunal had been put together from officers and other ranks of the British battalion, and the sentence was based on a general order on tribunals issued by Vicente Rojo, the chief of staff of the Army of the Centre, on 31 December.[88]

There had been pressure from the beginning, mainly from Soviet "advisers" or Republican generals, to execute those who disobeyed orders or deserted, but British officers like Fred Copeman or Commissar George Aitken, now no longer in Spain, had argued in 1937 that shooting volunteers would have disastrous

---

[87] McDougall, Voices, pp. 323-324.
[88] Bundesarchiv, Berlin, SAPMO, Signatur SGY 11/4/86/5, Sonderbefehl der 35. Division, 11.01.1938. For the Spanish language version of the same document see: RGASPI, f. 545, o. 3, d. 3, l. 103. Ironically, Glacken was granted home leave on 8th February, almost three weeks after his death (RGASPI, f. 545, o. 6, d. 140, ll. 3, 5, 5 reverse, 6). It is possible that the careful interrogation of Glacken by commissar Bob Cooney and the prisoner's confession led to the commutation of the death sentence – see D. Corkill/S. Rawnsley (eds), The Road to Spain. Anti-Fascists at War, Dunfermline 1981, pp.120-121 (Interview with Bob Cooney).

consequences on morale, and on the recruiting drive in Britain. Personally, they abhorred the practice.[89]

On the Ebro such mental reservations had less force. The battle was, in the words of Richard Baxell, "The Last Throw of the Dice", there could be no way out, it would be a fight to the finish. Serious disciplinary offenders could therefore expect no clemency in the heat of battle, as in any other army in a similar critical situation. But, of course, there is always an alternative to semi-judicial murder, some place of detention could have been found for Ryan. At this late stage in the war, the holding centres for military defaulters were being run down: the headquarters of the Brigades was now in Barcelona and many of the "hopeless cases" from the British battalion had been repatriated by the Spanish government shortly before. Because the battle was still going on, there could no general assembly, as in the case of Kemp and Glacken, to try a culprit. Besides, the evidence was not clear-cut, it was multi-facetted or downright contradictory, and Ryan was popular. Allegedly, Wild referred the matter to Division and received the order to have Ryan executed.[90] There are two versions of what happened next, either on 2 August, when the battalion drew back a few hundred yards but was still in the battle zone, or around 6 August when the battered remnants were taken out of the line during the night.[91] John Dunlop remembers:

If he [Ryan] *had been sent down the line to Barcelona, lawyers there would have appeared for him and he would have got off. He came back to the battalion with orders for him to be executed by his own comrades. I was told some time later that Sam Wild, the battalion commander, and George Fletcher, second in command, took Ryan for a walk and told him to go ahead and then they shot him in the back of the head. Apparently George Fletcher was in tears over that because he was very fond of this bloke.*[92]

---

[89] Judith Cook, Apprentices of Freedom, London 1979, pp. 82-83 (Interview with George Aitken); IWM, Interview 793 Fred Copeman, reel 5; Copeman, Reason in Revolt, pp. 108-109.

[90] Stradling, The Irish and the Spanish Civil War, p. 191, quoting IWM, Interview John Dunlop, reel 10.

[91] Rust (British Volunteers, p. 180) wrote that the battalion went into reserve on the night of 6 August. In Ryan's file the date is "missing 30.07.1938" and beside it in pencil "killed" (RGASPI, f. 545, o. 6, d. 195, l. 60)

[92] Stradling, The Irish and the Spanish Civil War, p. 191.

Shortly after the Spanish war, Sam Wild informed Jim Prendergast about that grisly task. Prendergast, on his return to Dublin in 1941 as CPI organizer, confided the following to Eugene Downing:

> *Sam Wild and George Fletcher had taken Ryan for a walk and informed him of the decision that had been taken. He responded calmly, "You wouldn't do that, Sam, would you?" But he was wrong. He was shot in the back of the head.*[93]

Downing heard about the execution while in hospital in Spain, as did, presumably, other wounded men like Michael O'Riordan and Michael Lehane. In all probability none of them believed that Ryan was a spy, Downing certainly did not: he was of the opinion that drink was the downfall of Maurice Ryan, a man who "unfortunately was always kicking against the pricks, in a manner of speaking".[94] Bob Clark, who lost an eye attacking Hill 481, summed up in old age what Maurice had meant to him:

> *Paddy, remarkably handsome, educated, of a wealthy family, a great linguist, about the best machine-gunner the British Battalion ever produced, with a supreme contempt for the enemy for which he was to pay with a bullet wound quite early in his part in the war, yet not to be killed by the enemy. Even after his execution nobody could really hate his memory.*[95]

Jim Jump, another machine-gunner, held similar sentiments, and dedicated a poem to Maurice Ryan ("For M.R. Fifty Years on"). The last lines read:

> *Though I do not condone what you did, Paddy*
> *I cannot forget our friendship.*
> *There were times when your sense of fun*
> *Did more to keep up our morale than all the slogans and sermonizing*
> *Of our political commissars*

---

[93] *www.irelandscw.com/ibvol-EDinterview1.htm.* Accessed 01.09.2013.
[94] Ibid.
[95] WCML, Interview Bob Clark, p. 43.

What is more, you were a fine machine-gunner
When you were not sleeping off the effects
Of drunkenness.[96]

Other potential informants were not alive when interest in the International Brigades spawned countless books from the late 1960s onwards. Johnny Power died in 1968, Bill McGregor and Jack Nalty were killed on 23 September, the very last day of IB participation in the Ebro battle. It is unknown if Sergeant Paddy Duff, Nalty's adjutant, who died in 1972, ever gave an interview. The same can be said for Paddy O'Daire, who died in Bangor, North Wales, in 1981. Others kept their counsel.

The "true believers", in this case those chroniclers determined to keep the narrative of the International Brigades a Communist one, obfuscated for decades. In 1939, Bill Rust placed Maurice Ryan on the "Roll of Honour of the British Battalion" with the comment:

Maurice Ryan. Ireland–August, 1938–Ebro [97]

In March 1941 Maurice Emmet Ryan's mother Mary, then resident in Rush, Co. Dublin, learned from the International Brigades Association in London that "it is unquestionable that he [Emmet] was shot by the Franco forces immediately after his capture during the Battle of the Ebro".[98]

In 1946 Edward C. Ryan, Maurice's older brother, visited the offices of the International Brigades Association in London enquiring about his sibling, whom he probably had not seen since the mid-1930s. In a written reply he was told that Sam Wild and Bob Cooney (battalion commissar at the Ebro) were "able to certify that your brother was killed and buried during the battle of the Ebro".[99] In the 1970s both Michael O'Riordan and Bill Alexander were preparing books on their respective IB national contingents. O'Riordan omitted the name of Maurice Ryan from his first Roll of Honour, compiled in September 1973. Alexander

---

[96] James R. Jump, With Machine Gun and Pen, Alf Killick Education Trust 1990 (deposited in MML, Box A12, File Pe/3). I am grateful to Ger McCloskey for the excerpt.
[97] Rust, Britons in Spain, p. 197.
[98] I thank Ger McCloskey and Eamon Ryan for a copy of this letter dated 07.03.1941.
[99] MML, Box 41, File A 43, letter to Edward Ryan, 17/19 Stratford Place, London W1, 21.03.1946.

told/reminded him of the Ryan case, and O'Riordan wrote on 2 September 1975 to Alexander:

Maurice Ryan – We agree with his inclusion on Roll.[100]

Ryan does indeed feature on O'Riordan's "Roll of Honour", but as a Tipperary man, and in the text as one of the Ebro fallen.[101] As regards Alexander, mention is made only on the "Roll of Honour".[102]

In a macabre twist, Maurice Ryan had the last word, at least in 1938. Days after his death, his friends and comrades read his article on teamwork in a machine-gun crew in the Brigade's propaganda sheet. He signed it with his initialed Christian names, a penchant of middle-class men of the time, for example army officers or rugby players.[103]

Maybe he had been both.

---

[100] MML, Catalogue 1994, vol. 3, Box C, „Special files", file 1/6.
[101] O'Riordan, Connolly Column, pp. 127, 163.
[102] Alexander, British Volunteers, p. 274.
[103] M.E. Ryan, „The Heavy Machine Gun", The Volunteer for Liberty, 06.08.1938, p. 5. (RGASPI, f. 545, o. 2, d. 363, l. 27)

6

Statistical data on Irish volunteers

The following list and biographies of the Irish enlisted in the International Brigades can be termed "work in progress". The original basis for the first data-bank was extracted from the personal files in Moscow (RGASPI, fond 545, opis' 6). The most important additions were files exchanged with Richard Baxell (especially RGASPI, fond 545, opis' 6, dela 90 and 91), the summarized data compiled by Ciaran Crossey and Jim Carmody[1] and personal enquiries answered by a score of people, especially Emmet O'Connor, Jim Carmody, Richard Baxell Nicky Cummins and Myron Momryk. I also accessed internet data on the volunteers from Canada,[2] the USA,[3] the British "Roll of Honour"[4] and Canadian immigration information.[5] The excellent series of articles on individual volunteers and the reprints from Irish leftwing periodicals provided by Crossey and Carmody were also of great assistance. Various biographical snippets were

---

[1] *www.irelandscw.com*
[2] *www.web.net/~macpap/volunteers.htm*
[3] *www.alba-valb.org/volunteers/browse/*
[4] *www.international-brigades.org.uk/content/roll-honour*
[5] *www.bac-lac.gc.ca/eng/search/Pages/ancestors-search.aspx*

garnered from the British and Irish archival stocks, books and articles cited in "Sources". It should be emphasised that I include only those for whom there is documentary proof that they served in the International Brigades. Irish serving in other units of the Republican forces have not been considered.

In contrast to Jim and Ciaran, I take a narrower view of who is an Irishmen, i.e. he has to have been born in Ireland and/or have lived there. I abandoned the "Jack Charlton" principle ("My granfawver came from Cork.") for several reasons, the main one being that it would be well-nigh impossible for a single researcher to check the Irish antecedents of volunteers bearing Irish names, even when they stated in Spain that they were "Irish" but had been born in an English-speaking country other than Ireland.

As regards the county of origin (birth-place) of the individual volunteers, Dublin and Antrim dominate:

Antrim 42, Armagh 9, Carlow 1, Cavan 3, Clare 2, Cork 12, Derry 12, Donegal 7, Down 8, **Dublin 55**, Fermanagh 2, Galway 5, Kerry 4, Kildare 2, Kilkenny 6, Laois 1, Leitrim 1, Limerick 6, Longford 1, Louth 5, Mayo 4, Monaghan 3, Offaly 1, Sligo 1, Tipperary 7, Tyrone 2, Waterford 10, Westmeath 2, Wexford 2, Canada 1, at sea 1, UK 3, unknown 10 = 230.

Striking about the flow of Irish volunteers (country of departure) is that only a quarter went direct from Ireland and almost half from Britain. The Irish contingent among the Canadian volunteers is surprisingly high, and that travelling from America relatively low, presumably because Irish Republican organisations in the USA were not enthusiastic about Irishmen fighting in "foreign wars":

Ireland 59, UK 123, Canada 30, USA 12, Australia 3, France 1, joined in Spain 1, unknown 1 = 230.

Concerning recruitment patterns in the Twenty-Six Counties, it emerges that the great majority left between December 1936 and February 1937. Thereafter enlistment seems to have been discouraged in Dublin, until a smaller, second wave arrived in Spain from late March 1938.[6] Not surprising to experts is the large contingent of at least 75 from the Six Counties of Northern Ireland.

At least four of the volunteers repatriated by Frank Ryan in 1937 returned to the Spanish battlefields after a few months: Jack Nalty, Paddy Duff, Michael Lehane and Jim O'Regan.

The date given for arrival in Spain is not always accurate to the day since Moscow files often do not distinguish between registration in Figueras or Albacete, and the date the men joined the British battalion. All Irish volunteers from Ireland or the UK, as mentioned earlier, who arrived in Spain after the battle of Brunete (July 1937), were assigned to the British battalion (57th). Information from Moscow on the early Irish arrivals is scanty because a cadres department was not established in Albacete for the English-speakers until March/April 1937.

The percentage of Communists among the British volunteers was about 75 per cent.[7] In the U.S. Abraham Lincoln and George Washington battalions the proportion was roughly the same, between two-thirds and three-quarters.[8] In the case of the Irish brigaders, this figure was much lower, totaling 42 per cent (101 persons) according to the incomplete data at our disposal. Some volunteers had been members of more than one CP (e.g. Peter O'Connor, Johnny Power and Ben Murray):

Communist Party of Ireland 37, Communist Party of Great Britain 34, Communist Party of Canada 19, Communist Party of the United States 10, Communist Party of Australia 1.

The figures collated for affiliation (usually in the past) to an Irish Republican organization are undoubtedly underestimates: IRA 34, Irish Republican Congress 25. It seems that the earliest contingent, that led by Frank Ryan in December 1936, contained a high number of serving IRA volunteers. Afterwards, Communists predominate in the groups that left Ireland for Spain. However, it is likely that a greater number of the Irish in Spain had been active in the IRA, the

---

[6] Eugene Downing, Hugh Hunter, Alec Digges, Tom O'Brien, Bill McGregor, Michael O'Riordan, James F. O'Regan and Liam Burgess.
[7] Richard Baxell, Unlikely Warriors. The British in the Spanish Civil War and the Struggle against Fascism, London 2012, p. 7.
[8] Peter N. Carroll, The Odyssey of the Abraham Lincoln Brigade. Americans in the Spanish Civil War, Stanford California 1994, p. 19.

CPI and the Congress movement than listed in these pages. It is also worth noting that many Irish who travelled from Britain on cross-Channel weekend tickets do not seem to have been politically active beforehand in Ireland or have known Frank Ryan, the recognized head of all Irishmen (Fr.: *responsable*) in Spain.

Approximately two-thirds of the Irish who fought in the International Brigades survived the war. At least three (Jim Haughey, Michael Lehane, Joe Ryan) were killed during the Second World War. Almost all Irish IB volunteers were wounded, many more than once.

The fatality rate at 30 per cent was enormous for a 20th Century war – the British Army figures, in per cent, for men killed in action or died of wounds or disease in the First World War was about 13 per cent (12 per cent enlisted men, 27 per cent for officers).[9] This was less than half the proportional losses of the Irish in the Spanish Republican Army. The British fatality rate in Spain was 25 per cent. Almost 300 volunteers from Britain deserted (one man in eight), although it is not clear how many could exit Spain undetected, usually with the help of British diplomats.[10]

The 69 Irish deaths occurred as follows:

59 killed in action or died of wounds in Spain, 1 died of disease, 2 were killed in accidents, 2 were executed, 5 missing believed dead. The fate of 9 volunteers remains unclear.

The 59 deaths in battle: Madrid front 4, Cordoba front 7, Jarama 17, Brunete 8, Aragon 8, Teruel 3, Ebro 12.

At least 26 Irish-born IB soldiers were taken prisoner by the troops of Franco and his ally Mussolini, mainly during the "March Retreats" of 1938. They were repatriated with the help of the British Government in 1938/39 and Dublin later reimbursed the British Foreign Office for the travel costs. The majority seems to have stayed in the United Kingdom.

The Irish contingent (it never formed a separate unit recognized by the IB leadership) had its share of "bad elements". Many of these, however, had cracked

---

[9] Denis Winter, Death's Men. Soldiers of the Great War, Penguin Books 1979, pp. 192-193.
[10] James K. Hopkins, Into the Fire. The British in the Spanish Civil War, Stanford 1998, pp. 254-255.

up in the appalling conditions of modern warfare or became demoralized because the promised repatriation was never sanctioned by Albacete. The number of what Communists called "lumpen elements" or what we would call "adventurers" is low, between ten and twenty. The number of desertions totals 32. Many of these, one must emphasise, returned to the British battalion after a stretch in a punishment unit, and merely twelve managed to abscond without being arrested, going home via France. Others were serial offenders and saw the war out in a Republican prison, half-starved and forgotten about.

A few Irish volunteers, obviously "not fit for purpose", were expelled or expatriated from Spain, i.e. allowed to cross the French border with an official permit before the Brigades were withdrawn from action. And, as has been described, Frank Ryan organized the repatriation of comrades, who he felt "had done enough", in the second half of 1937.

Further research is needed to find answers and add detail to these questions. All corrections and additions to the biographies of the Irishmen in the International Brigades are welcome. Please contact: *finbarr.mcloughlin@univie.ac.at*

No	Name	Year of birth	County of birth	Country of departure	Political affiliation	Arrival in Spain	Fate	Remarks
1	ANDERSON Samuel	1904	Down	Canada	CPCan	23.10.1937	Survivor	Repat. Canada 1938
2	ASH Francis	1909	Down	UK	CPGB	11.01.1938	Open	Deserter March 1938?
3	BAMBRICK Arthur	1915	Longford	Canada	CPCan	18.10.1937	Survivor	Sergeant, repat. Canada 1938
4	BAILIE Archie	1912	Antrim	UK		02.10.1937	Survivor	POW
5	BARR Victor	1916	Antrim	UK	YCL	13.01.1938	Survivor	POW
6	BARRY William	?	Dublin	Australia		1936	KIA	Madrid fatality
7	BEATTIE William	1908	Antrim	UK	CPGB	10.12.1936	KIA	Brunete fatality, July 1937
8	BLACK William	1913	Antrim	UK			Survivor	Repat. 1937
9	BLAKE Patrick	1916	Dublin	IRL	IRC	03.01.1937	Survivor	Repat. 1938/39
10	BONAR Henry	1897	Dublin	UK		07.01.1937	DOW	Madrid fatality
11	BONNER Hugh	1907	Donegal	IRL		14.12.1936	KIA	Platoon leader Lincolns, Jarama fatality, 05.04.1937
12	BOURNE E.J.	1908	Antrim	IRL	LP	10.11.1936	Survivor	Repat. 1937
13	BOYLE Daniel	1906	Antrim	IRL	IRA, CPI	07.12.1936	KIA	Ebro fatality
14	BOYLE George	1900	Antrim	UK	CPGB	21.12.1936	Survivor	Repat.
15	BOYLE Philip	1903	Donegal	UK	CPGB	20.09.1937	Survivor	Normal repat. 1938
16	BRADY Patrick	1904	Limerick	UK	CPGB	07.01.1937	Survivor	Repat. 1937
17	BRENNAN Michael	1910	Kilkenny	IRL	CPI	?	Survivor	No further data
18	BRENNAN Michael	1919	Kilkenny	IRL		11.02.1937	Survivor	May have been sent home for age reasons
19	BROWN Samuel	1912	Antrim	Canada		20.01.1937	Survivor	Repat. Canada July 1938.
20	BROWN George	1906	Kilkenny	UK	CPGB	01.02.1937	KIA	Brunete fatality
21	BROWN Michael	1900	Kilkenny	UK	CPGB	03.12.1936	Survivor	Deserted early 1937, home.
22	BURGESS William	1910	Cork	USA	CPUSA	24.08.1938	Survivor	Normal repat. 1938
23	BYRNE Edward	1914	Dublin	IRL		13.09.1937	Survivor	Deserted to France 1938
24	BYRNE Joseph Leo	1913	Dublin	UK	CPGB	07.02.1938	Survivor	POW
25	BYRNE Patrick C.	1899	Dublin	Spain	CPI	06.12.1937	Survivor	Jumped ship in Barcelona to join IB, POW
26	CAMPBELL James	1902	Derry	UK		27.01.1937	Survivor	POW
27	CAMPBELL John	1910	Antrim	UK		22.01.1937	KIA	Jarama fatality

No	Name	Year of birth	County of birth	Country of departure	Political affiliation	Arrival in Spain	Fate	Remarks
28	CARBERRY Dominic	1905	Dublin	Canada		20.01.1938	Survivor	Repatriated 1938, returned to Ireland
29	COADY Denis	1903	Dublin	IRL	IRC	08.12.1936	KIA	Madrid fatality
30	COCHRANE Vincent Patrick	1913	Dublin	UK	CPGB	17.02.1937	Survivor	Ambulance driver
31	COCHRANE Thomas	1885	Antrim	Canada	CPCan	15.06.1937	Survivor	Repat. 1937 because of wounds
32	COLMAN Charles	1906	Cork	IRL	IRA	22.12.1936	Survivor	Repat. 1937
33	COLEMAN John	1909	Antrim	UK		18.11.1937	Survivor	Normal repat. 1938
34	CONROY Frank	1914	Kildare	IRL	IRA, CPI	16.12.1936	KIA	Cordoba fatality
35	CONWAY Christopher	1899	Tipperary	IRL	IRA, CPI	12.12.1936	DOW	Jarama fatality. Company C.O.
36	COX Colum	1917	Dublin	IRL	IRC	17.02.1937	Survivor	
37	CULLEN Hugh O'Brien	1915	?	UK		01.11.1937	Survivor	Deserted, left Spain May 1938
38	CUMMINGS James	1899	Dublin	IRL	CPI	13.12.1936	Survivor	Repat. 1937 for family reasons
39	CURLEY Patrick	1890	Dublin	UK		26.12.1936	KIA	Jarama fatality
40	CURTIN Edward	1909	Tipperary	IRL		05.01.1937	Survivor	No further data
41	DALY Peter	1903	Wexford	UK	IRA	16.12.1936	DOW	Captain, C.O. British battalion. Aragon fatality, died 05.09.1937.
42	DAVIS William	1909	Dublin	UK	CPGB	1936	KIA	Brunete fatality
43	DELANEY Andrew	1912	Louth	USA	CPUSA	12.1937	Executed	POW, killed by fascists
44	DEVITT Thomas	1903	Dublin	Canada	CPCan	30.03.1938	Survivor	Repat. Canada 1939
45	DIGGES Alexander	1914	UK	IRL	CPI	06.04.1938	Survivor	SIM agent, repat. 1938
46	DOLAN John		Derry	UK		12.1936	KIA	Jarama fatality, 27.02.1937
47	DONALD James		Derry	UK		30.01.1937	KIA	Aragon fatality, March 1938
48	DOMEGAN James	1916	Louth	UK		14.04.1938	KIA	Ebro fatality, September 1938
49	DONNELLY Chas.	1914	Tyrone	UK	IRC	28.12.1936	KIA	Jarama fatality, killed 27.02.1937
50	DONOVAN Tom	1914	Cork	UK		10.12.1936	KIA	Aragon fatality, March 1938
51	DOOLEY Hugh	1910	Antrim	UK		01.01.1937	Survivor	Repat. August 1937
52	DORAN Gerry	1911	Antrim	IRL		12.1936	Survivor	Repat. 1937 because of wounds
53	DORAN Lester A.	1913	Louth	UK		01.01.1937	KIA	Jarama fatality
54	DOWLING John	1909	Kilkenny	IRL	CPI	11.02.1937	Survivor	Repat. August 1938

No	Name	Year of birth	County of birth	Country of departure	Political affiliation	Arrival in Spain	Fate	Remarks
55	DOWNING Eugene	1913	Dublin	IRL	IRC, CPI	30.03.1938	Survivor	Leg amputated, home 21.12.1938
56	DOYLE Gerrard	1908	Limerick	UK	CPGB	11.02.1937	Survivor	Sergeant, POW, repat. 10.1938
57	DOYLE Laurence	1902	Dublin	IRL		21.01.1937	Open	No further data
58	DOYLE Robert	1916	Dublin	UK	CPI	08.12.1937	Survivor	POW, repat. 1939
59	DUFF Patrick	1902	Dublin	IRL	CPI	08.12.1936	Survivor	Sergeant, repat. 1937, returned to Spain March 1938, repat. 1939
60	EDWARDS Frank	1907	Antrim	IRL	IRA, IRC, CPI	15.12.1936	Survivor	Platoon leader, repat., September 1937.
61	FENNELLY William	1897	Laois	UK	IRA	1936	Survivor	Deserted, home, second entry to Spain
62	FINNEGAN John	1909	Monaghan	Canada	CPCan	21.07.1937	MIA	Missing in action 03.04.1938
63	FLANAGAN Terry	1912	Dublin	IRL	IRA, CPI	21.12.1936	Survivor	Repat. 1937
64	FLYNN Jack	1914	Derry	UK		07.01.1937	Survivor	POW, captured at Jarama, released May 1937
65	FOLEY James	1903	Dublin	UK		23.01.1937	KIA	Cordoba fatality
66	FOX Anthony	1914	Dublin	IRL	IRA	1936	KIA	Cordoba fatality
67	FULTON Albert	1905	Antrim	Australia	CPAUS	27.04.1938	Survivor	Repat. 1938
68	GALLAGHER Edward	1898	Derry	UK		1936	Survivor	Repat. 1939
69	GIBSON Patrick	1906	Dublin	IRL	IRC	16.05.1937	Survivor	Lieutenant, repat. 1939 to Canada
70	GLACKEN Patrick	1913	Donegal	UK	LP	02.10.1937	KIA	Deserted, tried January 1938, Teruel fatality
71	GOFF John (Sean)	1910	Dublin	IRL		11.11.1936	Survivor	Repat. 1937
72	GOLDING Patrick James	1904	Offaly	UK	CPGB	24.02.1937	Survivor	Repat. 23.09.1938
73	GOULDNEY Fredrick G.	1909	Dublin	UK		01.01.1937	Survivor	No further data
74	GORMAN George	1900	Derry	UK		03.05.1938	KIA	Ebro fatality
75	GREEN Leo	1909	Dublin	IRL		1936	KIA	Jarama fatality, killed 12.02.1937
76	HAIRE William	1899	Armagh	UK		02.01.1937	Survivor	Deserted, caught, repat. 1939
77	HALL Patrick	1912	Down	UK	IRA	14.01.1937	Survivor	Deserted after Brunete
78	HAMILL Patrick	1905	Cavan	USA		04.01.1937	Open	No further data
79	HAUGHEY James	1919	Armagh	UK		16.05.1938	Survivor	Lieutenant, POW, released, repat. Canada 1939, killed WW2

No	Name	Year of birth	County of birth	Country of departure	Political affiliation	Arrival in Spain	Fate	Remarks
80	HAYES Thomas	1893	Dublin	IRL	IRA	19.12.1936	Survivor	Repat. 1937
81	HEANEY John	1913	Antrim	Canada		20.09.1937	Survivor	Deserted, caught, repat. 1939
82	HEANEY Thomas	1919	Galway	UK			Survivor	POW, captured March 1938
83	HENRY William	1896	Antrim	UK	NILP, CPI	19.12.1936	KIA	Jarama fatality
84	HEPBURN Robert	1913	Kildare	UK		10.02.1937	Survivor	Deserted to France July 1938
85	HILLEN James	1906	UK	UK	CPI	10.12.1936	Survivor	Repat. by F. Ryan 1937
86	HILLIARD Robert	1904	Kerry	UK	CPGB	22.12.1936	DOW	Jarama fatality, died 22.02.1937
87	HOLDEN Denis	1891	Carlow	UK		01.02.1937	Survivor	Repat. 1937
88	HUNT John	1911	Waterford	UK	IRA, IRC, CPGB	21.12.1936	Survivor	Repat. August 1938
89	HUNT Vincent	1906	Tipperary	UK		11.1936	KIA	Ambulance driver, Brunete fatality 10.07.1937
90	HUNTER Hugh	1904	Antrim	IRL	CPI	30.03.1938	Survivor	Normal repatriation 1938
91	JOHNSON William	1903	Down	UK		11.02.1937	Survivor	Repat. 1937?
92	JOHNSTONE John	1900	Antrim	UK	CPGB	10.03.1938	Survivor	Repat. December 1938
93	JONES James J.	1905	Dublin	UK			KIA	Ebro fatality
94	JONES Thomas	1910	Wexford	UK			Open	Medical assistant
95	KEENAN Patrick	1908	Dublin	IRL		22.12.1936	Survivor	Deserted February 1937, home
96	KEENAN Wm.	1901	Down	Canada		04.12.1937	KIA	Ebro fatality
97	KELLY Christopher	1906	Dublin	USA		29.08.1937	Open	Deserted, caught
98	KELLY John	1914	Waterford	UK		12.08.1937	Survivor	Normal repat. 1938
99	KELLY Joseph	1898	Donegal	Canada	CPCan	27.03.1937	Survivor	Lieutenant, died Canada 1977
100	KELLY Joseph M.	1918	Dublin	UK		20.12.1936	KIA	Brunete fatality
101	KELLY Michael	1905	Galway	UK	IRA, IRC	12.1936	KIA	Platoon leader Lincolns, Brunete fatality
102	KENNEDY David	1915	Armagh	UK	LP	27.02.1938	Survivor	POW
103	KENNEDY Harry	1909	Waterford	UK		06.09.1937	Survivor	Deserted, home
104	KERR Thomas	1910	Antrim	UK	SPNI	08.12.1937	DOS	Deserted, died of typhoid
105	LARMOUR Jas.	1910	Antrim	UK	CPGB	18.12.1936	Survivor	Repat. 1937

No	Name	Year of birth	County of birth	Country of departure	Political affiliation	Arrival in Spain	Fate	Remarks
106	LEESON George	1907	Cork	UK	CPGB	12.01.1937	Survivor	POW, released Sept. 1937
107	LEHANE Michael	1908	Kerry	IRL	CPI	12.12.1936	Survivor	Repat., returned, killed WW2
108	LEMON John	1918	Waterford	UK		12.08.1937	Survivor	POW, captured March 1938, repat. 1939
109	LEVITAS Maurice	1917	Dublin	UK	CPGB	23.01.1938	Survivor	POW, captured 31.03.1938, released 1939
110	LORD James	1916	Antrim	UK		20.03.1938	Survivor	Normal repat. 1938
111	LOWRY Joseph	1906	Armagh	UK		10.12.1936	Survivor	Repat. by Frank Ryan, September 1937
112	LYNCH Thomas	1913	Dublin	UK		22.12.1936	Survivor	Deserted or repat. 1937
113	MADERO Alex	1911	Louth	UK		20.12.1937	DIA	Shot in accident
114	MAGILL Joseph	1907	Armagh	UK		10.01.1937	Survivor	Deserted, caught, repat. 1939
115	MALONE John	1912	Dublin	Canada	CPCan	01.12.1937	Survivor	Repat. Canada, died 1972.
116	MARTIN Chris.	1907	Cork	Canada	CPCan	29.01.1938	Survivor	Normal repat. 1938
117	MARTIN Samuel	1912	Antrim	UK		14.04.1937	Open	Deserted at Brunete
118	MAY Michael	1916	Dublin	IRL	IRA, CPI	1936	KIA	Cordoba fatality, 28.12.1936
119	MC ALEENAN Richd.	1909	Down	UK	CPI, IRC, IRA	07.10.1937	Survivor	Normal repat. Brit. Batt.
120	MC ALISTER Patrick	1909	Antrim	Canada	CPCan	02.12.1937	Survivor	Re-settled in Belfast.
121	MC CARTHY Cormac	1893	Canada	Australia		1936	MIA	Deserted to France, April 1938
122	MC CHRYSTAL William	1905	Derry	Canada	CPCan	14.08.1937	Survivor	POW, captured 17.03.1938
123	MC CLURE George	1894	Down	UK	CPGB	31.01.1937	Survivor	Normal repat. 1938
124	MC DADE William	1897	Antrim	UK		22.12.1936	Survivor	Adjutant to Tom Wintringham at Jarama. Repat. 1937
125	MC ELLIGOTT John	1905	Kerry	Canada	CPCan	10.11.1937	Survivor	Repat. Canada 1939
126	MC ELROY Albert	1915	Fermanagh	IRL			KIA	Jarama fatality
127	MC ELROY Patrick	1911	Dublin	IRL		05.01.1937	Survivor	Repat. 1937
128	MC GOVERN Bernard	1914	Leitrim	?		10.01.1937	Survivor	No further data
129	MC GRATH Henry	1902	Antrim	UK	CPI	10.11.1936	KIA	Ebro fatality
130	MC GRATH Michael	1898	Cork	UK	IRA	23.01.1938	Survivor	POW, repat. 10.1938
131	MC GREGOR William	1914	Dublin	IRL	IRA, CPI	19.04.1938	KIA	Co. Commissar, Ebro fatality, 23.09.1938

No	Name	Year of birth	County of birth	Country of departure	Political affiliation	Arrival in Spain	Fate	Remarks
132	MC GROTTY Eamonn	1911	Derry	IRL		22.12.1936	KIA	Jarama fatality
133	MC GUINNESS Chas.	1893	Derry	IRL		1936	Survivor	Deserter 1936, home
134	MC GUINNESS Patk.	1910	Dublin	UK	CPGB	19.11.1937	Survivor	Deserted, caught
135	MC GUIRE Patrick	1900	Monaghan	Canada		25.04.1937	Survivor	Repat. 1939
136	MC KEEFREY James	1912	Antrim	UK		05.05.1938	Survivor	Repat. 1938/39?
137	MC LARNON Alan	1907	Armagh	UK	IRC	23.12.1936	Survivor	Deserted, caught
138	MC LAUGHLIN Matthew	1910	Derry	Canada	CPCan	06.1937	KIA	Aragon fatality, March 1938 at Belchite
139	MC LAUGHLIN Michael	1890	?	USA	CPUSA	08.04.1937	Survivor	No further data
140	MC LAUGHLIN Patrick	1902	Donegal	UK	CPUSA	04.01.1937	Survivor	Repat. March 1938
141	MC LAUGHLIN William	1903	Antrim	UK		10.12.1936	KIA	Killed Villaneuva 06.07.1937. Brunete fatality.
142	MC PARLAND Eugene	1915	Armagh	UK		10.10.1937	Survivor	Repat. August 1938
143	MEEHAN John	1912	Galway	IRL		17.09.1936?	DOW	Cordoba front fatality, died 02.01.1937
144	MITCHELL Charles	1914	Dublin	UK		22.12.1936	Survivor	Deserted, caught, repat. 1939
145	MOLYNEAUX Andrew	1906	Antrim	Canada	CPCan	15.07.1937	Survivor	Sergeant, repat. Canada 1939, died 1970
146	MONKS Joseph	1914	Dublin	IRL	CPI	15.12.1936	Survivor	Repat. July 1937. Died London 1988
147	MORAN Maurice	1910	Mayo	USA	CPUSA	04.01.1937	Survivor	Repat. 1937 because of family problems
148	MORONEY Brendan	1913	Clare	UK		10.12.1936	Survivor	Deserted, caught, expelled from Spain
149	MORRISON William A.	1910	Antrim	UK		22.12.1936	Survivor	Repat. Canada 1939, died 1970
150	MURPHY John	1902	Derry	UK		01.09.1937	Survivor	No further data
151	MURPHY Pat/ Cardiff	1897	?	UK		09.1936	Survivor	Repat. 1938
152	MURPHY Pat/Lvpl		?	UK		02.1937	Survivor	
153	MURPHY Th./Lvpl		?	UK			Survivor	
154	MURPHY Thomas	1903	Monaghan	UK	CPGB	04.02.1937	Survivor	
155	MURRAY Ben	1895	Fermanagh	UK	CPI, CPGB	11.02.1937	KIA	Political Commissar, Aragon fatality, March 1938
156	MURRAY Joseph	1886	Antrim	UK	CPGB	23.12.1936	Survivor	Repat. 1937
157	MURRAY Joseph	1911	Dublin	UK		1937	MIA	Missing Aragon, March 1938

No	Name	Year of birth	County of birth	Country of departure	Political affiliation	Arrival in Spain	Fate	Remarks
158	NALTY Jack	1902	Galway	IRL	IRA, IRC, CPI	08.12.1936	KIA	Lieutenant, repat. 1937, returned to Spain in March 1938. Ebro fatality, 23.09.1938
159	NOLAN Michael	1910	Dublin	IRL	IRC	12.12.1936	KIA	Cordoba fatality
160	O'BEIRNE John	1899	Galway	USA	CPUSA	1937	Survivor	POW
161	O'BEIRNE James	1887	Cavan	IRL		05.12.1936	Survivor	Repat. 1937
162	O'BOYLE Patrick	1894	Antrim	USA	CPUSA	11.1937	Survivor	Repat. 25.10.1938
163	O'BRIEN Francis D	1909	Louth	UK	CPGB	10.09.1937	KIA	Sergeant, Teruel fatality, 17.02.1938 Segura de los Banos
164	O'BRIEN John	1910	?	UK	IRA	03.12.1936	Survivor	Repat. 1937
165	O'BRIEN Thos.	1914	Dublin	IRL	IRC, CPI	14.04.1938	Survivor	Normal repat. 1938
166	O'BRIEN Thos.	1909	?	UK		16.12.1936	Survivor	Deserted, caught, repat. 1938
167	O'BRIEN Thos. T.	1911	Dublin	UK	CPGB	01.12.1936	KIA	Jarama fatality
168	O'CONNOR James	1905	Dublin	Canada	CPCan	28.08.1937	KIA	Aragon fatality 11.03.1938
169	O'CONNOR Peter	1912	Waterford	UK	IRA, IRC, CPI, CPGB	21.12.1936	Survivor	Repatriated August 1937. Sergeant, died 1999.
170	O'DAIRE Patrick	1905	Donegal	UK	CPGB	05.12.1936	Survivor	Captain, C.O. British Battalion, repat. Sept. 1938
171	O'DONNELL Vincent	1904	Dublin	UK	CPGB	26.01.1937	Survivor	POW
172	O'DONNELL Hugh	1899	Donegal	UK	CPGB	12.08.1936	Survivor	POW
173	O'DONNELL John	1915	Tipperary	UK		20.12.1937	Survivor	Deserted, home
174	O'DONNELL Wm.	1913	Tipperary	UK		11.08.1937	Survivor	Repat. 12.05.1938
175	O'DONOVAN Michael	1914	Westmeath	UK		22.12.1936	Open	No further data
176	O'FARRELL Thos.	1902	Dublin	UK		20.12.1936	Survivor	Deserted, caught, POW
177	O'FLAHERTY Thos.	1914	Kerry	USA	CPUSA	01.02.1938	KIA	Platoon leader, Ebro fatality
178	O'HANLON Wm.	1913	Antrim	UK	IRA, IRC	16.09.1937	Survivor	Normal repat. 1938
179	O'NEILL Richard	1910	Antrim	UK	NILP, CPI	10.12.1936	KIA	Platoon leader, Jarama fatality
180	O'NEILL Stewart	1900	?	Canada	CPCan	30.03.1937	KIA	Brunete fatality, sergeant
181	O'REGAN James F	1916	Cork	IRL	IRA, CPI	30.03.1938	Survivor	Normal repat. 1938

No	Name	Year of birth	County of birth	Country of departure	Political affiliation	Arrival in Spain	Fate	Remarks
182	O'REGAN James	1911	Cork	IRL	IRC	18.12.1936	Survivor	Repat. 1937, returned to Spain, normal repat. 1938
183	O'REILLY Domhnall	1903	Dublin	IRL	CPI	01.12.1936	Survivor	Political Commissar, repat. March 1937
184	O'REILLY John	1908	Tipperary	IRL		10.1936?	Survivor	Repat. Oct. 1938
185	O'RIORDAN Michael	1917	Cork	IRL	IRA, CPI	05.05.1938	Survivor	Died 18.05.2006
186	ORMSBY Hannah	1901	Sligo	UK		20.08.1936	DIA	Killed in fire, Barcelona
187	O'SHEA John (W)	1908	Waterford	UK	IRC	17.02.1937	Survivor	Sergeant, normal repat. 1938
188	O'SHEA John(Can)	1904	?	Canada		28.05.1937	MIA	Platoon leader Canadian Co. with Lincolns. Missing in Aragon March-April 1938 or killed in action May 1938
189	O'SULLIVAN John	1908	Cork	USA	CPUSA	11.11.1937	MIA	Believed killed, March-April 1938
190	O'SULLIVAN Patrick	1914	UK	IRL	CPI	08.02.1937	KIA	Lieutenant, Ebro fatality 31.7.1938
191	PATTEN Thomas	1910	Mayo	UK	IRC	10.10.1936	KIA	Madrid fatality
192	PATTERSON Edward	1904	Armagh	Canada		12.1937	KIA	Ebro fatality at Gandesa
193	PENROSE John	1905	Dublin	IRL	IRA	24.02.1937	Survivor	Repat. August 1937
194	PLAIN David	1908	Armagh	UK		14.04.1937	Survivor	Deserted, caught
195	POLLOCK Herbert	1899	Derry	Canada	CPCan	27.08.1937	Survivor	Repat. Canada 1939, died 1953
196	POWER John	1908	Waterford	UK	CPGB, CPI, IRC, IRA	21.12.1936	Survivor	Captain
197	POWER Patrick	1910	Waterford	UK	IRC, CPI	21.12.1936	Survivor	Repat. November 1937
198	POWER William	1912	Waterford	IRL	CPI	02.04.1937	Survivor	Repat. 1937
199	PRENDERGAST Jas.	1915	Dublin	IRL	CPI	12.12.1936	Survivor	Repat. July 1937
200	PRITCHARD David	1906	Down	Canada		28.10.1937	MIA	March 1938
201	PYPER Robert	1906	Antrim	UK		14.02.1938	Survivor	Deserted, home May 1938
202	QUINLAN Maurice	1911	Waterford	UK	IRA, IRC, CPI	01.12.1936	KIA	Jarama fatality
203	QUINN Sydney	1909	Antrim	UK	CPGB	02.12.1936	Survivor	Repat. October 1937
204	READ Patrick	1899	At sea	USA		17.03.1937	Survivor	Repat. 1938

No	Name	Year of birth	County of birth	Country of departure	Political affiliation	Arrival in Spain	Fate	Remarks
205	ROE Michael A.	1908	Westmeath	IRL		07.01.1937	Survivor	Repat. 1937, Adjutant 4 Co., British batt. Jarama
206	ROBINSON QUIGLEY John	1897	Antrim	USA	CPUSA	01.01.1937	Survivor	Company C.O. Lincolns, deputy Brigade Commissar, repat. 1937
207	RUSSELL Michael	1909	Clare	Canada		19.02.1937	KIA	Jarama fatality
208	RYAN Frank	1902	Limerick	IRL	IRA, IRC	15.12.1936	Survivor	Major, POW, died Dresden 1944
209	RYAN Joseph	1917	Limerick	UK	LP	28.12.1936	Survivor	Deserted, sent home. Killed WW2
210	RYAN Maurice	1915	Limerick	France		05.11.1937	Executed	Executed by Sam Wilde, C.O. British Battalion, August 1938
211	SCOTT Willoughby	1908	Dublin	IRL	CPI	20.09.1936	Survivor	Repat. 1937
212	SHEEHAN Thomas	1904	Cork	UK	CPGB	21.02.1938	KIA	Aragon fatality
213	SIMS Thomas	1904	Tipperary	Canada	CPCan	09.09.1937	Survivor	Ambulance driver. Repat. Canada, died 1983
214	SMITH Patrick	1910	Dublin	IRL	IRA	09.12.1936	Survivor	Repat. 1937
215	STANLEY Patrick	1916	Dublin	IRL	IRA	09.12.1936	Survivor	Deserted, caught
216	STEELE George	1913	Antrim	UK		14.01.1937	Survivor	Deserted, caught
217	STOKES Edward	1907	Kilkenny	IRL		10.11.1936	Open	No further data
218	STRANEY James	1915	Antrim	UK	IRA, IRC	20.09.1937	KIA	Corporal, Ebro fatality, 31.07.1938 Hill 481
219	THORNTON David	1905	Antrim	Canada		04.12.1936	Survivor	
220	TIERNEY Frank	1911	Antrim	Canada		27.07.1937	Survivor	Repat. Canada, died 1964.
221	TIERNEY John	1902	Dublin	UK	CPGB	10.07.1937	Survivor	Deserted, home
222	TIGHE Patrick	1914	Mayo	UK	IRA	08.12.1936	Survivor	Deserted, caught, normal repat.
223	TRAYNOR Thomas	1897	Tyrone	Canada	CPCan	04.04.1937	Survivor	Platoon leader
224	TUMILSON Wm.	1904	Antrim	UK	IRC, IRA	21.01.1937	KIA	C.O. MG Co. Lincolns. Jarama fatality
225	VALLELY Edward	1910	Cavan	UK		20.12.1937	Survivor	POW, aka "Peter Brady", repat. 1939
226	WALSH David	1904	Mayo	UK		20.09.1937	KIA	Teruel fatality
227	WARD Gerald J.	1909	Dublin	UK	CPGB	12.06.1937	Survivor	Deserted, caught, normal repat.
228	WATERS Michael	1913	Cork	IRL		06.01.1937	Survivor	Deserted, caught, normal repat.
229	WOOD Thomas B.	1919	Dublin	IRL	IRA	15.12.1936	DOW	Cordoba fatality
230	WOULFE James	1899	Limerick	Canada	IRA, CPCan	05.03.1937	DOW	Aragon fatality, Belchite 05.09.1937

7

Biographies of Irish volunteers

1. ANDERSON Samuel, born 06.03.1904 in Banbridge, Co. Down. Emigrated to Canada from Scotland and landed in Quebec 16.10.1927. Painter. Took part in "Regina Riots" in July 1935 when the RCMP attacked the unemployed trekkers, killing two and wounding 100. Anderson joined CPCan in Vancouver in June 1937. Arrived in Spain from Canada 03.10.1937. Repatriated. Died in Vancouver 25.11.1974.

2. ASH Francis, born 16.04.1909 in Dooey, Downpatrick, Co. Down. Emigrated with his parents to Glasgow as an infant. Tunnel worker, merchant seaman. CPGB since 1933, had served in the Canadian Reserve Rifles. Arrived in Spain 11.01.1938. Disappeared during the March/April retreats, posted as deserter from the line.

3. BAILIE Archibald F., born 28.03.1912 Belfast. Lived at 199, Connsbrook Avenue. Labourer. Arrived in Spain from London 02.10.1937. Taken prisoner in March 1938. Non-communist.

4. BAMBRICK Arthur James, born 14.10.1915 in Longford. Emigrated to Canada at 14 years of age, landing at Halifax 31.03.1930. Miner, no living

dependants, unemployed before Spain. Lived in Vancouver. Member of YCL 1936 and CPCan 1937. Arrived in Spain 18.10.37. In 2nd recruits company, Tarazona, 11.02.1938, later Sergeant in company No. 2 of Canadian battalion. Repatriated to Canada. Used Pseudonym "Pat O'Hara" while in Spain. Served in the Canadian Army in WW2.

5. BARR Victor, born 13.11.1916 Belfast, lived at 39, Swift Street. Labourer. Member of YCL in Birmingham. Arrived in Spain 13.01.1938. 6th recruits company, Tarazona, 11.02.1938. Missing in Aragon March 1938, taken prisoner.

6. BARRY William (Jack), Dublin, came via Melbourne and London, was in Barcelona for the workers' Olympics (19-26 July 1936), which was cancelled because of the fascist coup. Served in the Tom Mann Centuria from September 1936, which was later part of the Thälmann Battalion of the 12th International Brigade. Killed at Boadilla del Monte, probably on 14.12.1936.

7. BEATTIE William, born probably 1908 in Belfast, from 14, Wilton St., Shankhill Road, Belfast. Served 8 years in the Royal Irish (Ulster) Rifles, 1924-32. Was a member of the NILP, moved to Scotland. Joined the CPGB in Glasgow. Arrived in Spain, December 1936. Served at Lopera on the Cordoba Front, wounded by shrapnel 27.12.1936, still in hospital 11.02.1937. Killed in battle of Brunete, 23-25 July 1937.

8. BLACK William, born probably 13.02.1913 Belfast, from 99, Delhi Street, Belfast. Arrived in Spain in early December 1936 from London. Member of Nathan's Anglo-Irish Company in the 12th International Brigade, alleged trouble-maker and anti-Semite, gaoled. Repatriated in early 1937.

9. BLAKE Patrick Kevin, born 26.05.1916 North Dublin, lived at 13, Lower Gardiner Street, Dublin. Painter. IRC. Arrived in Spain 03.01.1937 from Dublin. Non-Communist. Wounded in left shoulder at Brunete. Recommended for repatriation by Frank Ryan 11.08.1937. Tried to desert, was arrested in Barcelona trying to board the ship SS Oregon in April 1938. Repatriated by order of 02.08.1938. Served as ambulance driver based at Huete hospital, together with Vincent (Paddy) Cochrane.

10. BONAR Henry, born 1897 in Dublin. Gardener. Arrived in Spain via Glasgow 14.12.1936, died of wounds in hospital, Colmenar de Oreja (Madrid front) in December 1936.

11. BONNER Hugh, Donegal, born 02.10.1907 in Falcorrib, Templecrone, Co. Donegal. His father was an agricultural labourer. Plasterer, he arrived in Spain 07.01.1937. Bonner was a platoon leader in the Lincoln Battalion when he was killed at Jarama 05.04.1937.

12. BOURNE Edward J., born 1908 Belfast. Labourer. Labour Party member. Probably from 20, Cranbourn St. Belfast. Arrived in Spain 10.11.1936. Wounded 16.02.1937. Recommended by Frank Ryan for repatriation, 11.08.1937. Repatriated 1937.

13. BOYLE Daniel, Belfast. Born 1906. Next of kin: Mrs McCaul, 169, Glenard Gardens, Belfast. Labourer, joined CPI in 1936. Ex-IRA. Left Ireland 05.12.1936 for Spain. Arrived in Spain 07.12.1936. Served in the MG Company of the British Battalion at Jarama. In hospital at Murcia in early 1938. One false report stated that he was killed on Cordoba front, 28.12.1936, another that he was a fatality at Jarama. Killed during Ebro battle, 1938.

14. BOYLE George, born probably 03.02.1900 Belfast, from 38, Lockhart Street, Germiston, Glasgow. Arrived in Spain 22.12.1936. Stated he was Irish-born, wanted to join Irish unit at Madrigueras. Jailed for disturbance and sent to penal unit. Repatriated because of wounds and TB 1937.

15. BOYLE Philip, born 05.10.1903 in Calhane, Falcarragh, Co. Donegal, carpenter. Gaelic speaker. IRA 1919-24, imprisoned from August 1920 to December 1921 in Strangeways and Parkhurst. Fought with the anti-Treaty IRA in the civil war in Co. Tipperary. Emigrated to Scotland in 1925, member of CPGB in Hammersmith, worked for a woodworking firm in Islington. Arrived in Spain 20.09.1937. Wounded at Teruel 19.01.1938, promoted to corporal. Company quartermaster, disciplined 28.06.1938 for drunkenness and reduced to the ranks, deducted ten days' pay and given 10 days guard duties. With British Battalion 30.09.1938. Normal repatriation.

16. BRADY Patrick born 07.03.1904 in Limerick, home at 65, New Road, Thomondgate. Bootmaker. Emigrated to Liverpool, married. Activist in

unemployed movement and CPGB. Went to Spain from Liverpool, arrived in Spain 07.01.1937. In MG Co. at Jarama. Group leader. Wounded in the shoulder by a sniper at Villaneuva de la Cañada, July 1937. Repatriated with his arm in a cast in 1937.

17. BRENNAN Michael, born probably 27.09.1919 Castlecomer, Co. Kilkenny. Miner. Arrived in Spain 11.02.1937, but was rejected as under-age. Later served in Republican air force. Survivor.

18. BRENNAN Michael, born probably 04.01.1910 Castlecomer. Co. Kilkenny, member CPI, arrived in Spain no date. Probably a miner from Castlecomer.

19. BROWN George, born 05.11.1906 in Ballyneale, Thomastown, Co. Kilkenny, the fourth child of Francis and Mary. His parents had settled in Manchester in the 1890s where his father Francis was a farrier. His mother Mary Brown, nee Lackey, went home to Ireland to have the first four of her children. Francis Brown worked for the local railway shoeing horses. After leaving school, George worked at a series of unskilled jobs and was often unemployed. He joined the CPGB in 1927, became a full-time party organiser for Manchester and Salford and stood as a Communist candidate at the local elections for the Openshaw Ward in 1934. He attended the International Lenin School in Moscow in 1931/32 and was elected to the Central Committee of the CPGB at its 13th congress in 1935. Shortly before leaving for Spain Brown married Evelyn Mary Taylor. Arrived in Spain 30.01.1937. At first responsible for British wounded at Albacete and assisting Commissar Peter Kerrigan. George Brown was killed as he lay wounded on the road 06.07.1937 at Villanueva de la Cañada. A memorial in his honour was unveiled in St. Mary's graveyard, Inistioge, Co. Kilkenny, 27.06.2008. His widow Evelyn married Jack Jones of Liverpool, the future trade union leader.

20. BROWN Michael, born 1900 in Co. Kilkenny, brother of George. Electrician in Manchester. CPGB 1930. Arrived in Spain 03.12.1936. Deserted at Lopera 1936, back in Britain early 1937. Allegedly gave an interview to the pro-fascist Daily Mail.

21. BROWN Samuel, born 02.05.1912 Belfast, machinist. Emigrated to Canada, lived in Winnipeg, Vancouver, joined the militia. Non-Party. Left for Spain 04.01.1937, served with Lincolns and MacPaps, wounded, returned 21.07.1938.

22. BURGESS William (Liam), born 15.07.1910 in Ballydaniel, Mallow, Co. Cork. Farming background. University education, school teacher in Ireland, emigrated to USA. U.S. citizen. Hospital orderly in New York. Joined CPUSA in 1936, party name "Bill O'Reilly". Arrived in Spain 24.08.1938. With British Battalion at Ripoll, 16.10.1938. It is not known whether he was repatriated to America, Britain or Ireland.

23. BYRNE Edward, born 18.10.1914 Holles St. Hospital, Dublin, mother's address: 64, Hollyfield Buildings, Rathmines, Dublin. Served 3 years in the Royal Artillery and 11 months in the Irish Free State Army before leaving for Spain. Said he lived in Peckham, London, but probably left Ireland in August 1937 via Liverpool. Arrived in Spain 13.09.1937. Served in anti-tank unit, saw action at Fuentos del Ebro and during the March-April retreats. Allegedly deserted with Welsh volunteer Tom Jones 04.04.1938, arrested at Castellfollit de la Roca (Girona) 12.04.1938 and sent to Figueras jail, escaped to France. Repatriated with the help of the Irish Legation in Paris in late April 1938.

24. BYRNE Joseph Leo, born 22.04.1913 North Dublin. Family moved to Liverpool in 1916. Seaman, welder. Joined CPGB 1937. Arrived in Spain 07.02.1938. Captured March 1938.

25. BYRNE Patrick C., born ca. 1899. Seaman, member CPI. Lived off Dame Street, Dublin. Deserted his ship "Florentina" on the London- Barcelona route and joined the IB 06.12.1937. Taken prisoner in March-April 1938.

26. CAMPBELL James, born 1902. From 22 Tyrconnell St., Derry. Arrived in Spain 27.01.1937. Arrested in Barcelona, July 1937. Said to have survived the war but did not return to Derry.

27. CAMPBELL John, born ca. 1910, from 39 Woodstock Road, Belfast. Left London for Spain, arrival 22.01.1937. British Battalion. Killed at Jarama, Pingarron Hill, 27.02.1937.

28. CARBERRY Dominic Patrick. Born 01.08.1905 in Dublin. Probably lived as the step-son of Michael and Kathleen Quinn in Pigeon House, South Dock, Dublin as a child. Emigrated to Canada at the age of 21, landing in St. John 27.03.1927, lived in Calgary. Left for Spain 30.12.1937, 6th recruits company, Tarazona, 11.02.1938. Served in the Canadian battalion and in the air force. Repatriated by order of 25.07.1938. Returned to Ireland.

29. COADY Denis, born 1903, lived at 4, Waterford St., Dublin. Labourer, member of the WUI and IRC. Left for Spain 08.12.1936, arrived at IB Base 12.12.1936. Killed at Las Rozas near Madrid 12.01.1937 by a shell-burst. Buried at Torrledones, north-west of Madrid on the Corunna road.

30. COCHRANE Vincent Patrick (Paddy), born 11.03.1913 in Dublin. Toolmaker. Arrived in Spain on 17 February 1937 as member of a medical team with four ambulances. Ambulance driver. Member of the CPGB.

31. COCHRANE Thomas ("Pop"), born 10.12.1885 in Belfast. 1911 census lists him living at 53, Balkan St., Falls Road. Probably oldest Irish volunteer. Emigrated to Canada, father of six children, electrician, member of CPCan from Windsor, Ontario. Left for Spain 28.05.1937. Wounded four times at Brunete. Transferred to censor's office, Valencia. Sent home in 1937.

32. COLMAN John Charles, born 1906. Lived at 132, Barrack Street, Cork. Moulder. IRA 1922-24, ITGWU since 1932. Arrived in Spain, 22.12.1936. Fought in the Irish section of the Lincoln Battalion. Repatriated 1937.

33. COLEMAN John, born 04.05.1909, Belfast. Labourer. Mother lived at 67, Grove Street, East Belfast. Joined British Battalion. 22.11.1937. Allegedly deserted from Taragona, repatriated October 1938.

34. CONROY Frank, born 25.02.1914 Naas, Co. Kildare. Ex-IRA, member of CPI, left Ireland for Spain 13.12.1936. Gave no next-of-kin. Killed at Cordoba front 28.12.1936.

35. CONWAY Christopher (Kit), born 03.12.1899 in Clogheen Workhouse near the village of Burncourt in south-west Tipperary. An orphan, he was raised in the workhouse and went to work for William English, a local farmer, at the age of fourteen. Enlisted in the British Army in 1915, but

realised his mistake almost immediately, feigned insanity and was discharged. He later joined D Company, 6ᵗʰ Battalion, 3ʳᵈ Tipperary Brigade of the IRA and became a member of the Flying Column under Sean Hogan. After the Truce Conway went back to farm work before joining the Free State Army. He was stationed in the Curragh, Clonmel and Cahir, but deserted after a few months. In later years he worked as a labourer in the building industry in Dublin and used the pseudonym "Kit Ryan" when in charge of IRA training. He emigrated to the USA in 1928, joined the National Guard for more military experience but returned to Ireland in 1932. Joined the CPI in Dublin 1933, member of the ITGWU. Arrived in Spain 12.12.1936. Fought at Lopera and Las Rozas. Conway was O.C. No. 1 Company British Battalion January-12 February 1937. Fatally wounded at Jarama 12.02.1937 and died in hospital in Orega on the same day. In 2005 a plaque was unveiled to his memory in Burncourt.

36. COX Patrick John Colum, (Colum) born probably 17.03.1917 North Dublin. Lived at 11, Grace Park Road, Drumcondra. Member of IRC, arrived in Spain 17.02.1937. Wounded at Jarama when serving with Lincolns, tried to desert and was sentenced to 3 months in the labour battalion in March 1937. Survivor.

37. CULLEN Hugh O'Brien, born probably 1916 Co. Down. Lived in Bathgate, West Lothian, before Spain. Seaman. Arrived in Spain November 1937. Joined British Battalion 11.11.1937, in 4ᵗʰ recruits company, Tarazona, 11.02.1938. Deserted after third day in action, April 1938. Left Spain 01.05.1938.

38. CUMMINGS James (Seamus), born 1899, from Dublin. Concrete worker. Member CPI, arrived in Spain 13.12.1936. Wounded in the shoulder 28.12.1936 at Lopera. In 1937 he sought repatriation because he father, who lived alone at 30, Hanbury Lane, Thomas St., Dublin, was gravely ill. Repatriated 1937.

39. CURLEY Patrick, born 1890 from Dublin or Limerick or Galway, came via Alexandria, Dumbartonshire, Scotland. Arrived in Spain 26.12.1936. Killed at Jarama, February 1937.

40. CURTIN Edward, born probably 19.04.1909 Nenagh, Co. Tipperary. Lived in Lancaster. Labourer, ITGWU. Arrived in Spain 05.01.1937. Wounded 23.02.1937. Possible deserter.

41. DALY Peter, born 1903 Killabeg, Enniscorthy, Co. Wexford. Took part in the Irish Civil War on the side of the IRA, was wounded and taken prisoner. Spent 17 months in internment. Emigrated to England afterwards and joined a Welsh regiment of the British Army, which he left after four years with the rank of sergeant. Said to have smuggled out arms to the IRA. For a while he worked as a miner at Gorseinon near Swansea. In the early 1930s Daly was training officer in the Wexford Brigade of the IRA. Unemployed, emigrated to England and worked for Wimpey builders in Hammersmith. Arrived in Spain from the UK, 21.01.1937. Wounded 12.02.1937 in the hip at Jarama. Discharged himself after one month in hospital. Returned to the base and was commissioned lieutenant. He then served in the 20th Battalion in March 1937 in Pozoblanco, where he was again wounded in the hip at Chimora. Attended OTS with Paddy O'Daire in July 1937. On the eve of the Aragon campaign promoted to captain and made O.C. of the British Battalion 12.08.1937. He was wounded in the stomach when attacking Purburrell Hill outside Quinto 25.08.1937 and died 05.09.1937 in hospital in Benicasim. A memorial to his honour was unveiled at Monageer, Co. Wexford, 03.09.2011.

42. DAVIS William, born 28.05.1909 Dublin. Spent two years in the Irish Guards. CPGB member in Camden Town. Left Britain for Spain. Killed in the storming of Villaneuva de la Cañada, Brunete, July 1937, by a burst of machine-gun fire.

43. DELANEY Andrew, born 21.07.1912 in Carlingford, Co. Louth, one of 9 children. His father was a RIC constable. Emigrated to the USA in 1930 and lived in Oakland California. CPUSA 1930. Seaman. Arrived in Spain in late 1937, in 1st recruits company, Tarazona 11.02.1938. Taken prisoner at Gandesa, 03.04.1938. Executed after capture.

44. DEVITT Thomas Francis, born Dublin 17.11.1903. Emigrated to Canada. Worked as truck driver in Windsor, Ontario. Single, CPCan member. Expelled from party because of habitual drunkenness. Arrived in Spain in March 1938. Returned to Canada 1939.

45. DIGGES Alexander Patrick (Alec), born 21.06.1914 in London. Freelance journalist. Joined Irish Labour Party in December 1936, CPI in May 1937. Member of Dublin Committee CPI. Lived at 75, Amiens St. Arrived in Spain in April 1938. Originally in 5th Company, British Battalion, later SIM agent in 15th Brigade in Valencia. Transferred to the MG Co. of the British Battalion before the Ebro battle. Was in hospital when the IBs were withdrawn. Repatriated. Lost a leg when serving during WW2. Leading official in the British IB veterans' organisation.

46. DOLAN John. Lived in Glasgow before Spain, killed at Jarama 27.02.1937.

47. DOMEGAN James C., born probably 06.01.1916 Drogheda Co. Louth. Single. Next of kin: Mrs Susan Domegan, 4, Leeson Street, Belfast. Labourer, arrived in Spain via London 14.04.1938. Killed in the Ebro battle, 23 September 1938.

48. DONALD James, born probably 12.01.1916 in Derry, lived in Methil, Fife. Miner. Arrived in Spain 24.01.1937. Served in the British Battalion, killed at Belchite, March 1938.

49. DONNELLY Charles. Born 10.06.1914 (according to birth cert.) in Killybrackey, Dungannon, Co. Tyrone, the eldest of eight children of Joseph Donnelly and Rose McCaughey. His father sold the farm in 1917 and bought property, including a large shop, in Dundalk. Charlie attended Dundalk CBS. His mother died in February 1927 and the family moved to Dublin two years later. Charlie was largely self-educated and entered UCD in October 1931 to study Arts. He failed his first year but repeated his English and Logic exams with success in 1933. Donnelly became active in the IRC, abandoned his studies and was arrested three times in Dublin for Republican or trade union activities. Forced to leave home by his conservative, conventional father, Donnelly emigrated to London in 1935 and began employment in an new agency in Fleet Street. He was the first chairman of the IRC London Branch and began to write and lecture. After the outbreak of the war in Spain, Donnelly helped out in the London office of the Spanish Medical Aid Committee. His last address was 21, Chaucer Road, Acton, London. Donnelly left for Spain 23.12.1936, arriving in Figueras on Christmas Day and at Albacete two days later. He arrived in Madrigueras 28.12.1936. He gave his age on enlistment as 26, but he was

just over 22. Donnelly was killed by a shot in the head at Jarama 27.02.1937 while serving in the Irish unit (Lincons), which he led on that day following the death of Bill Henry. His body was recovered 09.03.1937 by Peter O'Connor and was carried down by John Power, Paddy Power and Peter O'Connor and buried the following day beneath an olive tree. His family was informed of his death by a letter Johnny Power wrote to Tom Donnelly, Charlie's brother then living in London. Donnelly was not a Communist, he was indeed critical of Stalin following the death of Kirov (murdered in Leningrad, 01.12.1934). He can be said to have shared the politic tenets of James Connolly and left-wing Irish Republicanism generally. His impressive literary achievement includes poems, essays and writings on military tactics.

50. DONOVAN Thomas/John ('Paddy'), born, from Skibbereen, Co. Cork. Worked as a printer with the "Southern Star" in his home town. Emigrated to Britain. Arrived in Spain December 1936. Served initially with the Thälmann battalion, deserted. Moved to Barcelona and joined the Scottish Medical unit. Repatriated July 1937.

51. DOOLEY Hugh, born 13.06.1910, Belfast. Labourer. Arrived in Spain 01.01.1937. On the "Blacklist" at Madrigueras. Deserted from the front at Jarama and was arrested 04.03.1937 for twice refusing to go up the line. On the next day he requested to be sent back to the British Battalion. Repatriated to Britain in early August 1937 for health reasons.

52. DORAN, Lester Archibald, born 28.04.1913 Ardee, Co. Louth. Lived in Britain, ex-Pilot Officer RAF. Professional motor cycle racer. Arrived in Spain 01.01.1937. Killed at Jarama, February 1937.

53. DORAN Gerald, born probably 26.08.1911 Belfast, lived in Dublin. Wounded at Jarama, 15.02.1937. Repatriated 1937 because of wounds. Arrived in Dublin July 1937.

54. DOWLING John, born 26.03.1909 (15.11.1902?) in Co. Kilkenny, from Ardra, Castlecomer, Co. Kilkenny. Miner, married. CPI. Arrived in Spain 11.02.1937, worked as driver in the medical service on several fronts, also acted as guard at Huete hospital. Proposed for repatriation in August 1938.

55. DOWNING Eugene, born 13.09.1913 in Dublin, electrician. Member of CPI since September 1933, spent one month in Mountjoy Jail because of political activities. Arrived in Spain 30.03.1938. Wounded in the left foot 26.07.1938 in attack on Gandesa. Sent to Mataro and Sagaro hospitals, foot amputated because of gangrene. Arrived in Dublin 21.12.1938.

56. DOYLE Gerrard Bernard, born 08.10.1908 in Limerick and lived at 36, Upper William Street where his family kept a restaurant. His father was a cattle dealer. Attended CBS school in Sexton Street. He left home after his mother's suicide (1923) and the second marriage of his father. Apprenticed as moulder, sacked after two years because of a strike. Later worked in the building of Ardnacrusha power station, then Fords of Cork. 1930-34 driver in Irish Free State Army, then Dublin bus driver until he was made redundant in June 1935. In January 1936 Doyle moved to England, joined CPGB in Birmingham. Arrived in Spain 11.02.1937 from 2, Vale Road, Forest Gate, London E7. Wounded 14.02.1937. Promoted to rank of Sergeant, sent to OTS in April 1937. Was down for repatriation in September 1937. Taken prisoner in Caspe, 17.03.1938. After his release in October 1938 and marriage, Doyle moved to Cornwall, where he died at Liskeard in 1970. He is buried in St. Martin's Churchyard, Liskeard, Diocese of Truro.

57. DOYLE Laurence born 1902 in Dublin, member of Sinn Fein 1919-21, ITGWU 1930-34, possibly in Volunteer Reserve of Irish Army. Labourer. Gave his Irish address as 32, Lower Ormond Quay, Dublin, the office of the CPI. Arrived in Spain 21.01.1937. No further data.

58. DOYLE Robert, born 14.02.1916 (12.02.1916 on birth cert.) North Dublin. Family lived at 26, North Great George's Street. Labourer, seaman. Member of the IRC and CPI since 1935. Arrived in Spain 08.12.1937, entrained for Albacete 11.12.1937. 6th recruits company, Tarazona, 11.02.1938. Platoon instructor. "Deserted" to the front, taken prisoner Calaceite, 31.03.1938, with Frank Ryan, Jackie Lemon and Eddie Vallely ("Peter Brady"). Released from San Sebastian prison in early February 1939, repatriated with the help of the Irish Legation in Paris, arrived in Dublin 09.02.1939. Last surviving member of the Irish contingent in the IB, died 22.01.2009.

59.   DUFF Patrick, born 24.10.1902 Finglas, Co. Dublin, grew up in Rathmines-Terenure area, worked for farmers from 14 years of age, joined the Fianna in 1916, ITGWU in 1927, and the IRA in 1933. Member of CPI, family lived at 68, Monasterboice Road, Crumlin. Active in IRC, formed a branch in Tallaght, Co. Dublin. Building worker in Dublin. Arrived in Spain 08.12.1936. Promoted Sergeant February 1937. Fought in the battles of Cordoba, Las Rozas, Jarama, Brunete and Ebro. Platoon leader from May 1937 after OTS. Wounded three times (right leg, right foot, right and left arm) 12.02.1937, July 1937 and 19.08.1938. Recommended for repatriation by Frank Ryan 11.08.1937. Repatriated 14.09.1937, returned to Spain with Jack Nalty in April 1938 and re-joined British Battalion 07.04.1938. Served in MG Company as Sergeant, adjutant to O.C. of the Company, Jack Nalty. Again wounded Sierra Pandols 19.08.1938, in Figueras Hospital 19.09.1938. Interned with Spanish soldiers in St. Cyprien camp, France. Repatriated 1939. Later an official of WUI, died 1972.

60.   EDWARDS Frank, born 02.09.1907 Belfast. The family moved to Waterford. The father of the family was killed serving with the British Army in WW1, and Frank's older brother Jack, taken prisoner while fighting with IRA in the Civil War, was shot by a sentry in Kilkenny Gaol, September 1922. Edwards joined the Fianna in 1917, in 1924 the IRA city battalion, and was its adjutant in 1931. Trained to be a primary school teacher, INTO secretary in Waterford and member of the Trades Council. Edwards set up a branch of the IRC in the city. Because of this, Bishop Kinnane dismissed him from his teaching post in January 1935 at Mount Sion, a cause célèbre in 1930s Ireland. And Frank's mother, a public health nurse, was forced out of her job. A member of the CPI, Edwards left for Spain from Dunlaoghaire with Frank Ryan 11.12.1936. Fought at Lopera on the Cordoba front before Christmas, then at Las Rozas near Madrid where he was wounded 12.01.1937. Later fought in the south in the 2nd company of the 20th International Battalion as platoon leader. Repatriated to Ireland in September 1937. Died in Dublin 07.06.1983.

61.   FENNELLY William, born 12.08.1897 in Abbeyleix, Co. Laois, lived in Carlisle before Spain. Married. Cobbler, later miner. Ex-member of IRA. Wounded 27.02.1937 at Jarama while attached to Lincolns. Deserter.

Arrested by French police in Amiens, returned to Britain mid-January 1938. It seems that Fennelly was refused re-entry to Spain by IB staff at Figueras 31.01.1938. Other sources state that he joined the IB again on 05.02.1938 and left Spain 30.04.1938.

62. FINNEGAN John, born 18.03.1909. From Castleblaney, Co. Monaghan. Blacksmith. Emigrated to Canada, landing at Halifax 21.04.1929. Joined Canadian YCL in 1935. Arrived in Spain via Canada 21.07.1937. Missing in action 03.04.1938, on Canadian Roll of Honour.

63. FLANAGAN Terence, born 25.07.1912 South Dublin, from 49, Portland Row, Dublin. Ex-IRA, CPI. Member of Bakers' union. Arrived in Spain 21.12.1936. While Frank Ryan was at the Madrid front, Terry Flanagan was in charge of the Irish at Madrigueras when the row developed with the British officers. He was accused of "sabotage" and gaoled. Frank Ryan had him released. Flanagan was wounded at Jarama 17.02.1937 (shoulder) and spent 23.04.-25.07.1937 in Orihuela hospital. On 21 April Flanagan had approached Dave Springhall, Political Commissar, and asked to be sent to Ireland for propaganda purposes. He was categorically refused. Flanagan was repatriated to Ireland in 1937, after a recommendation from Frank Ryan 11.08.1937.

64. FLYNN Jack, from Derry. Born 1914. Went to Spain from Liverpool after deserting from the British Army. Arrived in Spain, 07.01.1937. Member of MG Company, British Battalion. Captured at Jarama. Sentenced to 20 years by a court in Salamanca, 18.05.1937. Released with 23 other prisoners in May 1937 and returned to Britain the same month.

65. FOLEY James, from Dublin, born 14.10.1903 Dublin. He lived in London. Killed on Cordoba front, Lopera, December 1936.

66. FOX Anthony, born 1914, lived in Goldenbridge Avenue, Inchicore, Dublin. He was a member of A Company, 4th battalion of the Dublin Brigade IRA. Killed on Cordoba front 28.12.1936 while dressing the wounds of his comrades Sean Goff and Seamus Cummings.

67. FULTON Albert, born 17.09.1905 Belfast, plumber. Fulton was a member of the Plumbers' Union in Belfast, emigrated to Australia in 1927. He joined CP Australia in July 1928 in Perth, short jail terms in Freemantle for

assault and obstruction of traffic in August 1929. Lived and worked in North Queensland as a railwayman. Arrived in Spain 27.04.1938. Sent to MG battalion of 15th Corps in June 1938, wounded during Ebro battle, in hospital at Mataro when the IB were withdrawn. Repatriated.

68. GALLAGHER Edward, born in Derry 1898. Arrived in Spain 1936. Stationed in garrison kitchen, Figueras, from January 1937. Later served in the 129th artillery division. Repatriated 1939.

69. GIBSON Patrick, born in Dublin 26.08.1906, Irish address 36, Bride St., Dublin. Salesman. Member of IRC. Arrived in Spain 16.05.1937. Listed as volunteer from Canada, lieutenant, on Brigade staff February 1938, later in artillery, anti-tank and anti-aircraft units. In November 1938 was still stationed in Valencia. Repatriated in January 1939 to Canada, landing 04.02.1939.

70. GLACKEN Patrick, b. 24.09.1913 Inishowen, originally from Moville, Co. Donegal. Lived in Greenock, his mother lived at 40, Holmscroft Street, Greenock. Labourer, member of Scottish Baker's Union. Joined the Labour Party in 1933. Arrived in Spain, 02.10.1937. Deserted at Teruel with Sergeant "Allen Kemp" (i.e. Donald B. Morris from Port Glasgow, Scotland) 04.01.1938, caught by Republican troops crossing the lines, both arrested 08.01.1938 and sentenced to death by a tribunal of their comrades and on the basis of an army order of 31.12.1937. Kemp was shot on 10.01.1938 but in the case of Glacken the death sentence was commuted. He was degraded, sent back to Brigade and served in a labour unit. Reported killed in action 20.01.1938.

71. GOFF Sean, born probably 1911, from Dundrum, Co. Dublin. House-painter. Arrived in Spain 11.11.1936. Wounded in the neck on the Cordoba front, 31.12.1936. Repatriated, returned to Dublin, July 1937.

72. GOLDING Patrick James, born probably 04.05.1904 in Tullamore, Co. Offaly. Lorry driver in Hayes, Middlesex. CPGB 1936, TGWU. Arrived in Spain 24.02.1937. Repatriated 22.09.1938.

73. GORMAN George F., born 1900, lived at Long Tower, Derry. Spent 12 years in the British Army, including WW1 and was posted to India and Iraq. Went to Spain from Folkestone, Kent, arriving 03.05.1938. Joined

No. 4 Company, British Battalion. Promoted Sergeant. Allegedly taken prisoner in the Sierra Caballs or, according to fellow prisoner George Wheeler, killed by Republican artillery in "friendly fire" incident 22.09.1938.

74. GOULDNEY Frederick G., born Dublin 1909, medical orderly, gave his address as 15, Holles Street (hospital). Arrived in Spain 01.01.1937 and sent to medical service. Fate unknown, possible deserter.

75. GREEN Leo James, born 08.12.1909 Dublin, from 2a, Bride Street Dublin. Motor driver, member of No. 1 Branch ITGWU since 1925. Arrived in Spain 16.12.1936. Killed at Jarama, 12.02.1937 when bringing in a wounded comrade. Michael Lehane was wounded in the same incident. His family was issued with a Spanish death certificate in February 1938.

76. HAIRE William John, born 1902 in Lurgan. Lived 23, Anne St., Lurgan, Co. Armagh. Arrived in Spain, 02.01.1937. Not a member of a political party, was unemployed. Deserted from the Jarama front 05.03.1937. According to IB records was a heavy drinker, proposed for deportation, 17.03.1938. Haire spent time in several gaols (Alicante, Valencia) and labour camps, including Camp Lukacs, Villamaruja and in the prison of Casteldefells. In Disciplinary Company, June-July 1938. With the British Battalion at Ripoll, 16.10.1938. Normal repatriation.

77. HALL Patrick., born probably 01.09.1912 Belfast. Labourer. IRA 1932-35. Arrived in Spain 14.01.1937. Probably deserted after Brunete, in gaol July 1937, afterwards absconded to Britain.

78. HAMILL Patrick, born ca. 1904 or 1906, originally from Knappagh, Co. Cavan. Emigrated to the USA. Lived in New York. Arrived with the first contingent of Americans in Figueras 04.01.1937, fought in the Lincoln Battalion. No further data.

79. HAUGHEY James Patrick, born 06.12.1919 Lurgan, Co. Armagh. Family lived at 82 Lower North St. Arrived in Spain via London 16.05.1938. Non-Party. British Battalion. Promoted Lieutenant on the day he was taken prisoner during last day of the Ebro battle, 23.09.1938. Badly beaten after capture. Emigrated to Canada on release from San Pedro de Cardeña, landing 06.05.1939. Joined the Royal Canadian Air Force (407 Squadron)

and was a warrant officer Class II. Haughey was killed serving as a wireless-operator/gunner when his plane (Wellington bomber) crashed in North Devon 12.09.1943. He was buried in Dougher Catholic Cemetery, Lurgan.

80. HAYES Thomas, born 1893, from 11, Tower View Road, Dublin. Member of ITGWU. Arrived in Spain 19.12.1936. Served in the Irish unit of the Lincolns. Recommended for repatriation by Frank Ryan 11.08.1937.

81. HEANEY John Hugh, born 03.04.1913 in Belfast. Emigrated to Canada, landing at Quebec 22.08.1929. Worked in cafes as cook in Edmonton, Alberta. Arrived in Spain 03.09.1937. Sent to Torcilla for MG training, joined the Mac-Paps at Fuentes del Ebro (October 1937), short time leader in light MG unit but handed back the command because of bad nerves. Fought also at Teruel. Deserted from battalion at Mora de Ebro in April 1938 with another Canadian volunteer, caught 17 April by carbineros at Massanet trying to cross the border into France. Brought to IB Delegation Barcelona but escaped, caught same day and brought to Figueras, sent back to Battalion. In June 1938 deserted from disciplinary company, was apprehended in Barcelona, sent to Castelldefels in August. He was with the Canadians at Ripoll in December 1938. Allegedly wanted to join anarchist FAI. Repatriated.

82. HEANEY Thomas, born 14.08.1919 Galway. Second youngest Irish volunteer. Worked in family butcher shop, Upper Abbey Gate Street, Galway. Emigrated to London in August 1937 and worked as a van guard at Bishopsgate Station, left for Spain in September 1937. Taken prisoner in March 1938. Repatriated normally. Stayed in Britain.

83. HENRY William, born 1896. From 31, Bradford St., Old Lodge Road, Belfast Veteran of WW1. Member of NILP, later of CPI and Irish Distributive Workers' Union, street dealer. Arrived in Spain 17.12.1936. Leader of Irish platoon in Company No. 1 of Lincoln Battalion, killed at Jarama 27.02.1937. He left a widow, Rosina.

84. HEPBURN Robert Charles, born 13.03.1913 in Naas, Co. Kildare, from 78, Iveagh Gardens, Crumlin, Dublin. Tailor's presser. Served in the Royal Army Medical Corps of the British Army 1931-1934. Arrived in Spain from London 06.02.1937. Sent to the front on 18.02.1937, nervous breakdown

after 6 days. Sent to the cook-house to rest, but refused after a week to return to the frontline. Jock Cunningham sent him to the base at Albacete for a medical examination. Doctors found him fit for the front, but he still refused. Arrested 03.03.1937, sentenced 05.03.1937 to one month in the labour column, requested 08.03.1937 to return to his unit in the line. Served in an anti-aircraft unit. Caught deserting second time on ship in Alicante, June 1937. Later sent to Battalion at Brunete, and for punishment to Camp Lukacs. In late June 1938 at Denia Hospital. Proposed for repatriation in 1938 before withdrawal of IB. Deserted by stowing aboard S.S. Wisconsin in Alicante and landing at Marseilles 18.07.1938. Repatriated with the help of the Irish Legation and British Embassy in Paris.

85. HILLEN James Isaac, born 1906 in Greenock, Scotland. Lived in Belfast. Member of CPI. Arrived in Spain 10.12.1936. Served in "Commune de Paris battalion" of the 11th Brigade, fought on Cordoba front and was wounded in the shoulder, fought at Jarama and Brunete, where he was again wounded in shoulder and wrist. Sought repatriation in June 1937. Recommended for repatriation by Frank Ryan 11.08.1937. Survivor.

86. HILLIARD Robert Martin, born 07.04.1904 in Moyeightragh near Killarney, the son of a wealthy leather merchant in the town. Educated at Cork Grammar School and Mountjoy School, Dublin. Studied at TCD where he revived the hurling team. Left without taking a degree, returned later and studied for the priesthood. Ordained as deacon in 1931. Served as a Church of Ireland pastor in Co. Antrim and Belfast. Left the clergy largely because of financial problems and joined the CPGB in 1935. Later worked as a journalist and as a driver. Member of the NUJ. Robert Hilliard married in 1926 and had four children. Arrived in Spain 22.12.1936. He was wounded at Jarama, admitted to hospital 17 February 1937 and died on 22 February 1937 in Benicasim. Buried by his comrades. Personal effects included British passport, pocket book and CPGB card.

87. HOLDEN Denis, from 7, Brown St., Carlow. Born in 1891, Holden lived in Liverpool and arrived in Spain 19.12.1936. He was in the Irish section of the Lincolns, was posted to the transport section in Albacete and repatriated in June 1937.

88. HUNT John, born 1911, from 14, New St., Waterford. Left London 19.12.1936 with Peter O'Connor, Paddy Power and Johnny Power. Arrived in Spain 21.12.1936. Wounded in the ankle at Jarama, 27.02.1937. Served in the artillery, repatriated August 1938. Died in London, 1980.

89. HUNT Vincent Joseph, born 28.09.1906 in Carrick-on-Suir, Co. Tipperary. Onetime inspector of cotton plantations, arrived in Spain from London in November 1936 with British Medical Unit. Served in the hospital of the Thälmann battalion (11th Brigade) in El Escorial and in Benicasim. Killed when a bomb hit the ambulance he was driving at Brunete, 17.07.1937.

90. HUNTER Hugh Stewart, born 1904 near Ballyclare, Co. Antrim, gave Irish address as J. O'Hagan, 20, Grove Street off Queen Street, Belfast. Labourer, member of CPI since September 1935. Arrived in Spain 30.03.1938. Joined British Battalion 20.05.1938. Wounded three times, the last time 08.09.1938. In Vich hospital 14.10.1938. Repatriated. Active Belfast Communist up to his death in 1972.

91. JOHNSON William, born 01.04.1903, Newry, Co. Down. Married, one child, 12 years in British Army as sergeant, unemployed since 1933, non-Party, non-trade union. Arrived in Spain from Liverpool 05.01.1937. Arrested 11.02.1937 and sentenced to three months in labour battalion by judicial commission. Possibly repatriated in September 1937.

92. JOHNSTONE John A., born 03.02.1900, Belfast. Metalworker. Served 1918-1920 in the British Army, married with 1 child. CPGB since 1923. Lived in Hayes, Middlesex. Arrived in Spain 10.03.1938. No further data.

93. JONES James J., born 1905, from Dublin. Lived in London. Arrived in Spain. Killed during Ebro battle, July 1938.

94. JONES Thomas, born probably 30.08.1910 Carrickbyrne, Co. Wexford, said to have come from Gorey, Co. Wexford. Served as a stretcher bearer at the battle of Brunete. No further data.

95. KEENAN Patrick, born 02.02.1908 Dublin, metal worker, lived before Spain at 39, Bolton Street, next-of-kin an uncle in Basin St. Left Ireland 19.12.1936. Allegedly worked in Albacete as a mechanic, arrested for sabotage 10.02.1937, escaped from custody 14.02.1937, fled to Valencia,

joined ship 20.02.1937, arrived in Marseilles 21.02.1937. Deserted from Spain. Repatriated with help of Irish Legation in Paris.

96. KEENAN William, born 1901 in Bangor, Co. Down. Emigrated to Canada in 1934. Left for Spain 19.11.1937. Arrested in France, spent 20 days in prison. Joined Mac-Paps battalion and was killed by a Stuka dive-bomber during the Ebro battle in July 1938. On Canadian Roll of Honour.

97. KELLY Christopher Joseph, born 01.11.1906 in Dublin. Radio-telegraphist. Served five years in the British Army. Lived in New York. Arrived in Spain 29.08.1937, attached to 1st company, Lincoln Battalion. Instructor at Tarazona, three times arrested for drunkenness, sent back to battalion 07.12.1937, deserted from depository company, 17.07.1938. Later a transit soldier in the barracks Cuartal de Rectorat in Las Planas, Barcelona. Kelly's mother in Dublin (20, Greenville Terrace, S.C. Road) asked the Irish Department of External Affairs to locate her son in January 1939 but this was impossible due to the end of the Spanish Civil War in March 1939. His fate remains unknown.

98. KELLY John, born probably 22.10.1914 Waterford, lived in Grady's Lane, of Barrack Street, Waterford. Arrived in Spain 12.08.1937 via London. Stonemason. Instructor at Tarazona, September 1937. Wounded Teruel, January 1938, and Sierra Pandols, 26.08.1938. With battalion 16.10.1938. Normal repatriation after withdrawal of IB. Died in London 1980.

99. KELLY Joseph, born 10.03.1898, perhaps from Drumcarbit, Malin, Co. Donegal. Emigrated to Canada, lived in Vancouver, single, lumberjack, trade union organiser, joined CPCan in 1932. Canadian citizen. Arrived in Spain 14.02.1937 from Canada. Promoted Lieutenant in November 1937, instructor in Tarazona, wounded first at Brunete, and then in an accident at Tarazona. Arrived in Canada 03.02.1939. Died in Kamloops, British Columbia, 02.01.1977.

100. KELLY Joseph M., originally from Dublin. Born probably in 1918/19 and lived at 14, Leinster Square, Rathmines. Apprentice engineer. Later lived in London. Arrived in Spain 20.12.1936. Killed at Brunete, July 1937.

101. KELLY Michael J., born 1905, from Kilconnell near Ballinasloe, Co. Galway. IRA 1928, IRC 1933. Arrived in Spain from Britain in December

1936. IRC activist in London. Caterer. Kelly trained the Irish platoon of the Lincolns and was appointed its first leader in February 1937. Wounded in the chest 27.02.1937 but left hospital prematurely. Attached to Brigade staff. Killed at Brunete, 07.07.1937, by a sniper while acting as battalion runner and out on reconnaissance with the Brigade observation officer.

102. KENNEDY David, born probably 30.03.1915 Co. Armagh. Lived in Greenock, Scotland, and worked as a painter. LP 1935. Arrived in Spain 27.02.1938. Taken prisoner at Calaceite, 31.03.1938.

103. KENNEDY Harry, born 21.06.1909 in Waterford and lived at 12, Cook Lane, Waterford. Emigrated to England around 1930 to work as a house decorator, returned and worked for a builder in Waterford. Moved back to London and went from there to Spain. Arrived in Spain 06.09.1937. Soon deserted and was sent to a penal battalion. Took part in the battle for Teruel, January 1938. Member of Brigade Staff, worked as an instructor under Major Johnson in Tarazona. Deserted January 1938 and reached Algiers on a Greek ship as a stowaway. Again as a stowaway reached Marseilles, where the British Consul loaned him the train fare to Paris. Kennedy turned up at the Irish Legation, where he made claims about his life being in danger. Travelled to London at the expense of the British Charitable Fund in Paris.

104. KERR Thomas, Belfast, born 1910, lived 49, Sunny Side St., Ormeau Road. Seaman, joined Socialist Party 1930, arrived in Spain via Liverpool 05.01.1937. Entrained for Albacete, 11.12.1937. At some stage storeman in Huete hospital. Probably wounded at Brunete, in hospital in Barcelona in September 1937. 5th recruits company, Tarazona, 11.02.1938. Arrested at the docks in Barcelona 22.05.1938, sent to brigade jail, then Castelldefels. Due to be repatriated in September 1938, died from typhoid in hospital at Vich 10.10.1938.

105. LARMOUR James (Johnny), born 1910, originally from 15, Torrens Gardens, Belfast. Seaman. Member of CPGB since 1933. Arrived in Spain from Liverpool 18.12.1936. Wounded in the left arm at Lopera, 28.12.1936. Repatriated, later member of the selection committee for outgoing volunteers from London.

106. LEESON Harold George, born 23.09.1907 in Clonakilty, Co. Cork, where his father was in the Coastguard service. His mother was a Liston from Limerick. His middle-class family moved to Scotland in 1916. Served in the Royal Navy, bought himself out in 1930 and later worked as a sailor and railway clerk. Joined the CPGB in London in 1935, left for Spain 07.01.1937.Taken prisoner at Jarama, released from captivity September 1937 after most of fellow British captives were already back in Britain and due to a campaign and questions asked in the House of Commons. Helped later with the repatriation of the wounded from Spain via France. Afterwards CPGB organiser in North London, left the party after WW2.

107. LEHANE Michael, born 27.09.1908 at Morley's Bridge, Kilgarvan, Co. Kerry. After secondary school he attended an agricultural college in Clonakilty, Co. Cork, but had to leave for financial reasons. Afterwards worked as a builder's labourer in Dublin. CPI member. Arrived in Spain 12.12.1936. Fought in Cordoba, Las Rozas near Madrid, Jarama and Brunete. Recommended for repatriation by Frank Ryan 11.08.1937. Repatriated for work in Ireland, September 1937. Again Lehane worked on Dublin building sites, but arrived in Spain again 22.03.1938. Wounded during Ebro battles, on Hill 481, 31.07.1938 and was carried to safety by Michael O'Riordan. Sent to Santa Coloma hospital, was still there 14.10.1938. Lehane received a citation for bravery for his conduct during the last battles. He arrived back in Dublin with Eugene Downing, 21.12.1938. Lehane went to Birmingham in search of work in 1939. During WW2 he enlisted in the Norwegian Merchant Navy and was killed when his ship, "Brant County", on a convoy to Halifax, was sunk by a German submarine in the Atlantic 11.03.1943. Twenty-four passengers and crew, including Michael Lehane, perished. A memorial in his honour was unveiled at Morley's Bridge 07.05.1989.

108. LEMON John (Jackie), born 04.07.1918 Waterford. Mother lived at 2, Olaf Street. Fitter's mate. Worked at HMV gramophone company in London. Arrived in Spain 12.08.1937. In light machine gun team with 'Peter Brady' (real name: Edward Vallely) and Bob Doyle when captured 31.03.1938 at Calaceite. Repatriated with 66 of British Battalion 06.02.1939, arrived in Ireland 27.02.1939. Died 03.09.1975.

109. LEVITAS Maurice, born 01.02.1917 at 8, Warren Street, S.C. Road, Dublin, of Jewish parents. Family emigrated to Glasgow in 1927 and to East End of London in 1931. YCL 1933, CPGB 1937 in Bethnall Green. Lived at 78, Brady Mansions, Brady St. Plumber by trade. Arrived in Spain 23.01.1938. 6th recruits company, Tarazona, 11.02.1938. Captured with Frank Ryan, 31 March 1938. Released in February 1939 with Bob Doyle and Maurice Levitas. Repatriated with the help of the Irish Legation in Paris. Served in Royal Medical Corps during WW2. Levitas was later a university sociologist and emigrated to the GDR in 1985, where he defended the reputation of Erich Honecker after the latter's arrest and conviction in 1992. Maurice Levitas died 24.02.2001 in London.

110. LORD James Arthur, born probably 1916 Carrick Hill, Belfast. Motor driver. Gave his address as 128, Upper Library Street, Belfast. Arrived in Spain from Liverpool, 20.03.1938. Joined British Battalion, 23.03.1938, with the battalion at Ripoll, 16.10.1938. Normal repatriation.

111. LOWRY Joseph, born probably 02.09.1906 Co. Armagh. From 21, Hanover Street, Belfast. Married, fitter's helper. Arrived in Spain 10.12.1936. Recommended for repatriation by Frank Ryan 11.08.1937, sent home September 1937.

112. LYNCH Thomas, Dublin, born 1913, arrived in Spain 22.12.1936. He was from 26, Our Lady's Road, Maryland, Dublin, and may have deserted from the British Army, in which he may have enlisted under the name of "Walsh". IB records in London state he returned from Spain in September 1937.

113. MADERO Alexander, born 02.11.1911 in Dundalk, Co. Louth. Gave Irish address as 6, Union St., Dundalk, c/o Hayes. Glassworker. Arrived in Spain 20.12.1937. Third recruits company, Tarazona, 11.02.1938. Captured 17.03.38 Caspe-Belchite. Other reports state he was accidentally shot at Figueras, where he died of wounds, April 1938. On British Roll of Honour. Said to have been "demoralised" in Spain.

114. MAGILL Joseph, born in Lurgan, Co. Armagh, 07.06.1907. Lived 56 Tobergill St., Belfast. British address 67, Edgware Road, London. Arrived in Spain, 10.01.1937. Possibly lived in Canada beforehand. Deserted on three

occasions. Villa Maruja 1937, Brigade prison 09.09.1938, sent to military tribunal 12.10.1938. Proposed for repatriation, 03.11.1938. Seen in Castelldefels by Canadian Consul, 21.01.1939, repatriated to Britain shortly afterwards.

115. MALONE John, born Dublin 17.02.1912, father James lived at 320, St. Michael St., Dublin. Emigrated to Canada, lived in Vancouver, taxi-driver. Canadian citizen. Imprisoned three times for political activities. Joined CPCan in January 1937. Arrived in Spain via Canada 01.12.1937. Served in Canadian battalion, wounded, was in Mataro Hospital at withdrawal of IB. Returned to Canada 1939, died 22.10.1972.

116. MARTIN Christopher, born 25.12.1907 Cork, served in the Irish Free State Army, later fitter's mate. Canadian militia. CPCan 1937. Arrived in Spain 29.01.1938, served in the British Battalion. Deserted 23.09.1938 and returned to Britain with the British Battalion.

117. MARTIN Samuel, born 26.08.1912 Belfast, from 108, Lepper Street, Belfast. Scrap iron employee, arrived 14.04.1937 in Spain. Deserted during battle of Brunete, 07.07.1937.

118. MAY Michael, born 23.11.1916 in Coombe Hospital, lived at 37, Connolly Avenue, Inchicore, Dublin. Member of A Company, 4th battalion, Dublin Brigade IRA, later joined CPI. Killed in action at Lopera, Cordoba front, 28.12.1936, while covering the retreat of his comrades.

119. MC ALEENAN Richard, born 16.12.1909 Banbridge, Co. Down. Parents small farmers. Labourer. Spent the years 1927-32 in Britain. In Ireland he was a cyclist sportsman, joined CPI in Dublin, February 1934, North Dublin Branch. Ex-member of the IRA. Arrested 02.03.1934 in Belfast, sentenced to 6 months hard labour, released September 1934. Member of ITGWU in Newry. Worked in London in a hotel and as building worker for McAlpine before departure to Spain. Member IRC London Branch. Arrived Spain 07.10.1937. In 1st recruits company, Tarazona, 11.02.1938. Served with Battalion observers, never wounded. Went missing during retreats of March-April 1938. At Ripoll with British Battalion 16.10.1938. Normal repatriation.

120. MC ALISTER Patrick, born 08.01.1909 in Belfast. Family lived at 81, Lincoln St., Belfast. Next-of-kin lived 1937 in Carrickmacross, Co. Monaghan. Member of the Fianna, joined the IRA in 1926. McAlister emigrated to Canada, landing in Quebec 04.08.1928. Worked as a waiter and logger in Vancouver region. Single. Joined CPCan in 1935, arrested twice for political activities. Arrived in Spain via Canada 02.12.1937. 5th recruits company, Tarazona, 11.02.1938. Corporal, wounded in right forearm during the Ebro battles 10.09.1938. Returned to Belfast 24.12.1938. Died 16.09.1997. There is a plaque in his honour erected by the Workers' Party in Belfast.

121. MC CARTHY Cormac, born on Vancouver Island in 1893 as one of 15 children of Irish immigrants. When he was two, the family returned to Ireland, and he started work (probably in England) from the age of twelve. Served in an Irish regiment during WW1 as a machine-gunner. McCarthy emigrated to Australia in 1923, where he worked at a series of unskilled jobs. In 1936 he worked his ship's passage from Melbourne to Britain as a fireman. The date of his arrival in Spain is unknown, but he fought with the Canadians and was reported as missing during the retreats on 16 March 1938. Deserter. He was arrested in Paris in April 1938 for burglary.

122. MC CHRYSTAL William, born 28.12.1905. Irish address: 36, Cross St., Waterside, Derry. Tailor, single. Emigrated to Canada, landing in Halifax 09.04.1928. Member of CPCan since January 1936. In Vancouver organiser of unemployed. Arrived in Spain 14.08.1937 from Canada. 5th recruits company, Tarazona, 11.02.1938. Graduate of OTS, Tarazona. Taken prisoner Caspe-Belchite 17.03.38. Repatriated after withdrawal of Brigades 1939.

123. MC CLURE George, born Donaghadee, Co. Down, in 1894. Lived in Liverpool and worked as a journalist and seaman. Married with 2 children. Member of CPGB since 1935. Arrived in Spain 27.01.1937. Probably served in the medical service. In gaol at IB base in Badalona, Barcelona, 1938. Re-joined battalion 14.10.1938. Normal repatriation.

124. MC DADE William, born 1897 in Belfast, lived in Dundee. Woodworker. Arrived in Spain 22.12.1936. Ex-British Army, served as battalion adjutant

at Madrigueras to Wilfred Macartney. Wounded at Jarama and Brunete. Repatriated August 1937.

125. MC ELLIGOTT John (Jack, Paddy) born 21.05.1905, Annascaul, Co. Kerry, parents lived in Killarney. Member No. 2 Kerry Brigade IRA 1918-24. Emigrated from Ireland in 1924 and again in 1929, landing in St. John's 21.04.1929. He settled in Canada and lived in New Westminster, British Columbia. Worked 1934/35 as a miner in the Yukon. Single, joined CPCan in November 1934. Organiser of YCL. Arrested four times for political activities. Arrived in Spain from Canada 20.10.1937. Sergeant training recruits at Tarazona, later demoted for insubordination and gaoled because of a dispute about the siting of machine-guns in the Ebro battles. Criticised lack of military training in brigades. Repatriated to Canada, arriving 18.02.1939, later active in the veterans' association. McElligott served in the Merchant Navy in WW2. Died 23.08.1984.

126. MC ELROY Albert E. (Bert), born probably 08.09.1915 Enniskillen, Co. Fermanagh. Later lived in Co. Louth. Killed at Jarama 1937.

127. MC ELROY Patrick J., born 22.05.1911 South Dublin. Lived at 20, Nash St., Inchicore, Dublin. Machinist, Engineers' Union. His brother Christopher took part in the Easter Rising. Member of Sinn Fein/IRA, 1932/33. He joined the IB 07.01.1937 and was seriously wounded at Jarama. Repatriated, arrived in Dublin in late November 1937.

128. MC GOVERN Bernard, born probably 02.03.1914 Manorhamilton, Co. Leitrim, lived at Glenfarne, Co. Leitrim. Arrived in Spain early 1937. No further data, probably deserted.

129. MC GRATH Henry, born 1902 Belfast. Home at 56, Tobergill Street, Belfast. CP. Fireman. Arrived in Spain 10.11.1936, transferred to the Republican Navy at Cartagena 11.12.1936, served as a stoker on an armed trawler. Transferred to infantry. Deserted during second day of battle of Brunete, July 1937, sent to Camp Lukacs. Proposed for deportation, 17.03.1938. Killed September 1938 during Ebro battle.

130. MC GRATH Michael Aloysius, born 30.06.1898 in Fermoy, Co. Cork, said to be from Ardnalee, Crosshaven, Co. Cork. Civil servant, ex-IRA. Arrived in Spain 23.01.1938. Taken prisoner in Aragon, March 1938. Gave

his Irish address as 13, South Mall, Cork. Repatriated from San Pedro in the first release of British prisoners, October 1938.

131. MC GREGOR William Scott, born 27.08.1914 North Dublin. Electrician and clerk, secondary school education. Lived at 68, Kickham Road, Kilmainham. ITGWU since 1931, member of B Co., 4th battalion, Dublin Brigade IRA. He was a delegate to the inaugural congress of CPI in June 1933, and was expelled from the IRA in January 1934 because of CPI membership. Attended the International Lenin School 1935-37. Organizer of CPI Dublin branches. Arrived in Spain 19.04.1938, joined British Battalion June 1938. Accidentally wounded by grenade 22.07.38. Killed on last day of action, 23.09.38. Commissar of No. 1 Company, British Battalion. Posthumous citation for bravery in Ebro battle.

132. MC GROTTY Eamon, born 12.07.1911 Limavady, Co. Derry, lived at 4, Mount St., Rosemount, Derry, Christian Brother 1925-32. Moved to Dublin with family when his father died in 1932 and lived at 9, Upper Drumcondra Road. Worked for the Irish language paper An t-Éireannach. Member of NUJ. Arrived in Spain 22.12.1936. Adjutant of the Irish unit in the Lincolns. Killed in Pingarron Hill assault, 27.02.1937.

133. MC GUINNESS Charles J., born 1893. Lived at 5, Clarence Avenue, Derry. Sea-captain, gun-runner and adventurer. Date of arrival in Spain not known, soon deserted.

134. MC GUINNESS Patrick Bryan, born 31.10.1910 North Dublin, lived probably at 21, Merchants Quay, Dublin. Labourer. Worked in London as kitchen porter, member of YCL since 1936. Arrived in Spain via London 19.11.1937. 4th recruits company, Tarazona, 11.02.1938. Deserted from Mac Paps, 07.08.1938. Major Jose Valledor, the successor to Čopić as Commander of 15th Brigade, urged his expulsion from Spain. In Brigade prison 09.09.1938 at Badalona. No further data.

135. MC GUIRE Patrick, born 17.05.1900 Castleblaney, Co. Monaghan. According to Canadian immigration records, one Patrick Maguire, aged 27, arrived in Quebec from Scotland 28.04.1928. Lived in Vancouver, B.C. Sailed for Spain 06.04.1937, served in Canadian battalion, machine-gunner. With Canadians at Ripoll, repatriated 1939.

136. MC KEEFREY James J., born probably 15.12.1912 Co. Antrim. Lived in Glasgow. Arrived in Spain via London early May 1938 and was sent from Figueras to British Battalion 08.05.1938. Wounded at the Ebro and still in Vich hospital 14.10.1938. No further data.

137. MC LARNON Alan Fredrick, born 16.12.1907, Lurgan, Co. Armagh. The family later moved to 50 Eaton Square, Terenure, Dublin. He was a member of IRC in London where he worked as a waiter. Arrived in Spain, 23.12.1936. First in the MG Company of British Battalion, then with the Lincolns. Wounded at Jarama, 23.02.1937. Four months in hospital. Assigned a post as truck driver in June and attached to 14th Brigada Mixta (Tren de Combat) near Madrid. Suffering from fever and abdominal complaints, McLarnon requested he be sent to Albacete for a thorough medical examination. Proposed for repatriation, he fought at Brunete and was in Valencia prison in September 1938. Died in 1960 in Britain.

138. MC LAUGHLIN Matthew. Born ca. 1908. Probably from Hamilton Street, Derry. Emigrated at the age of 19 to Canada, landing at Quebec 07.08.1927. Lived in Hamilton, Ontario. Left for Spain 04.06.1937. Killed during the retreats at Belchite, March 1938.

139. MC LAUGHLIN Michael P., born ca. 1890. Emigrated to the USA where he worked as a miner. Member CPUSA since 1935. Arrived in Spain 08.04.1937. Fought at Brunete and Aragon, wounded in the head and hip. Served finally with the Canadians. In Brigade prison in Barcelona in summer 1938. No further data.

140. MC LAUGHLIN Patrick Roe, born 17.12.1902 in Lecamey, Moville, Co. Donegal. Member of the IRA during the War of Independence. Emigrated to America in 1925, worked as lorry driver in New York on subway construction. Member of the Irish Workers Club and the CPUSA since 1934. Left London 04.12.1936. Another source states he sailed with the first American contingent from New York on 26.12.1936 and arrived in Figueras on 01.01.1937. Spent four months on the Jarama front, assistant commander of American MG Co. then transferred to OTS, which he left voluntarily and served later with the artillery at Almanza in the Brown Battery on 155mm guns. Served in the IB from 26.12.36 to January 1938. Repatriated (via Ireland) in February 1938. Tried to have his Irish passport

renewed at the Paris Legation but was given a document valid for travel to Ireland only. Lived later in Liverpool, where he married the fiancée of Liam Tumilson. McLaughlin and his wife were members of the CPGB. During WW2 McLaughlin worked as a mechanic in the RAF. He died in Liverpool in 1974.

141. MC LAUGHLIN (Laughran), William P., born probably 1903, from 162, Conway Street, Belfast. Married. Spent 13 years in the British army, Irish Guards. Worked afterwards as a labourer. Arrived in Spain December 1936. Fought at Lopera, Las Rozas and Jarama. MG instructor at Madrigueras. Wounded at least once. Killed in the storming of Villaneuva de la Cañada, 06.07.1937.

142. MC PARLAND Eugene. Born 1915 Northern Ireland. British Battalion. Arrived in Spain from Birkenhead, 30.07.1937. Mistakenly arrested by SIM in May 1938 when serving as an ambulance driver. Spent three months in the labour battalion. Repatriated August 1938.

143. MEEHAN John, born 1912, from Carrowmanagh, Dunmore, Co. Galway. Arrived in Spain 17.09.1936. Fatally wounded at Lopera, Cordoba front, 28.12.1936, by a machine gun burst. Died in hospital in Ciudad Real, 02.01.1937.

144. MITCHELL Charles B., in Spain used the name "John Doyle". Born 21.09.1914 South Dublin. Home at 9 Golden Vale, Emmet Road, Inchicore, Dublin. Lived in Whitechapel, London. In Ireland member of the WUI, in London joined the CPGB. Arrived in Spain via England 22.12.1936, allegedly deserted from British Army. Wounded slightly 27.02.1937 at Jarama when serving in the 4th Company. On 7 March tried to escape with another patient from Tarracon hospital, arrested in the vicinity. Sentenced by Juridical Commission (11.03.1937) to serve in the labour battalion for duration of war and permanent exclusion from British Battalion. After hospital transferred to artillery at Almansa. Passed by the medical commission at Benicasim as fit for the front. Sent to medical service 45th Division 13.09.1937. Deserted from Aragon front with car in November 1937. Captured, sent to Albacete, spent a week in Albacete military prison, then at Villamaruja. Deserted again, caught in Barcelona after visit to British Consul and attempt to board a British ship,

27.06.1938. Sent to fortifications 45th Division, Castelldefels. Proposed for repatriation, 03.11.1938. Seen in Castelldefels 29.01.1939 by Canadian Consul, repatriated to Britain shortly afterwards.

145. MOLYNEAUX Andrew, born 22.10.1906, Belfast and lived as a child at 14, Silvio Street, Shankill Road. Emigrated to Canada, landing in Quebec 31.07.1926. He joined CPCan in April 1935. Labourer. Arrived in Spain from Canada 15.07.1937. Sergeant, platoon leader, good characteristic, repatriated 1939. Lived in Vancouver. Died 21.12.1970 in Vancouver.

146. MONKS Patrick Joseph (Joe), born 10.08.1914, from 16 Park St., Inchicore, Dublin. Member of RWG and CPGB after he had emigrated to London. Worked as a machine-operator in the Lucas factory in Acton. Monks contacted CPGB head office on 08.12.1936 and left London with a group four days later. Arrived in Figueras. 15.12.1936, Albacete 17.12.1936. Served with the English-speaking Company No. 1 of the Marseillaise battalion of the 14th Brigade IB on the Cordoba front. Wounded in the chest 28.12.1936. After hospital joined 2nd (English-speaking) Company of the 20th Battalion of the 86th Brigade, again sent to the Cordoba front. Repatriated to Ireland July 1937. Wrote an interesting memoir, "Reds in Andalusia" (1985). He died in London 06.01.1988.

147. MORAN Maurice, born 11.10.1910, Ballina, Co. Mayo and probably lived as an infant at 9 Arbuckle Row, Ballina, Co. Mayo. Emigrated to America, joined CPUSA 1936. Engineer. Arrived in Spain 06.01.1937. Recommended for repatriation to the USA 27.06.1937 by Bill Lawrence, American Political Commissar, because of family problems. Obtained an Irish passport in Paris for return to the USA but was refused re-entry in 1938.

148. MORONEY Brendan, born 30.10.1913, Co. Clare. Irish address 62, Parnell St., Ennis. Served in Irish Guards 1934-36, then factory worker in London. Arrived in Spain via London 10.12.1936. Notorious trouble-maker. Expelled from British Battalion 18.01.1937 for "insubordination and mutiny". Imprisoned from 06.07.1937 for ten days, then handed over to Spaniards. Tried by civilian court in Orihuela (near Murcia) because he attacked a civilian. Recommended for expulsion from Spain and categorized an "undesirable element" for refusing to go to the front, 29.07.1937. In

early February 1938 Moroney was in the 3rd recruits company, Tarazona, and in detention. Sent to labour battalion from Tarazona, 12.02.1938. Short sojourn at the front where he helped to bury Ben Murray, March 1938. Disappeared after another stay in hospital, April 1938. Placed on British ship at Barcelona by British consul, landed at Marseilles and proceeded to Paris. Repatriated via Irish Legation in mid-June 1938. Moroney lied repeatedly to the Irish diplomats, stating that Frank Ryan was a communist who "deserved to be shot". After his return to Ireland he wrote a pro-fascist account of his experiences for the Irish Catholic periodical "Hibernia", which also appeared in the pro-Franco periodical "Spain" in New York. Lived afterwards in London.

149. MORRISON William A., born 10.02.1910 Belfast. Emigrated to Canada in 1925, worked as a waiter and variety artist. Returned to Ireland 1931. Moved to London in 1936. Arrived in Spain via London 22.12.1936. Wounded at Jarama 23.02.1937, assistant platoon leader while in the American battalion, in hospital until May. Joined British Battalion, worked in the cookhouse, rejected by OTS, characterized as "disruptive" in the repatriation question. In February 1938 in personnel office, Tarazona, proposed for deportation, 17.03.1938. Returned to Canada, died 21.12.1970.

150. MURPHY John, born about 1900 in Derry, lived at 8, Mountjoy St., Derry. Worked as a fruit-seller in London. Arrived in Spain 01.09.1937. No further data.

151. MURPHY Patrick, born in Belfast. Lived in Liverpool. Arrived in Spain February 1937. Bricklayer, deserted once, returned to IB. No further data.

152. MURPHY Patrick, born Ireland 1897, lived in Cardiff. Arrived in Spain September 1936, badly wounded at Brunete, allegedly deserted, repatriated 1938.

153. MURPHY Thomas, born 1903 in Newbliss, Co. Monaghan, son of a sergeant in the RIC. Ex-Irish Guards. Member of CPGB in Camden Town. Arrived in Spain 04.02.1937. Badly wounded in the left arm during the Battle of the Ebro, which necessitated amputation. In Vich hospital 14.10.1938. Repatriated 1938.

154. MURPHY Thomas, originally from Belfast, lived in Liverpool, brother of Patrick (Liverpool). Ex-British Army soldier. Excellent record in Spain. Probably Belfast-born.

155. MURRAY Benjamin Fredrick ("Ben"). Family originally from Rockcorry, Co. Monaghan. Born 19.07.1895 in Maguiresbridge, Lisnaskea, Co. Fermanagh. His father was in the RIC and the family moved to Moy Bridge, Aughnacloy, Co. Tyrone. Ben emigrated with his father to Canada in 1912, served in Canadian army in WW1, worked as literature salesman in Canada after 1919 and founded radical journal. Returned to parents' farm in Ireland in 1932. Activist in CPI. Emigrated to Britain 1935 and joined CPGB. Lived at 21, Winchester Avenue, London NW6. Arrived in Spain 09.02.1937. Fought at Jarama, wounded at Brunete 06.07.1937. Afterwards Political Commissar in Camp Lukacs and in Investigation Dept. at Tarazona. Compiled material for 15th Brigade book. Gifted linguist. Volunteered again for the front, killed by a bomb blast in Abalate, Aragon, 14.03.1938. A memorial was unveiled in his honour in Aughnacloy, 09.03.2013.

156. MURRAY Joseph, born. ca. 1886, arrived in Spain 23.12.1936. CPGB, fought at Jarama and Brunete, heart trouble. Recommended for repatriation in September 1937.

157. MURRAY Joseph, born 05.11.1911 Dublin. British Army 1928-37. Missing since Belchite 17.03.1938. Came to Spain from Rochdale. No further data.

158. NALTY Jack, born 08.09.1902 Ballygar, Co. Galway, father in RIC. Family moved to Dublin and Jack attended CBS secondary school, joined Fianna 1918 and later C Co., No. 1 Battalion Dublin IRA. He worked in the Anglo-American Oil Co. from 1919, yard foreman, member of No. 1 Branch ITGWU. Took part in the War of Independence and Civil War, arrested March 1923, released November 1923. Nalty was dismissed from the IRA in May 1934 because he had joined CPI in 1933. IRC member. He was also a shop steward, spent six weeks prison in 1935 because of mass-picketing and later brought to the Curragh Camp for trial before a military tribunal. The sentence of one month's imprisonment had already been served and Nalty was released. He lived at 1, Merville Villas, Fairview. Left

for Spain 08.12.1936 with six other comrades. Wounded in the chest and arm at Lopera 31.12.1936. Sent to OTS in May 1937, promoted sergeant. Repatriated to Ireland in July 1937, returned to Spain in April 1938 with Paddy Duff. Nalty was the commander of the MG Company, British Battalion, from 07.04.1938. Killed 23.09.1938, last day of action. Posthumous citation for bravery.

159. NOLAN Michael, born 1910 Dublin. Member of IRC. His mother lived at 14, Emerald Terrace, Inchicore. Labourer. Arrived in Spain 12.12.1936. Killed on the Cordoba front, 28./29.12.1936.

160. O'BEIRNE, Patrick James. Born in Bawnboy, Co. Cavan 1887. Said to have come from Belturbert, Co. Cavan and is probably the "Seamus McBroin" mentioned in "Reds in Andalusia" by Joe Monks. On his arrival in Spain on 05.12.1936 O'Beirne gave his age as 49 and said he was an agricultural labourer from Carrick-on-Shannon, Co. Leitrim, and had served in the IRA from 1919 to 1925. He may have lived in Belfast before going to Spain. Repatriated 1937.

161. O'BEIRNE, William John. Born 23.08.1899, Portumna, Co. Galway. His mother hailed from Co. Tipperary and following the death of her first husband who kept a business in Cloughjordan, she married a RIC man, Nicholas Hobin, in Roscrea. The family lived in Dundrum, Co, Tipperary at the time of the 1901 Census. Nicholas Hobin was later posted to Balbriggan, Co. Dublin as station sergeant. W.J. O'Beirne (Jack) was educated in Tipperary and Dublin and was active in the IRA in Balbriggan during the Irish War of Independence. In 1924/25 he emigrated to America and lived in Edgewater, New Jersey. Member CPUSA from 1937. Seaman. Arrived in Spain in 1937 and served in the Lincoln-Washington battalion. Wounded in the hip 10.03.1938, taken prisoner. Released in February 1939 while posing as another man (an American citizen), and returned to Balbriggan. He was so incapacitated on arrival at Balbriggan Station that his brother brought him the short distant to his home in the sidecar of a motorbike. Later worked for a while in Scotland, died in 1966.

162. O'BOYLE Patrick, born probably 1894 in Belfast or Ballina. Also used the names William Henry Preston and Jim Steward. Fought in the Great War and emigrated to Canada in 1920. He joined the "Mounties", but deserted

to the USA. Worked in the lumber industry. Member CPUSA. Left for Spain from the USA, November 1937. 5th recruits company, Tarazona, 11.02.1938. Corporal, badly wounded when run over by a tank during the March retreats 1938. Not organised politically, repatriated 25.10.1938. Died in New York 1978.

163. O'BRIEN Francis, used the name Duffy in Spain. Born 1909, Dundalk. Bus-driver and mechanic in London, lived at 21, Langby Lane, SW8. CPGB since 1937. Ex-British Army. Arrived in Spain 10.09.1937. Sergeant in MG unit, killed at Segura de los Baños, 17.02.1938.

164. O'BRIEN John, born 1910. Labourer, IRA member to 1936. Lived in Rotherhithe in the East End of London. Arrived in Spain 03.12.1936. Probably served in a signallers' unit. Repatriated 1937.

165. O'BRIEN Thomas, born 24.04.1914 North Dublin, lived 225, Phibsborough Road. Free-lance journalist and writer. Joined the IRA in 1932, later expelled after joining IRC and CPI in 1934. Gaoled for 6 weeks in 1935 because of strike activity (together with Denis Coady and Charlie Donnelly). Arrived Spain 14.04.1938. 4th company, British Battalion. Arrived home 10.12.1938 with Johnny Power and Mick O'Riordan. Founder of The O'Brien Press publishing house, died 07.12.1974 in Dublin. A book about his war in Spain was published in1994.

166. O'BRIEN Thomas, born probably in Dublin 1909, emigrated to England 1926, hotel clerk. Not politically involved in Ireland or England. Arrived in Spain 16.12.1936. Deserted at Brunete, caught near French border and confined in Garda Nacional in Albacete for 14 days. Later sent to Camp Lukacs, stayed three months, from there to Villa Maruja and finally to training base at Tarazona. Arrived in Albacete for medical treatment, January 1938, tore up his military book and refused to go to the front. Sent from Tarazona to labour battalion, 12.02.1938. Proposed for repatriation. Left Spain 22.05.1938.

167. O'BRIEN Thomas T., born 1911. Originally from Dublin, lived 22, July Road, Anfield, Liverpool, went from Liverpool to Spain in December 1936. Member of CPGB. Killed at Jarama 27.02.1937.

168. O'CONNOR James, born in Dublin 1905, lived at 98, Lower Gloucester St. Emigrated to Canada. Labourer, single. Lived in Vancouver, B.C. Joined CPCan in 1937 and arrived in Spain August 1937. Served as instructor, killed in action 11.03.1938.

169. O'CONNOR Peter, Waterford. Born 31.03.1912. His father and three brothers were carpenters, Peter was a labourer. Joined IRA 1929, CPI 1933, IRC activist. Emigrated with Billy Power to London in November 1934 and found work in Woolf's rubber factory in Willesden, and were soon joined by the other Power brothers Paddy and Johnny. Joined CPGB in Southall with Johnny Power. Left London for Spain on 19.12.1936 with Johnny Power, Paddy Power and Jackie Hunt. Arrived in Spain 21.12.1936. Firmly against the Irish moving to the Lincoln Battalion in January 1937 but obeyed the majority vote. Sergeant, assistant platoon leader in the Lincolns. Took part in the battles of Jarama and Brunete. Recommended for repatriation by Frank Ryan 11.08.1937 and arrived in Waterford on 19.09.1937. Afterwards labourer, then insurance agent. Joined the Labour Party in October 1938. Councillor on Waterford Corporation for the Labour Party. Died 19.06.1999.

170. O'DAIRE Patrick, born 22.05.1905, Co. Donegal. One and a half years secondary school education. Service in Irish Free State Army (6th, 9th, 14th, 17th, 23rd battalions) 1922-29, sergeant. Emigrated to Canada in August 1929 on a government scheme to become a farmer. The Great Depression put an end to his farming hopes and O'Daire began to organise the unemployed. He was jailed for 15 months in Saskatchewan for provoking a riot. Deported to Britain in 1934, O'Daire joined CPGB in Bootle, Liverpool, in 1934. Jailed twice for short periods in Britain after demonstrations. Worked as a miner in Norfolk, arrived in Spain from Britain 05.12.1936. Wounded at Lopera, in hospital in Ciudad Real. Later served in the 20th International Battalion on the Cordoba front. On the recommendation of Will Paynter, representative of the CPGB in Albacete, Peter Daly and O'Daire were put in charge of the British Battalion after the battle of Brunete. Adjutant of British Battalion 12-24 August 1937 and O.C. 24 August-29 September 1937 and 6 November-9 November 1937. In February 1938 sent to OTS Pozorubio, which he left of his own volition and then transferred to Tarazona as second in command. This was a

political decision because of his difficulties with Čopić and the British Battalion commissar. Returned to British Battalion April 1938 as Captain, O.C. No. 1 Company, British Battalion 30.03.-01.09.1938. Repatriated, he left Spain with Jack Jones on 14 September 1938. Served as a major in the Pioneer Corps during WW2 in Italy. After 1945 he lived in Coventry and then moved to North Wales. He died in 1981 and was buried in Bangor, North Wales.

171. O'DONNELL Vincent Francis William, born 27.08.1904 in South Dublin, known as "Vincent". As a child probably lived at 78, Lower George's Street, Kingstown (Dun Laoghaire). Before Spain he lived at 15C, Gour Rd, London SE16 and worked as a waiter at 5, Camden Square W1. Member of the YCL and CPGB. Arrived in Spain via London 26.01.1937. Served with the Lincolns at Jarama. Recommended for repatriation by Frank Ryan, 11.08.1937. Served in a supply unit in Murcia, taken prisoner during March retreats 1938 and incarcerated in San Pedro de Cardeña.

172. O'DONNELL, Hugh, born 1899. Originally from Burtonport, Co. Donegal and said to have worked as a stoker. Left Ireland in 1918. Member of CPGB. Hugh O'Donnell served with the British Medical Unit while acting as an agent for the Catalan CP. He was involved in the surveillance of George Kopp and George Orwell of the ILP contingent fighting with the POUM, and of Orwell's wife. Taken prisoner during March retreats 1938. Repatriated 1938.

173. O'DONNELL John, born probably 1916. His family lived at 32, Cashel Road, Clonmel, Co. Tipperary. Deserted from the British Army after 6 months. Seaman. Arrived in Spain 20.12.37. Attached to 3rd company recruits, Tarazona, 11.02.1938. Deserted, left Spain 29.04.1938.

174. O'DONNELL William, born 08.04.1913 Tipperary town. Emigrated to London in 1929 and worked as a waiter for a French family, later in a hotel. Arrived in Spain 11.08.1937. Had a psychiatric problem according to IB records. Repatriated by order of 12.05.1938, discharged on grounds of ill-health. Repatriated via Irish Legation in Paris in June 1938.

175. O'DONOVAN Michael, Irish, born 1914 Athlone, address 28, St, Kieran's Terrace, Athlone. Driver, TGWU 1934. Arrived in Spain from Britain 22.12.1936. Wounded 19.02.1937. No further data.

176. O'FARRELL Thomas, called himself "James Farrell" in Spain. Born in Dublin 04.07.1902, gave Irish address as 81, Prussia St. Arrived in Spain 20.12.1936 from London. Motor mechanic for Green Line coaches in London. Among his fantastic statements, he said he had attended TCD, served in the IRA (Easter Rising), the British Army (India, Russia, Shanghai) and had been a member of the ITGWU in Ballinasloe, Co. Galway. Also claimed he was a member of the CPI in Dublin and the CPGB in the East End of London. Deemed "suspicious and a liar" by IB staff, because he had stated he was a member of the CPGB and had served with the POUM militia. Posted to MG Company, British Battalion. Left Jarama front without permission and stayed away for four days. Sentenced to 10 days in the labour section. In Albacete military gaol 26.12.1937. Missing in Aragon in March 1938, taken prisoner. Repatriated to UK 1938.

177. O'FLAHERTY Thomas, born in Ireland 08.08.1914, possibly in Dingle, Co. Kerry. Lived in Waterbury, Connecticut. Seaman, worked for the Grace Line out of Santa Clara, California. Joined CPUSA in North Carolina, September 1935, also member YCL. At one time professional boxer (welterweight), Golden Gloves champion of North Carolina. Arrived in Spain February 1938. Platoon leader. Wounded and taken prisoner during Ebro battle, 6-12 September 1938 in Corbera. Another source claims that he was killed in the last days of conflict on the Ebro, 23.09.1938.

178. O'HANLON William (Liam), born 04.11.1913, from 13, Woodsback St., Belfast. Lived in Birmingham, labourer. Ex-IRA, IRC. Arrived in Spain via England 16.09.1937. Served with the anti-tank battery. Wounded at Brunete, proposed for repatriation. Later with the British Battalion as an infantryman from 12.04.1938. Again wounded in attack on Hill 481, 30.07.1938. In hospital at Santa Coloma 14.10.1938. Normal repatriation.

179. O'NEILL Richard. Born 1910. Lived at 5, Colinward Street, Belfast, with his father, a tailor. Worked as a machine presser/printer, member of the typographical union since 1929. Member NILP, joined CPI 1936. Arrived in Spain 10.12.1936. Killed at Jarama 14.02.1937 by a stray bullet.

180. O'NEIL Homer (Stewart,Paddy), born 28.12.1900. Served in the British Army, 1917-26, in France, India and Mesopotamia. Emigrant in Canada, lumberjack. Member of CPCan. Took part in Ottawa trek. Lived in Vancouver, B.C. Arrived in Spain via Canada, 30.03.1937. Promoted sergeant 06.05.1937 in 3rd platoon, 3rd company of the Lincolns. Platoon leader, killed at Brunete, 06.07.1937.

181. O'REGAN James Francis, born 17.09.1916 Cork city, joined IRA in 1932 and CPI in December 1934, factory worker in Dunlops, Cork. From 1, Park View, Wellington Road, Cork. Arrived in Spain 30.03.1938. Joined company No. 4 of the British Battalion, 21.05.1938. Wounded during attack on Hill 481, 27.07.1938, in hospital three days, wounded again 07.09.1938 in Sierra Caballs, in hospital again 08.09.1938. Deserted just prior to last action. With British Battalion 30.09.1938. Mother lived at 1, Park View, Wellington Road, Cork. She carried out a lengthy, and unsuccessful, correspondence with the Dept. of External Affairs to have her son repatriated at once for family reasons. He was with battalion 16.10.1938. Normal repatriation. Arrested afterwards in Britain for IRA activities and sentenced to 12 years' hard labour.

182. O'REGAN, James, born 16.05.1911 Cork. Irish address 9, St. Finbarr's Avenue, Cork. Married. Window glazier. Member of ITGWU since 1929, also of IRC. Arrived in Spain, 18.12.1936. Served in the Lincolns. Recommended for repatriation by Frank Ryan, 11.08.1937. He was allowed home in September 1937, returned and arrived at Figueras 20.02.1938. On British Battalion list, April 1938 and 30.09.1938. Wounded 26.07.1938 Ebro, rejoined battalion 05.09.1938, wounded again 07.09.1938 with battalion 16.10.1938. Normal repatriation.

183. O'REILLY Domhnall, born 30.12.1903 in Dublin. Plasterer. Father and brothers fought in the Easter Rising and he ran errands for the GPO garrison. Took part in the War of Independence and was a member of the IRA garrison in the Four Courts in 1922. Joined RWG and was sent to the International Lenin School in Moscow 1931/32. CPI 1933. Arrived in Spain 14.12.1936. Political Commissar in the Anglo-Irish Company of the 14th Brigade at Lopera, wounded. Sentenced to 2 months in the labour battalion for disobeying an order, 11.02.1937 in Albacete, but released on

intervention of Frank Ryan. Returned to Ireland with Frank Ryan at the end of February 1937.

184. O'REILLY John. Born 29.03.1908 in Thurles, Co. Tipperary, parents lived at 17, Sarsfield Avenue, Thurles, in 1936. Member of the IRA since 1922, of the ITGWU in Thurles, Co. Tipperary, since 1934. Book-binder. May have served in Spain as early as October 1936. Worked as an ambulance driver. At Sagaro repatriation centre 12.09.1938, repatriated 25.10.1938. Return to UK facilitated by Irish Legation in Paris. Wrote to his family that he was not returning home for fear of discrimination but intended staying in Britain or emigrating to the USA.

185. O'RIORDAN Michael, born 12.11.1917 Cork. Shop assistant. Joined Fianna in 1933, company adjutant of IRA, CPI member from May 1936. Left Ireland for Spain via Liverpool, 28.04.1938, arrived in Figueras 05.05.1938. Joined British Battalion 15.05.1938. Sent to corporal school. Light machine-gunner in Ebro battle, citation for bravery. Wounded. In hospital at Mataro. Repatriation after withdrawal of IB, arrived in Dublin 10.12.1938. Interned in the Curragh Camp during WW2. Long-time secretary of the Communist Party in Ireland. Died 18.05.2006. His mother Julia O'Riordan carried out a lengthy correspondence with the Department of External Affairs immediately after her son's departure from Cork in order to have her son repatriated. As in the case of James F. O'Regan, Irish diplomats could do nothing to help her.

186. ORMESBY Hannah (Ruth), born 1901, nurse, went to Spain with British Medical Unit. Originally from "Belleville", Drumore West, Co. Sligo. Arrived in Spain 18.04.1937. Accidentally killed in a fire in Barcelona.

187. O'SHEA John, born Waterford probably 02.07.1903, lived 35, John's St., his immediate family in Kilmeaden. Plasterer. Emigrated to London where he worked for Bovis builders. Member of TGWU. First emigrated to Britain 1926, member of IRC. Served two years in the 12th Battalion of the Irish Free State Army 1924-26, MG training. Arrived in Spain 17.02.1937 via England. Sergeant. Allowed 10 days leave November 1937. Left Battalion for repatriation 29.09.1937, re-joined Battalion 23.02.1938. Wounded 16.03.1937 at Jarama and at Caspe 16.03.1938. Sergeant,

citation for bravery during Ebro battle. With British Battalion, 30.09.1938. Repatriated after withdrawal of IB.

188. O'SHEA John. Born 03.06.1904. He was a shoe maker by trade and single. Irish emigrant, lived in Toronto, Ontario. Came to Spain via Canada June 1937. O'Shea, known as "Paddy", was a member of the CPCan since 1936. Left for Spain 10.05.1937. He was promoted platoon leader in the Canadian company of the Lincoln Battalion in June 1937. Wounded at Teruel. Missing believed killed during the retreats of March-April 1938.

189. O'SULLIVAN John, born 30.03.1908 in Bandon, Co. Cork. Emigrated to USA. Member of CPUSA since March 1935 in Seattle. Arrived in Spain from USA November 1937. Reported as missing during retreats in March/April 1938.

190. O'SULLIVAN Patrick, born 03.09.1914 in London. Single, tile-layer (terraza), no next of kin. Served 2 ½ years in the Volunteer Force of the Irish Free State Army. Joined CPI, June 1936. Based in Rathmines, Dublin, member of No. 5 branch ITGWU since 1935 and on arrival in Spain gave the contact address: C. O'Lenaghan, 54, Connolly Avenue, Inchicore. His last Irish address was in Mallow, Co. Cork. Arrived in Spain from Dublin 08.02.1937. Joined British Battalion 16.02.1937, wounded at Brunete 26.07.1937. Lieutenant and company OC at Tarazona training camp, executive officer of Tarazona OTS. Commander No. 1 Company British Battalion 10-15 March 1938. Wounded Aragon 16.03.1938, killed 31.07.1938 Ebro.

191. PATTEN Thomas, born 18.12.1910, Achill Island, Co. Mayo. One of 14 children, Patten, whose first language was Irish, emigrated to London in 1932 and worked as a labourer in Guinness's brewery. He was involved in the London branch of IRC. One of the first Irish volunteers, he arrived in Spain in October 1936, joined the militia and was killed at Boadilla on the Madrid front on the night of 16/17 December 1936. In September 1986 a monument to his honour was unveiled at Dooega, Achill.

192. PATTERSON Edward Theodore (Jackie), born 28.08.1904 in Armagh, from Dee St., in East Belfast. Harness maker. Emigrated to Canada, landing at Quebec 27.08.1927. Lived in Vancouver, B.C. Left for Spain in

December 1937. Killed with four comrades in a bomb blast near Gandesa, 30.07.1938.

193. PENROSE John (Sean) Thomas, born 26.11.1905 South Dublin. Arrived in Spain from Dublin 24.02.1937. Ex-IRA. Served on the Jarama front. Badly wounded, losing an eye. Had heart and nervous trouble. Recommended for repatriation by Frank Ryan for "health and conduct reasons" 11.08.1937. At that time he had been posted from the punishment unit in Camp Lukacs to the supply depot.

194. PLAIN David, from Armagh. Born 1909. Cinema operator. Labour Party member since 1930. Arrived in Spain from Glasgow 14.04.1937. Often disciplined for drunkenness and insubordination, seen as a "ringleader" in Tarazona in the repatriation question. According to a report from Albacete of 25.03.1938 he had family problems, was weak physically but a "good comrade". Deserted at least once. Re-joined British Battalion 12.09.1938. Repatriated after the withdrawal of the IB.

195. POLLOCK Herbert, born 1899 in Derry, lived with his eight siblings and parents at 22, Bennett Street, Derry, in 1911. Boilermaker. Emigrated to Canada. Member of CPCan since 1935. Arrived in Spain 27.07.1937, served with the Canadian battalion. Died in Canada 12.08.1953.

196. POWER John, born 09.04.1908 Waterford. Labourer. Brother of William and Patrick Power. All lived at Waterpark Lodge, Newtown Road, Waterford. 1932 Battalion Adjutant IRA, Waterford city. Member of Irish Labour Party and IRC in Ireland. Moved to England and was member of Southall Trades Council in London. Joined CPGB in May 1936. Arrived in Spain via London 21.12.1936. Joined British Battalion 22.12.1936, transferred to Lincolns 20.01.1937. Runner for Company commander Paul Burns. Company commissar from May 1937. He was wounded in the thigh and leg at Brunete, 09.07.1937. Recommended for repatriation by Frank Ryan 11.08.1937. Then commissar in Tarazona. Joined British Battalion 17.03.1938. Commander of No. 2 Company from 31.07.1938. Promoted from lieutenant to captain during the Ebro battle. Three citations for bravery. With British Battalion at Ripoll 16.10.1938. Arrived in Dublin 10.12.1938. Interned in the Curragh Camp, 1940-43. Died in Southampton, December 1968.

197. POWER Patrick, born 1909 in Waterford. Labourer, arrived in Spain 21.12.1936. Served with the Irish in the Lincoln Battalion. Repatriated by Frank Ryan in 1937. Died in London, 06.05.1983.

198. POWER William, born ca. 1912, from Waterford. Friend of Peter O'Connor, emigrated to England 1934, joined the CPGB in Southall in May 1936. Arrived in Spain, 04.02.1937. Member of CPI, with Lincolns at Jarama and Brunete. Recommended for repatriation by Frank Ryan, 11.08.1937, repatriated November 1937. Served in the merchant navy during WW2. Died in Harrow, Middlesex, 1978.

199. PRENDERGAST James, born probably 06.02.1915, Dublin, worked in mineral water factory from age of 14. Member of WUI, joined RWG in 1932, attended International Lenin School 1934/35. Afterwards unemployed. CPI activist. Moved to London, joined Acton branch CPGB in 1936, worked at Lucas Engineering. Arrived in Spain 12.12.1936, Irish Section of No. 1 English Company, 14th IB, on Cordoba front. Elected political delegate of Irish at Las Rozas, wounded 12.01.1937, hospital. Attended OTS June-July 1937, said to have no capacity for military leadership, repatriated to Ireland in 1937. Later leading official in railway union NUR in Britain. Died in 1974.

200. PRITCHARD David Frederick, born 10.12.1906 Newtownards, lived originally at 97, South St., Newtownards, Co. Down. Emigrated to Canada, landing in Quebec 28.07.1928. Lived in Saskatoon, left for Spain 08.10.1937, in 1st recruits company, Tarazona, 11.02.1938 being trained as a scout. Said to have "gone missing" during the retreats of March 1938. Another source states he was captured at Caspe-Belchite, March 1938.

201. PYPER Robert Bertram, born 12.11.1906, Belfast. Lived as a child at 30, Derg Street, Clifton, Belfast. Carpenter. Emigrated to Britain and lived at 4 Price St., Birkenhead. Married with two children. Arrived in Spain 14.02.1938. Missing 05.05.1938, probably crossed the French border.

202. QUINLAN Maurice Patrick, born 17.03.1911 in Waterford. Salesman. Gave as his Irish address that of his grandmother: 27, The Glen, Waterford. Emigrated to London ca. 1932. Arrived in Spain December 1936, killed

while serving with the British Battalion at Jarama, 15.02.1937, by a sniper. His remains were interred in a cemetery at Morata de Tajuna.

203. QUINN Sydney, born Co. Antrim 01.11.1909 as the 13th of 14 children. The father, a plasterer, moved the family to Glasgow in 1914 in search of work. During the 1920s Sydney's mother and several of his siblings died of TB. Sydney worked first as a grocer's boy, was laid off and became unemployed again in 1931. Member of CPGB. He joined the Royal Artillery in 1934 and served until 1936. Took part in hunger marches. Left for Spain 30.11.1936, in a group which included George Nathan. Fought in the battles of Lopera, Las Rozas, Jarama and Brunete. Repatriated October 1937.

204. READ Patrick. Born on a ship between Dublin and Britain 25.02.1899 so that the birth was never recorded. Baptised in London. The family (both parents were Dublin-born) settled in Liverpool but left for Canada in 1912 and returned to Britain in 1915. Pat Read stayed in Canada, served as a signaller with the Canadian Expeditionary Force in France. On his demobilisation in 1919, Read went from Canada to the USA. In 1921 he travelled to Ireland, working as a freelance journalist in Cork and Dublin and joining the CPI. He was a member of the CPI unit who fought in the early phase of the Irish Civil War, as the garrison of Bridgman's Tobacco Store in O'Connell St. Read emigrated to Britain in 1924, and to the USA in 1932. Until his departure for Spain in 1937 he lived in Chicago. Arrived in Spain 17.03.1937. In Spain he led a signallers' unit, but as a self-proclaimed anarchist (member of the IWW) who criticised the CPUSA, he was removed from the Lincoln Battalion in March 1938 on the orders of Brigade Commissar Dave Doran, sent to the rear and repatriated to the USA. He applied for an Irish passport at the Irish Legation in Paris in 1938, but the request was refused. He returned to America and died 16.11.1947 in Chicago.

205. ROE Michael A., born 1908 in Athlone. Lived in Dublin at 13 Jane Place, off Seville Place. Butcher. Arrived in Spain 07.01.1937. Second in command of No. 4 Company, British Battalion, at Jarama. Wounded. Repatriated, returned to Dublin, July 1937.

206. ROBINSON QUIGLEY John, born 1897 in Belfast. Served four years in the British Army (cavalry) during WW1. Emigrated to the USA and was an organizer in the International Seamen's Union, lived in New York. First company commander, then commissar of the Lincoln Battalion and deputy Brigade Commissar. Repatriated 1937. Served in the Merchant Marine during WW2. Known in the American battalion as "Robbie" or "Popeye".

207. RUSSELL Michael, born 05.09.1909 Ennis, Co. Clare, lived at Simms Lane, Ennis, Co. Clare. Emigrated to Canada, lived in Montreal. According to immigration data, a Michael Russell, aged 19 years from Ireland, landed in Quebec 06.07.1929. Left for Spain 05.02.1937. Killed at Jarama, February 1937.

208. RYAN Frank, born 11.09.1902, from Bottomstown, Elton, Knocklong, Co. Limerick. Fifth of nine children, both parents were teachers. Joined the 4th battalion of the East Limerick Brigade of the IRA and took part in the Civil War. Interned 1922-23. Received a MA in Celtic Studies from UCD in 1925, where he joined the Republican Club. Ryan was active in the Gaelic League and the Dublin IRA, in which he was adjutant, becoming editor of An Phoblacht, the Republican weekly, in 1929. Arrested many times, and charged before the Military Tribunal in 1931. Released from Arbour Hill Prison by the incoming Fianna Fáil government in March 1932. Resigned from the IRA 1934. Active in the IRC, later secretary and editor-printer of its paper. Left Dublin with about 25 volunteers, 11.12.1936. Arrived in Spain 15.12.1936. Wounded at Jarama, 15.02.1937. On leave in Ireland March-June 1937. Stood as a candidate in the 1st July 1937 Irish general election and received only 875 votes. Served in IB Political Commissariat, mainly based in Madrid, editor of "Book of the 15th Brigade". On his return to Spain in mid-June 1937, Ryan was appointed to the Political Commissariat of the 15th Brigade as the officer responsible for the Irish. Captured outside Calaceite, Aragon, 31.03.1938. Died in Dresden 1944.

209. RYAN Joseph, born ca. 1917, lived at 9, Mungret Street, Limerick. Attended Sexton Street CBS. Shoemaker. Immigrant in London from an early age. Member of the ITGWU since 1935. Member of the Labour Party, lived near Edgware Road. Arrived in Spain 28.12.1936. Arrested in

Madrigueras January 1937, again with the British volunteer Joseph Moran by police at Valencia without papers 06.05.1937, repatriated as "useless" in July 1937. Joined the Merchant Navy at the outbreak of WW2, served as a fireman. Joe Ryan died when his ship, "Dunvegan Castle", was torpedoed by U-Boot 46 off the west coast of Ireland 26.08.1940. The ship sunk the following day. There were 27 fatalities.

210. RYAN Maurice Emmett, born 06.05.1915 at 41, Upper Catherine Street Limerick as the fourth of six brothers. His father was a draper, his mother owned "The Desmond Hotel". He alleged he had been an officer in the Irish Free State Army and had studied law at Oxford, further that one of his brothers was a leading Blueshirt fighting with O'Duffy's unit on the side of Franco. Supported by parents when living in Portugal and Spain from 1933. Came direct from Paris to Spain, arrived at Figueras from Massanet (Girona) on 5 November 1937 and left for Albacete on 9 November. Joined British Battalion 11.11.1937. Docked ten days pay and served ten days imprisonment for insulting Commander Fred Copeman. Wounded in the shoulder at Teruel, late January1938. Caused disruption when recuperating in Benicasim, brought to Vladimir Čopić, O.C. of 15th Brigade. Sent from Tarazona training base to SIM at Albacete for his case to be investigated where he fell ill. Re-joined British Battalion, good machine-gunner. It was alleged that he fired on his own comrades while drunk during Ebro battle. In early August 1938 Ryan was assassinated by the British CO Sam Wilde, who was accompanied by the adjutant George Fletcher. George Murray, the battalion commissar of the MG Company in which Maurice served under Jack Nalty, presumably also had a hand in the decision, and the battalion commissar Bob Cooney was also undoubtedly consulted.

211. SCOTT Willoughby (Bill), b. 1908 in Dublin into a Protestant working class family, lived at 17, Ring St., Inchicore. His father William was a member of the ICA and fought in the College of Surgeons garrison during the Easter Rising. All males in the family followed the bricklaying trade. Bill Scott was a member of the IRA and the CPI and was imprisoned in the Military Detention Barracks in the Curragh in 1934. He travelled to Barcelona in September 1936 on his own to attend the workers' Olympiade. Joined the Tom Mann Centuria and later the Thälmann Centuria of the German 11th Brigade (3rd Section, No. 1 Company), fighting in Aragon and

in the defence of Madrid. Wounded in the neck. Scott returned to Ireland with Frank Ryan, arriving 11.03.1937. He reputedly returned to Spain and sustained a serious leg wound. Repatriation date unknown. Resigned from CPI because of Hitler-Stalin Pact but re-joined in 1941. Lived in the 1970s at Alvingham, Lincs. Died 1988.

212. SHEEHAN Thomas John, born probably 27.09.1904, originally from Skibbereen, Co. Cork. Worked as a shop assistant. Lived in Brighton, arrived in Spain 21.02.1938. Member of CPGB since 1935. Killed in Aragon, March 1938.

213. SIMS Thomas Patrick, born 15.05.1904 Templemore, Co. Tipperary, ex-IRA, ex-British Army. Went to Spain in August 1937 with the Canadian Spanish Medical Aid unit. His family lived in North Westminster, British Columbia. He was a miner, and a member of CPCan since 1936. Ambulance driver. Returned from Spain 27.04.1938. Died in Vernon, British Columbia, 25.09.1983.

214. SMITH Patrick, Dublin, born probably 12.04.1910 North Dublin. Arrived in Spain December 1936. Received shrapnel wound in the ankle at Lopera 31.12.1936, wounded in the head and arm at Jarama, February 1937. Recommended by medical commission for repatriation 11.06.1937. Arrived in Dublin, July 1937. Interned in the Curragh Camp during WW2.

215. STANLEY Patrick, born 1915/1916 lived at 11, Francis St., Dublin. Member of the Gaelic League and the IRA. Arrived in Spain 16.12.1936. Served with the Lincolns at Jarama as a machine-gunner and was granted two days leave to Madrid. Went afterwards to Alicante in an effort to board a ship going to England. Arrested 27.05.1937, turned over to IB HQ in Albacete. Survived the war.

216. STEELE George, born probably 1914. Lived at 2, Cheston Street, Carrickfergus, Co. Antrim. Labourer, non-Party. Arrived Spain 14.01.1937 from London. Wounded at Jarama and Brunete, sent to training base at Tarazona, deserted 02.12.1937. Caught in Valencia and sent to punishment camp at Villamaruja. Held to be "thoroughly demoralised".

217. STOKES, Edward, born probably 22.08.1907, Urlingford, Co. Kilkenny. Gave his Irish address as New Cottages, Wood Quay, Galway. Electrician. Arrived in Spain 10.11.1936. No further data, probably deserted.

218. STRANEY James, born 31.05.1915 Belfast, milkman in Ballymacarret. Father lived at 10, John Street, Belfast. Member of IRA, active in 1932 Outdoor Relief Movement. IRC activist. Later worked in factory in Birmingham. Arrived in Spain 20.09.1937 with Willie O'Hanlon and David Walsh, served in anti-tank unit until April 1938, then in infantry. Promoted corporal 20.05.1938. Killed in attack on Hill 481, Battle of the Ebro, 31.07.1938.

219. THORNTON David. Born 1905. Probably from Watson Street, Portadown, Co. Armagh. Pipe fitter by trade. Emigrated to Canada at the age of 22, landing in Quebec 04.08.1928. He lived in Calgary. Arrived in Spain 04.12.1937 from Canada, entrained for Albacete 11.12.1937. Trained as a sapper at Tarazona, February 1938. Fought at Belchite, Caspe, Ebro. Wounded 01.08.1938. No further data.

220. TIERNEY Frank, born 26.10.1911 Belfast. Emigrated to Canada, landing in Halifax 14.04.1930. Worked in the lumber industry, British Columbia. Arrived in Spain 27.07.1937, fought with Lincolns. Corporal, machine-gunner, wounded three times. Normal repatriation after withdrawal of IB, arriving in Canada 18.02.1939. Died 26.05.1964 in Pemberton, British Columbia.

221. TIERNEY John, born in Dublin 13.06.1902. Seaman. Lived in London, member of CPGB since 1931. Married. Arrived in Spain 16.05.1937. Wounded in the right arm at Brunete, he deserted on the way to hospital with Fred E. Clark from Acton. Sailed to Marseilles, from where they took a ship for Britain, arriving 20.11.1937. Tierney lived before and after Spain at 8A, Palace Road, Upper Norwood, London SE 19 (beside Crystal Palace). In an undated letter (July 1938) Tierney complained to Harry Pollitt that Fred Copeman and Bert Overton should have been brought to trial for their mistakes at Brunete and Jarama, respectively. Tierney remained in the CPGB and died in the early 1980s in London.

222. TIGHE Patrick, born probably 22.02.1914 Ballina, Co. Mayo. Family lived 13, Brook St., Ballina. Stone-cutter. Stated he had served in the IRA and in the British Army for two years. Worked in Leeds and later in Manchester, arrived in Spain 08.12.1937. Arrested in Figueras for drinking and fighting. Left for Albacete 11.12.1937, in Albacete military gaol, 26.12.1937. Served 10 days in prison for drunkenness in January-February 1938 at Tarazona. Sent to labour battalion, 12.02.1938. Rifleman and later machine-gunner in British Battalion. Commended for bravery at Belchite in April 1938. Later fought in Ebro battle, deserted 28.08.1938. Brigade prison from 09.09.1938. With British Battalion at Ripoll, 16.10.1938. Normal repatriation.

223. TRAYNOR Thomas, born July 1897 in Monaghan or Tyrone. Emigrated to Canada, landing in Quebec 09.08.1925. He worked as a time keeper and joined CPCan in 1936. Arrived in Spain via Canada 29.04.1937. During the Brunete campaign Traynor took over the command of the Canadian platoon in the American battalion after the death of Stewart O'Neil. But he was himself wounded in the face on Mosquito Ridge during the Brunete battle and was withdrawn. Served also in the battles at Fuentes del Ebro and Teruel. Popular platoon leader. Normal repatriation. Canadian citizen.

224. TUMILSON William James (Liam), born 10.11.1904 Belfast. From 9, Thorndyke Street, Belfast. Ex-IRA, IRC. Emigrated to Liverpool, worked as a crane driver. Arrived in Spain 21.01.1937. Adjutant, later commander, in MG Company of the Lincolns. Killed by a sniper, Jarama, March 1937. He was buried by his comrades in Morata de Tajuna. He may have emigrated to Australia as a young man.

225. VALLELY Edward, (known in Spain as BRADY, Peter), born 02.08.1910 at Aughdrumgullin, Butlerstown, Co. Cavan. His father was a shoemaker. On arrival in Spain he gave his sister's address: 5, Breffney Terrace, Cavan, Ireland. Joined British Battalion 25.12.1937. 3rd recruits company Tarazona, 11.02.1938. Taken prisoner at Calaceite 31.03.1938 together with Bob Doyle and Jackie Lemon. Repatriated 1939. Lived in the Limerick area from the 1940s.

226. WALSH David, born 12.06.1904, Ballina, and lived as a child at 9, Knox Street, Ballina, Co. Mayo. Labourer, his mother lived in 1936 at 35, St.

Muredach's Terrace, Ballina. Arrived in Spain 17.09.1937 with Jim Straney and Willie O'Hanlon, probably from England. Killed at Teruel, 19.01.1938.

227. WARD Gerald, born Dublin 15.09.1909. Originally from 13, Upper Kevin Street. Emigrated to Britain and worked as a miner. Lived in Wolverhampton, married with a son aged seven. CPGB. Arrived in Spain 12.06.1937. Wounded at Brunete and again at Teruel. Cook at Tarazona training base. Deserted for family reasons, caught in Barcelona, sent to Disciplinary Company June 1938, and was incarcerated in Castelldefels from 28.06.1938. Later in anti-aircraft unit. With British Battalion at Ripoll, 16.10.1938. Normal repatriation.

228. WATERS Michael, born probably 12.05.1913 Cork, family lived at 66, Barrett's Buildings. Metal polisher. Single. Arrived in Spain 06.01.1937, served first with Lincolns, wounded at Jarama 15.02.1937. Transferred to British Battalion in July 1937, deserted after Brunete. Gaoled several times in Tarazona for drunkenness, insubordination and desertion. Characterised as "demoralised". Proposed for deportation, 17.03.1938. Wounded in Battle of the Ebro, 29.07.1938. At Mataro hospital 03.09.1938. Joined British Battalion again at Ripoll, 18.10.1938. Normal repatriation.

229. WOOD Thomas B., born 21.07.1919 Dublin. Youngest Irish volunteer. Joined the Fianna at seven and was later in B Co., 2nd Battalion, Dublin Brigade IRA. Worked for Dublin Gas Co. One of his uncles was hanged by the British in Mountjoy (Patrick Doyle), another killed in the attack on the Customs House in May 1921 (Sean Doyle). Left Dublin on 11 December 1936 with Frank Ryan's group. Died from wounds inflicted (leg and head) on the Cordoba front 27. or 29.12.1936. Buried in Andujar. Letter of 18.06.1937 from father John Wood at 16, Buckingham Place, Portland Row, Dublin to IB about whereabouts of his son. Answer sent 07.07.1937 (not in Moscow file). His name is incorrectly given in all accounts as "Woods" and this confusion may have caused the delay in conveying the news of his death to Dublin, also the fact that he had been confused with a Dutchman named "Wools".

230. WOULF(F)E James, born 10.06.1899 in in Athea, Co. Limerick, into a farming family who kept a draper's shop. Joined Irish Volunteers in 1916,

IRA 1918, battalion signaller in 'G' Company (Athea) of 2nd battalion, West Limerick Brigade. Fought in the War of Independence and the Civil War, captured October 1922, released December 1923. Emigrated to Canada in 1924, worked as logger 1924-29, joined the CPCan in 1932, Party organiser of sailors. Lived in Vancouver. Arrived in Spain via Canada March 1937, fatally wounded by grenade in Belchite, 05.09.1937. He died in hospital the same day. A Spanish death certificate was issued to his mother in April 1938 following a request from Fr. Chawke, catholic curate in Athea.

List of maps and photographs

Sources

Archives

State Archive for Social and Political History (RGASPI), Moscow
Fond 545, International Brigades (IB)
Opis' 1: Documents of IB War Commissariat
Opis' 2: Documents from headquarters of IB at Republican Ministry for Defence
Opis' 3: Documents of 35th, 45th Division (10th-15th and 129th International
Brigades)
Opis' 6: Personal files of the Volunteers.

National Archives of Ireland (NAI), Dublin
Department of Foreign Affairs
Department of Justice
Department of the Taoiseach

Imperial War Museum, London (IWM) Interviews with IB veterans
Accessed online: Charles Bloom, Syd Booth, Jim Brewer, Fred Copeman, Walter
Greenhalgh, George Leeson, Tom Murphy, Charles Picard, Sydney Quinn

South Wales Miners' Library (SWML), Swansea
Ms. of interview with Jim Brewer

Southampton City Archives
Merchant navy papers of Maurice Emmet Ryan

Working Class Movement Library (WCML), Salford
Bob Clarke Ms.; Ms. of interview with Syd Booth

Marx Memorial Library (MML)London
Catalogue 1994, Box C, Special files 2, 3, 5, 7, 8, 9, 10, 11, 12, 17, 19, 24, 41;
Box 50, Ms. Joe Monks; Catalogue 1986, Box 21.

National Museum of Labour History, Manchester (NMLHM)
CP/Ind/Misc./18/6; CP/Ind/Poll/2/ 5 and 6

Newspapers

Limerick Chronicle, 1932-33
Limerick Leader, 1936-37
Irish Times, 1933-38
Irish Press, 1931-38

Books and articles

Bill Alexander, British Volunteers for Liberty: Spain 1936-39, London 1982

Michael Alpert, The Republican Army in the Spanish Civil War, Cambridge University Press 2007

Michael Alpert, "The Clash of Spanish Armies: Contrasting Ways of War in Spain, 1936-1939", War in History, 6 (3) 1999

C.S. Andrews, Man of No Property, Dublin , 2001 edition

Richard Baxell, Unlikely Warriors. The British in the Spanish Civil War and the Fight against Fascism, London 2012

Richard Baxell, British Volunteers in the Spanish Civil War. The British Battalion in the International Brigades, 1936-1939, London and New York 2004

William C. Beeching, Canadian Volunteers. Spain 1936-1939, University of Regina 1989

Anthony Beevor, The Battle for Spain. The Spanish Civil War 1936-1939. Penguin Edition London 2006

Angela Berg, Die Internationalen Brigaden im Spanischen Bürgerkrieg, Essen 2005

J. Bowyer Bell, The Secret Army. A History of the IRA 1916-1970, London 1970

Gerald Brenan, The Spanish Labyrinth. An Account of the Social and Political Background to the Spanish Civil War, Cambridge, 1976 edition

Charles Burdick, „'Gruen' German Military Plans – Ireland 1940", An Cosantóir, Vol. XXXIV, No. 3, March 1974

Patrick Byrne, Memoirs of the Republican Congress, London n.d.

Joseph T. Carroll, Ireland in the War Years, New York 1975

Peter N. Carroll, The Odyssey of the Abraham Lincoln Brigade. Americans in the Spanish Civil War, Stanford 1994

Bob Clark, No Boots to My Feet. Experiences of a Britisher in Spain 1937-38. With a Foreword by Jack Jones, Stoke-on-Trent 1984

David Convery, "Ireland and the Fall of the Second Republic in Spain", Bulletin of Spanish Studies, Vol. LXXXIX, nos. 7-8, 2012

David Convery, Cork and the Spanish Civil War, U.C.C. 2006 (online)

Judith Cook, Apprentices of Freedom, London 1979

Fred Copeman, Reason In Revolt, London 1948

D. Corkill/S. Rawnsley (eds), The Road to Spain. Anti-Fascists at War, Dunfermline 1981

Peter Costello, Liam O'Flaherty's Ireland, Dublin 1996

Sean Cronin, Frank Ryan. The Search for the Republic, Dublin 1980

Horst Dickel, Die Deutsche Aussenpolitik und die Irische Frage von 1932 bis 1944, Wiesbaden 1983

Gabriel Doherty /John Borgnovo, „Smoking Gun? RIC Reprisals, summer 1920", History Ireland, March/April 2009

Joseph Donnelly, Charlie Donnelly. The Life and Poems, Dublin 1987

Bob Doyle, Brigadista. An Irishman's Fight against Fascism. Notes and Additional Text by Harry Owens, Dublin 2006

John P. Duggan, Neutral Ireland and the Third Reich, Dublin 1989

Cecil Eby, Between the Bullet and the Lie. American Volunteers in the Spanish Civil War, New York-Chicago-San Francisco 1969

Fridrikh Firsov, Sekretye kody istorii kominterna 1919-1943, Moscow 2007

Harry Fisher, Comrades. Tales of a Brigadista in the Spanish Civil War, University of Nebraska Press 1999

Robert Fisk, In Time of War. Ireland, Ulster and the Price of Neutrality 1939-45, Paladin Books London 1987

Carl Geiser, Prisoners of the Good Fight. The Spanish Civil War 1936-1939, Westport Conn. 1986

George Gilmore, The Republican Congress (New York 1935), reprinted by The Cork Workers' Club, 1974

Greater Manchester International Brigade Memorial Committee (Ed.), Greater Manchester Men Who Fought in Spain, Manchester 1983

Walter Gregory, The Shallow Grave. A Memoir of the Spanish Civil War, London 1986

Jason Gurney, Crusade in Spain, London 1976

Brian Hanley, The IRA 1926-1926, Dublin 2002

Brian Hanley, "The Storming of Connolly House", History Ireland, vol. 7 (2), Summer 1999

Brian Hanley, „The Irish Citizen Army after 1916", Saothar 28, 2003

James K. Hopkins, Into the Heart of the Fire. The British in the Spanish Civil War, Stanford 1998

Victor Howard (with Mac Reynolds), The Mackenzie-Papineau Battalion. The Canadian Contingent in the Spanish Civil War, Carleton University Press 1969, 1986

Gerald Howson, Arms for Spain. The Untold Story of the Spanish Civil War, London 1998

Angela Jackson, At the Margins of Mayhem. Prologue and Epilogue to the Last Great Battle of the Spanish Civil War, Pontypool 2008

Michael Kennedy et al. (eds), Documents on Irish Foreign Policy, vols. 5 to 8 (1937-1948), Dublin 2006-2012

Harvey Klehr et al (eds), The Secret World of American Communism. New Haven and London 1995

Arthur H. Landis, The Abraham Lincoln Brigade, New York 1968

Joachim Lerchenmüller, Keltischer Sprengstoff. Eine wissenschaftliche Studie über die deutsche Keltologie von 1900-1945, Tübingen 1997

Maurice Levine, Cheetham to Cordoba. A Manchester Man of the Thirties, Manchester 1984.

Luigi Longo, Die Internationalen Brigaden in Spanien, West Berlin n.d. (original version Rome 1956)

Tom Mahon/James J. Gillogly, Decoding the IRA, Cork 2008

Igor-Philip Matič, Edmund Veesenmayer. Agent und Diplomat der nationalsozialistischen Expansionspolitik, München 2002

Uinseann Mac Eoin (ed.), Survivors, 2nd edition Dublin 1987

Ian McDougall, Voices from the Spanish Civil war. Personal Recollections of Scottish Volunteers in Republican Spain 1936-39, Edinburgh 1986

Ian McDougall, "Tom Murray: Veteran of Spain", Cencrastus (Edinburgh), no. 18, 1984

Fearghal McGarry, Irish Politics and the Spanish Civil War, Cork 1999

Fearghal McGarry, Frank Ryan. Historical Association of Ireland. Life and Times Series No. 17, Dundalk 2002

Michael McInerney, Peadar O'Donnell. Irish Social Rebel, Dublin 1974

Michael McInerney, Frank Ryan Profile – Parts 1-5, Irish Times, April 1975

Barry McLoughlin, Left to the Wolves. Irish Victims of Stalinist Terror, Dublin 2007

F.M. McLoughlin, Irish Neutrality During World War II, with Special References to German Sources, M.A. thesis, UCD 1979/80

Marion Merriman/Warren Lerude, American Commander in Spain. Robert Hale Merriman and the Abraham Lincoln Brigade, Reno 1986

Joe Monks, With the Reds in Andalusia, London 1985

Patrick Murray, Oracles of God. The Roman Catholic Church and Irish Politics, 1922-37, Dublin 2000

Steve Nelson, James R. Barrett and Rob Ruck, Steve Nelson, American Radical, University of Pittsburgh Press 1981

Aodh Ó Canainn, interview with Eilís Ryan, Saothar 21, 1996

Emmet O'Connor, Reds and the Green. Ireland, Russia and the Communist Internationals, 1919-43, Dublin 2004

Emmet O'Connor, James Larkin. Radical Irish Lives, Cork 2002

Emmet O'Connor, A Labour History of Waterford, Waterford Trades Council 1989

Emmet O'Connor, "Behind the Legend: Waterfordmen in the International Brigades in the Spanish Civil War", Decies, Journal of the Waterford Archaeological and Historical Society, vol. 61, 2005

Emmet O'Connor, "Mutiny or Sabotage? The Irish Defection to the Abraham Lincoln Battalion in the Spanish Civil War". Working Papers in Irish Studies, Winthrop University, South Carolina 2009, working paper 09-3

Emmet O'Connor, "Anti-Communism in twentieth century Ireland", Twentieth Century Communism, Issue 6, 2014.

Peter O'Connor, A Soldier of Liberty: Recollections of a Socialist and Anti-fascist Fighter, Dublin 1996

David O'Donoghue, Hitler's Irish Voices. The Story of German Radio's Wartime Irish Service, Belfast 1998

Eoghan Ó Duinnín, La Niña Bonita agus An Róisín Dubh, Baile Atha Cliath 1986

Eunan O'Halpin, Defending Ireland. The Irish State and its Enemies since 1922, Oxford 1999

Kate O'Malley, Ireland, India and Empire. Indo-Irish Radical Connections 1919-64, Manchester 2008

Michael O'Riordan, Connolly Column. The Story of the Irishmen who fought in the Ranks of the International Brigades in the national-revolutionary war of the Spanish People 1936-1939, Dublin 1979

Paul Preston, The Spanish Holocaust. Inquisition and Extermination in Twentieth-Century Spain, London 2012

John Quinn, Irish Volunteers for Spain. A Short History of the Northern Irish Volunteers who fought in Defence of the Republican Government of Spain 1936-1939, Belfast 2011

Ronald Radosh/Mary R. Habeck (eds), Spain Betrayed. The Soviet Union in the Spanish Civil War, New Haven and London 2001

Julius Ruiz, „'Work and Don't lose Hope': Republican forced Labour Camps during the Spanish Civil War", Contemporary European History, Vol. 18, no. 4, 2009

William Rust, Britons in Spain. The History of the British Battalion of the XVth International Brigade, 2nd edition, London 1939

Meda Ryan, Tom Barry, IRA Freedom Fighter, Cork 2003

Iurii Rybalkin, Sovetskaia voennaia pomoshch' respublikanskoi Ispanii (1936-1939), Moscow 2000

Michail Vital'evič Škarovskij, „Die Russische Kirche unter Stalin in den 20er und 30er Jahren des 20. Jahrhunderts", in: Manfred Hildermeier (Ed.), Stalinismus vor dem Zweiten Weltkrieg. Neue Wege der Forschung, München 1998, pp. 233-253.

Enda Staunton, "Frank Ryan & Collaboration: a reassessment", History Ireland, 5 (3), autumn 1997

Enno Stephan, Spies in Ireland, Four Square Books, London 1965

Robert A. Stradling, The Irish and the Spanish Civil War. Crusades in Conflict, Manchester 1999

Rob Stradling, „English-speaking Units of the International Brigades. War, Politics and Discipline", Journal of Contemporary History, Vol. 45, no. 4, 2010

Robert Stradling, Wales and the Spanish Civil War. The Dragon's Dearest Cause, Cardiff 2004

Francis Stuart, „Frank Ryan in Germany", The Bell, November, December 1950

Fred Thomas, Tilting at Windmills. A Memoir of the Spanish Civil War, Michigan State University Press 1996

Hugh Thomas, The Spanish Civil War, 3rd edition, London 1977

John Tisa, Recalling the Good Fight. An Autobiography of the Spanish Civil War, South Hadley, Mass. 1985

Thomas Toomey, The War of Independence in Limerick 1919-1921, self-publishing 2010

Sean Ua Cearnaigh, "From Tipperary to Jarama...The Story of Kit Conway, volunteer hero of the Spanish Republic", Ireland's Eye, March 2006

Sandor Voros, American Commissar, Philadelphia and New York 1961

Barrie Wharton/Des Ryan, „The Last Crusade: Limerick's role in the Spanish Civil War", Old Limerick Journal, Summer Edition 2001 (online)

George Wheeler, To Make the People Smile Again. A Memoir of the Spanish Civil War, Newcastle upon Tyne 2003

J.H. Whyte, Church and State in Modern Ireland, 1923-1979, 2nd edition, Dublin 1980

Howard Williamson, Toolmaking and Politics. The Life of Ted Smallbone – an Oral History, Birmingham 1987

Tom Wintringham, English Captain, Penguin Books, 1941 edition

Milton Wolff, Another Hill. An Autobiographical Novel, University of Illinois Press 1994

James Yates, Mississippi to Madrid. Memoir of a Black American in the Abraham Lincoln Brigade, Seattle 1989